THE RUSSIAN CHURCH UNDER
THE SOVIET REGIME,
1917-1982

VOLUME ONE

DIMITRY POSPIELOVSKY

THE RUSSIAN CHURCH UNDER THE SOVIET REGIME, 1917-1982

VOLUME ONE

ST. VLADIMIR'S SEMINARY PRESS
CRESTWOOD, NEW YORK 10707
1984

Library of Congress Cataloging in Publication Data

Pospielovsky, Dimitry, 1935-
   The Russian church under the Soviet regime,
1917-1982.

   Bibliography: p.
   Includes index.
   1. Russkaia pravoslavnaia tserkov—History—20th
century. 2. Orthodox Eastern Church—Soviet Union—
History—20th century. 3. Soviet Union—Church history—
1917-   I. Title.
BX492.P67   1984   281.9'3   84-5336
ISBN 0-88141-015-2 (v. 1)
ISBN 0-88141-016-0 (v. 2)
ISBN 0-88141-033-0 (set)

THE RUSSIAN CHURCH UNDER
THE SOVIET REGIME
1917-1982

© Copyright 1984

by

ST. VLADIMIR'S SEMINARY PRESS

ISBN 0-88141-015-2 (v. 1)
ISBN 0-88141-016-0 (v. 2)
ISBN 0-88141-033-0 (set)

PRINTED IN THE UNITED STATES OF AMERICA
BY
ATHENS PRINTING COMPANY
New York, NY 10018

Let this effort be a modest contribution to the remembrance and reverence of the countless new martyrs for their faith in Russia and in other lands dominated by regimes of militant atheism. In particular, it is dedicated to the sacred memories of the martyr Venyamin, the Metropolitan of Petrograd; Patriarch Tikhon; and the martyred priest and professor Pavel Florensky.

Preface

The year 1917 was marked not only by the collapse of a political system that governed the largest country on earth and claimed to be inspired by Christian teachings, but also by the beginning of a lasting confrontation between an Orthodox Church struggling for survival and a new totalitarian state that affirmed atheism as a precondition of social progress. Thousands of Russian Orthodox clergy and laity experienced martyrdom. Other thousands left Russia and established Russian Orthodox communities in Western Europe, America and Australia. The administration of dioceses of the Church of Russia beyond the borders of the country was disrupted. And the position of the Russian Church within the family of world Orthodoxy was blurred by confusion—especially since, within the Soviet Union in the 1920s and 1930s, the government supported the uncanonical schism of the "Renovationists" (sometimes also referred to as the "Living Church").

Many authors have undertaken the study of particular aspects of these tragic events. The value of these various publications, which are abundantly quoted by Professor Pospielovsky, is unequal. While many western authors, especially in the past two decades, show authentic objectivity in presenting the situation of religion in the Soviet Union, many of their predecessors were so hostile ideologically to the tsarist regime that they tended to sympathize with the Soviet persecution of Orthodoxy. On the other hand, Russian émigré authors tended to write apologies for their own particular political stands.

With the present book, we at last have an attempt at objective synthesis, within which historical facts are described and interpreted by a specialist in modern Russian social thought who also possesses true competence in and sensitivity to Orthodox canonical and spiritual traditions. Professor Pospielovsky makes truly exhaustive use of a great wealth of sources, including many *samizdat* documents that only recently became accessible. Of course, in the turmoil that followed the revolution, many documents perished; and in the 1920s and 1930s, records relevant to religious matters could only be kept in a clandestine manner, and the situation in this respect has not really changed even today.

The present book deserves to become the standard reference for any comprehensive understanding of modern Russian church history. And since the Church of Russia, by evangelizing the Alaskan natives and, later, by establishing the missionary, canonical and administrative basis for the development of a united Orthodoxy in the new world, has left an indelible mark upon the Orthodox witness in America, there is no doubt that Professor Pospielovsky's monumental work will contribute to a better self-understanding of those who today inherit the task, the responsibility and the enthusiasm of the first missionaries.

John Meyendorff

Contents

Abbreviations Used for Frequently Cited
Books and Periodicals

APV	*Amerikanskii pravoslavnyi vestnik* (New York-Cleveland, 1896-)
AS	Samizdat Archives, Radio Liberty (Munich)
Bogolepov, *Tserkov'*	Alexander A. Bogolepov, *Tserkov' pod vlast'yu kommunizma* (Munich, 1958)
Chrysostomus	J. Chrysostomus, *Kirchengeschichte Russlands der neusten Zeit,* 3 vols. (Munich-Salzburg, 1965-1968)
Curtiss, *Russian Church*	John S. Curtiss, *The Russian Church and the Soviet State, 1917-1950* (Boston: Little, Brown, 1953)
Dallin	Alexander Dallin, *German Rule in Russia, 1941-1945* (London: Macmillan, 1957)
Demyanov	A.I. Demyanov, *Istinno-pravoslavnoe khristianstvo* (Voronezh, 1977)
Dublyansky	A. Dublyansky, *Ternystym shlyakhom* (London: The Ukrainian Autocephalous Church Publications, 1962)
EMIRA	*Ezhegodnik muzeya istorii religii i ateizma.* (Moscow-Leningrad, 1957-1962)
Evlogy, *Put'*	Evlogy (Georgievsky), *Put' moei zhizni* (Paris: YMCA Press, 1947)
Fletcher, *Church Underground*	William Fletcher, *The Russian Orthodox Church Underground, 1917-1970* (Oxford: University Press, 1971)

11

Fletcher, *Nikolai*	William Fletcher, *Nikolai* (London: Collier-Macmillan, 1968)
Fletcher, *Study in Survival*	William Fletcher, *A Study in Survival* (New York: Macmillan, 1965)
Florovsky, *Puti*	G. Florovsky, *Puti russkogo bogosloviya* (Paris: YMCA Press, 1937)
Great Revival	W. Alexeev and T. Stavrou, *The Great Revival* (Minneapolis: Burgess Publishing Co., 1976)
Heyer	Friedrich Heyer, *Die orthodoxe Kirche in der Ukraine von 1917 bis 1945* (Cologne, 1953)
Leonty	Leonty, Bishop of Chile, "Political Controls over the Orthodox Church in the Soviet Union," ms. in Bakhmeteff Archives, Columbia University (New York)
Levitin-Shavrov	Anatoly Levitin-Krasnov and Vadim Shavrov, *Ocherki po istorii russkoi tserkovnoi smuty,* 3 vols. in 1 (Kuesnacht, Switzerland, 1978)
OC	*The Orthodox Church* (Syosset, N.Y., 1965-)
Orthodox America	Constance J. Tarasar, et al., eds., *Orthodox America, 1794-1976* (Syosset, N.Y.: OCA, Department of History and Archives, 1975)
Patriarch and Prophets	Michael Bourdeaux, *Patriarch and Prophets: Persecution of the Russian Orthodox Church Today* (London: Macmillan, 1969)
Patriarkh Sergii	*Patriarkh Sergii i ego dukhovnoe nasledstvo* (Moscow, 1947)
Polsky	Mikhail Polsky, *Kanonicheskoe polozhenie vysshei tserkovnoi vlasti v SSSR i zagranitsei* (Jordanville, N.Y.: Holy Trinity Monastery, 1948)

Rahr	Gleb Rahr, *Plenennaya tserkov'* (Frankfurt am Main, 1954)
RAPV	*Russko-amerikanskii pravoslavnyi vestnik* (Cleveland-New York)
RCL	*Religion in Communist Lands* (Keston College, Kent, England, 1973-)
Regelson	Lev Regelson, *Tragediya russkoi tserkvi, 1917-1945* (Paris: YMCA Press, 1977)
Shafarevich	Igor Shafarevich, *Zakonodatel'stvo o religii v SSSR* (Paris: YMCA Press, 1973)
Simon, *Church, State*	Gerhard Simon, *Church, State and Opposition in the USSR* (London: C. Hurst & Co., 1974)
Spinka	Matthew Spinka, *The Church in Soviet Russia* (New York: Oxford University Press, 1956)
Stratonov, *Smuta*	Irinarkh Stratonov, *Russkaya tserkovnaya smuta, 1921-1931* (Berlin, 1932)
Struve	Nikita Struve, *Christians in Contemporary Russia* (London: Harvill Press, 1967)
TsV	*Tserkovnye vedomosti* (Karlovci, 1922-)
VRKhD	*Vestnik russkogo khristianskogo dvizheniya* (Paris, 1974-)
VRSKhD	*Vestnik russkogo studencheskogo khristianskogo dvizheniya* (Paris-Germany-Paris, 1926-1974)
VS	*Vol'noe slovo* (Frankfurt am Main,
VSS	*Vestnik Svyashchennogo Sinoda pravoslavnoi rossiiskoi tserkvi* (Moscow, 1923-)
Zakonodatel'stvo	*Zakonodatel'stvo o religioznykh kul'takh: Sbornik materialov i dokumentov dlya slu-*

     zhebnogo pol'zovaniya (Moscow, 1971; re-
     print New York: Chalidze Publications,
     1981)

ZhMP   *Zhurnal Moskovskoi Patriarkhii* (Moscow,
     1931-1935, 1943-)

Author's Foreword and Acknowledgments

This book grew from an introductory historical chapter for a study of the interrelationship between the religious revival and the upsurge of Russian nationalism in the Soviet Union of the last few decades. While compiling information for this chapter, I was overwhelmed with material, some of it still unused by previous church historians. I also realized that, despite the numerous books on the Church under the Soviets published in the West in the course of the last forty years, some important aspects of the story have been ignored or only scantily covered. It might, perhaps, be possible to arrive at a quite comprehensive and well-balanced understanding of the history of the Russian Orthodox Church under the Soviets up to, say, 1965, if one had the language skills and the perseverance to read all the books on the subject published in the West in Russian, German and English. But even then, émigré church history would be either outside the picture or treated incompletely and subjectively by interested authors, and most of the latest *samizdat* material, which sheds additional light on many aspects of the Russian Church and her history, and the post-Khrushchev period of the story would likewise remain unknown.

I have therefore attempted to draw together the testimonies and material of the already published works, archival material, the periodical press of the periods concerned, *samizdat* works and documents and the newest and still somewhat controversial material on the last decade and a half to produce a reasonably comprehensive history of the Russian Orthodox Church under the

15

Soviet regime. I have limited my study to the history of the Russian Orthodox Church, avoiding the other major religions of the Soviet Union, not only because it would be impossible to treat all of them in a scholarly manner in a single volume, but because I am primarily interested as a historian in the historical-national Church of the Russians and other Slavs of the USSR—its core nations, as it were. For the time being however, I leave aside the question of national identities and possible frictions between the other two predominantly Orthodox Slavonic nations of the area (the Ukrainians and the Belorussians) and the Great Russians. This book is concerned with the Russian Orthodox Church. Inasmuch as she administers to the Ukrainians and the Belorussians the story of the book is relevant to them. But the history of separatist church attempts in the Ukraine and, to a much weaker degree, in Belorussia lies basically outside the scope of this study, and therefore is treated only in brief summaries.

As a member of the Orthodox Church and as a close student of internal societal developments in the USSR, I have tried to convey an insider's view of the subjects treated, occasionally adding a theological and canonical perspective on the most controversial issues, particularly those dealing with schisms and splits in the Orthodox Church after the revolution. Émigré church affairs are included in the volume inasmuch as they relate to the fate of the Church inside the USSR (the reader will see for himself how relevant they have been, particularly in the 1920s). In the chapters dealing with the most recent church history I depend to some extent on interviews with and oral information supplied otherwise by Soviet citizens active in contemporary church life inside the USSR. Despite all the subjectivity of such sources, they have true value in the directness and personal witness character of the facts and opinions supplied. This information has been used only for additional illustrations, details or confirmations of general facts and/or phenomena learned through other sources.

Besides the many authors of books and articles on the religious situation in the USSR on whose research I have heavily drawn, I am deeply indebted and particularly grateful to the following institutions: the Canadian Social Sciences and Humanities Research Council, which generously supplied me with annual grants beginning with the sabbatical year 1978-1979 to continue my research on the Church and Russian nationalism, making possible repeated journeys to the libraries and archival collections of the US and Europe; the Harvard University Russian Research Center, whose grant helped me through my research fellowship stay there in 1979; the University of Western Ontario Faculty of Social Sciences, who subsidized several brief journeys to the libraries of New York; and the University's Smallman Foundation for its grant subventing a part of the publication costs of this work.

I likewise extend my appreciation to the staff of Keston College; the Oeffentliche Bibliothek of the University of Basel (Switzerland), where the invaluable Lieb collection is to be found; the Istituto Orientale in Rome; the libraries of the London School of Economics and of the School of Slavonic Studies, University of London; the Widener Library at Harvard; the Columbia University Library and its Bakhmeteff Russian Émigré Archives; the Archives of the Orthodox Church in America (Syosset, N.Y.); and the Fr. Georges Florovsky Library of St. Vladimir's Orthodox Theological Seminary. To all these institutions and their staffs I owe my heartfelt gratitude.

I am particularly indebted to the Very Rev. Professor John Meyendorff, who carefully read my manuscript, suggested numerous important corrections and kindly agreed to preface this study. I am also very grateful to the following persons: Professor Bohdan Bociurkiw, for sending me invaluable offprints of his erudite works on the Church in the Ukraine and for encouraging my work; Professor Kazimir Papmehl, for his advice and editorial work; Mr. Anatoly Levitin-Krasnov, a "walking memoir" of Russian church history, who kindly invited me to his home in Switzerland and generously shared his knowledge and memories; and Prince Sergei G. Trubetskoy, who had originally collected and systematized the archives of the OCA, and who gave me invaluable help in finding my way through the files and illustrated much of the material by his own priceless reminiscences. I owe my heartfelt gratitude to Mr. Paul Kachur of SVS Press for his excellent final editing touches, stylistic advice and meticulous reading for technical accuracy. I am indebted to my wife, Mirjana, and our children, Darya, Andrei and Bogdan, for their patience and consideration for my work. My wife has always been the first reader and a highly qualified critic of all my writings. I am likewise grateful to Miss Joan Lemon and the University of Western Ontario History Department secretaries for the excellent typing of all the versions of the manuscript.

Naturally, all mistakes and flaws in this work are my own.

Introduction

The secular reforms of Peter the Great, forced upon the Church, turned her into a department of the state, headed by a secular bureaucracy appointed by the tsar. The bishops in this system, living in an external luxury, were in fact like captive birds in a golden cage: a hierarch could not leave his residence to visit peripheral parishes in his diocese without theoretically having the tsar's and practically the overprocurator's special permission, requested and granted via the channels of the Ruling Synod in St. Petersburg.[1] The priests were in a particularly contradictory position. On the one hand, they depended for most of their livelihood on the donations of their parishioners (which in many rural areas were extremely meager because of the poverty of many peasants) and on the harvests from the piece of land allotted to the parish, which they farmed like any other peasant. On the other hand, legally and according to the oath given at the time of their ordination, they were ex officio agents of the state, required to supply the Ministry of Defense with information on prospective recruits for the armed forces and, in theory, obliged to inform the authorities on all confessions of an antistate character—even though the church canons ban this on the pain of immediate defrocking.[2] Obviously, in this constrained position the Church as an institution could offer little moral leadership to the nation.

After the nationalization of the monastic estates by Catherine

---

[1] Evlogy, *Put'*, 194-232.

[2] *Polnoe sobranie zakonov rossiiskoi imperii,* 6:1720-2 (St. Petersburg, 1830), pp. 685-9, article 4012 and Ordination Oath. Apparently this stipulation fell into disuse and was not applied after Nicholas I, because the subsequent fifteen-volume Codes of Laws (*Svody zakonov*) containing all the laws currently in use appeared without it. Rev. Georges Florovsky says that theoretically the articles ("The Spiritual Regulation") remained in force to the end of the empire, while the oath of the members of the Holy Synod calling the emperor "the Supreme Judge" of the Synod was discontinued in 1901. Florovsky, *Puti,* 89.

II in 1763-1764, the Church as an institution became economically poor, receiving from the state but 10 percent of her former annual income from those properties as compensation. It was only since the 1890s that a substantial, regular state subsidy to support the clergy in the poorer parishes began to be paid. By 1916 it reached 18.8 million rubles—58 million short of making the Russian clergy economically independent from their parishioners.[3]

Externally, the prerevolutionary Church appeared to be very powerful. She was the official state Church, and until 1905 other religions were legally tolerated only as faiths of national minorities. Orthodox religion was an obligatory discipline in all general schools for all pupils born of members of the Orthodox faith, and children born of mixed marriages in which one of the parents was Orthodox had to be baptized Orthodox. Yet the philosopher Vladimir Soloviev said that the Orthodox priests were the least free subjects of the empire, because no one was legally allowed to enter into religious disputes with them—in other words, priests were deprived of the right of dialogue.

In 1914 the Orthodox Church of the empire officially had 117 million members organized into 67 dioceses with 130 bishops and 48,000 functioning parish churches with a total of over 50,000 clergy of all ranks.[4] It ran 35,000 primary schools; 58 seminaries, which in Russia meant a combination of secondary general education with incomplete undergraduate theological education; and four graduate theological academies. These figures, however, are highly misleading. For instance, the vast majority of the intelligentsia were either atheists or agnostics,[5] although its partial

[3]Gerhard Simon, "Church, State and Society," in G. Katkov, et al., eds., *Russia Enters the 20th Century* (London, 1971) 204-5.

[4]This figure includes only *parish* churches and the three ranks of the clergy: bishops, priests and deacons. In 1916, in addition, there were 6,000 parish churches not in use and over 23,000 monastic and institutional churches and chapels of all sorts (in hospitals, barracks, schools, etc.). Spinka, 118-20; A. Veshchikov, "Vekhi bol'shogo puti," *Nauka i religiya*, no. 11 (1962).

[5]As a university student, Alexander Vvedensky, one of the future founders and leaders of the Renovationist schism in the Russian Orthodox Church, carried out a survey of the religiosity of Russian intelligentsia by publishing a questionnaire in the liberal Russian press. Most of the readers mistook him for a well-known professor also named Alexander Vvedensky, and hence about a thousand responses were received. Of these, some 95 percent claimed to be either atheists or extreme freethinkers. Vvedensky, however, rather inaccurately extrapolated this figure as representative of the whole Russian intelligentsia, whereas the vast majority of the

return to the Church began in the last two prerevolutionary decades and would continue into the 1920s. But the prevalent mood in Russian educated circles of the post-Petrine era was that of indifference or atheism to the extent of a general loss of faith: "there was no faith in reason either. . . . There remained only a faith in the West. The West was saving our souls, because it possessed reason, which we did not."[6] This contempt for the Church on the part of the post-Petrine secular state and society was reflected in the fact that, for instance, no religion was taught in Russian secondary schools until 1832, and when it was introduced teachers of fencing and dancing received higher pay than those of religion.[7] To the Church's attempts to benefit from the era of the Great Reforms by proposing autonomy and greater freedom and independence from the state, the latter responded by pushing the Church further into isolation from society, closing university doors to graduates of the secondary theological seminaries in 1879. This practically barred sons of the clergy from advanced secular careers and practically forced them into ordination even when their faith was weak.[8] This was the main reason why the clergy and bishops were constantly requesting reforms in theological education and its status. The contemptuous attitude toward the Church of the largely positivistic and agnostic intelligentsia likewise did not strengthen the position of the Church in her confrontation with the authoritarian state. The liberal secular

church-going intelligentsia did not subscribe to liberal newspapers and conversely Russian liberalism was highly secular and mostly anticlerical. See Vvedensky's *Tserkov' i gosudarstvo* (Moscow, 1923) 23.

[6]This sarcastic remark by N.M. Sokolov, a prolific lay theologian, would be echoed fourteen years later by the great Russian religious philosopher Semen Frank, who said that the tragedy of Russian Westernism was that, not being an organic development of Russian culture, it uncreatively absorbed ready-made ideas from the West—and since positivism and materialism were the most primitive ideas, they were most readily assimilated and transplanted onto the Russian soil by the imitative Westernists. See Sokolov's *Russkie svyatye i russkaya intelligentsiya* (St. Petersburg, 1904) 51; and Frank's "De Profundis," in P.B. Struve, ed., *Iz glubiny* (Paris: YMCA Press, 1967) 328-30.

[7]N.P. Antonov, *Russkie svetskie bogoslovy i ikh religiozno-obshchestvennoe mirosozertsanie* (St. Petersburg, 1912), xxvii.

[8]Bishop Mikhail of Minsk, in *Otzyvy eparkhial'nykh arkhiereev po voprosu o tserkovnoi reforme* (St. Petersburg, 1906) 1:37. This was one of the sources of radicalism and atheism in the seminaries during roughly the last three prerevolutionary decades. See also the comments of Bishop Ioakim of Orenburg in the same volume, 170-4.

press generally reacted with hostility to the Church's yearning for a greater independence and a conciliar structure.[9]

The Edict of Toleration of April 30, 1905, followed by the ukaz of October 30, 1906, granting the status of legal persons to schismatics and sectarians, instilled hopes among the Orthodox that their Church would at last be allowed to regain a canonical conciliar structure. In fact, as early as February 1905, the intelligent and liberal Metropolitan of St. Petersburg Antony (Vadkovsky), in collusion with the Chairman of the Council of Ministers Sergei Witte and his Extraordinary Commission, instructed the scholars of the St. Petersburg Theological Academy to draft proposals "on the desirability of Church reforms . . . and on granting the Orthodox Church more freedom in administering her internal affairs" by emancipating her "from state functions."[10] At the end of March, the Synod presented a report to the tsar requesting permission to: (1) expand the Synod by including members from among the diocesan bishops in addition to the permanent members and to put an elected patriarch at its head; and (2) convoke a "national council made up of all diocesan bishops of the Russian Orthodox Church . . . which should deliberate on all ecclesiastical questions and should elect the patriarch."[11]

The tsar's response of March 31 was favorable, but suggested a postponement of the *sobor* (council) owing to the current revolutionary turmoil. But the reforming zeal continued: some diocesan bishops began to convoke diocesan assemblies in preparation for the national sobor, while the Synod requested all the bishops to send in reports on their ideas regarding reforms in the Church. A careful reading of these memoranda, which were published in three huge volumes, will dissipate most of the preconceived opinions as to the reactionary character of the Russian higher clergy of the time. Of all the bishops, only one, of Turkestan, was against restoring the patriarchal system. The majority proposed major reforms in the organizational structure of the Church—e.g., reintroduction of the patriarchal-conciliar system of

---

[9]Antonov, xxiii-xxiv; S.D. Babushkin, *Tserkovno-prikhodskaya obshchina i zemskii sobor* (Kazan, 1905).

[10]I. Smolitsch, "Predsobornoe prisutstvie 1906 g.," *Put'*, no. 38 (1933) 65-75.

[11]Ibid., 67-9; and N.D. Kuznetsov, *Po voprosam tserkovynkh preobrazovanii* (Moscow, 1907) 5.

administration with wide autonomy from the state, decentralization of the Church into self-governing metropolitan districts formed in accordance with either geographic or national-ethnic criteria, major reforms in clerical and theological education, greater autonomy for and activization of the parish, a gradual return to the apostolic tradition of election of clerical candidates by the parishes and replacement of the bureaucratic church administration by one made up of the bishops assisted by councils of priests and laymen. Some liturgical reforms were likewise suggested. Most bishops recognized the necessity of at least some lay representation in the central national sobors of the Church; only a small minority wanted to limit them to bishops alone, while on the other extreme there was the minority headed by Metropolitan Antony Vadkovsky, who wanted equal voting and decision-making rights for the lower clergy and laymen in the councils on all questions except those of canons and dogma.[12] All these hopes and dreams of a sobor that would at last return the Russian Orthodox Church to the canonical path after two centuries of canonical irregularity were, however, dealt a heavy blow by the refusal of Nicholas II to permit its convocation in the foreseeable future. This resolution by the tsar was issued on April 25, 1907, in response to the report of the Preconciliar Commission, which had met between March 8 and December 15, 1906 and which had requested the convocation of a constituent national sobor.[13]

[12]See the *Otzyvy*, in particular Tikhon (Belavin), 1:530-7; Antony (Vadkovsky), 3:83-108; Sergii (Stragorodsky), 3:259-90; and, on the extreme right, Antony (Khrapovitsky), 1:112-48 and 3:186-94. See also Smolitsch, 65-75; and Kuznetsov, 5. On the diocesan assemblies and the enthusiasm evoked by the same, see Bishop Mikhail of Minsk in *Otzyvy*, 1:37; and A. Vasiliev, *Pervoe yavlenie voskresayushchei sobornosti* (St. Petersburg, 1906) 3-13. The latter discusses the Riga Diocesan Assembly, which had set up foundations for autonomous, self-governing parishes and had given the right to each parish to decide the role that women may play in the activities and governing bodies of the parish, etc.

[13]Smolitsch, 75. The original, March 1905 Synod report to the tsar, requesting only a council of bishops rather than of the whole clergy and lay representatives, caused a heated public controversy with many published attacks on the Synod for trying to replace a genuine sobor with a bureaucratic *ersatz*. Church fathers and theologians were cited to affirm the canonicity of laity-clergy councils. For example, N. Aksakov cited Athanasius the Great to the effect that "a sobor consists of an assembly of people and bishops"; the theologian N.P. Gilyarov-Platonov wrote as far back as 1871 that an immediate convocation of a laity-clergy sobor was necessary to settle the most topical common problems and doubts; and the St. Petersburg Academy theology professor Fr. Mikhail (Semenov) suggested that in

Consequently, as pointed out by many authors, a paradoxical situation prevailed: the legalized schismatics and sectarians, now independent of the state, began to hold conferences and councils resulting in their activization, greater dynamism and an offensive of sorts against the national Church.[14] The latter, deprived of such privileges, remained static, lacking a horizontal cohesiveness and local dynamism in her bureaucratized, pyramidal subordination to a Synod consisting of almost powerless bishop-figureheads and a secular bureaucratic overseer, an outsider. It has been argued that the greatest defect of the synodal structure was this duality and the absence of an integrated, responsible master-administrator at the top.[15]

This governmental stifling of the Church's dynamic forces and potentials, as well as occasional ordinations of Rasputin's favorites on the tsar's orders,[16] caused considerable resentment toward the monarchy within the Church. This was further enhanced by the general frustration with the unsatisfactory progress of World War I and its heavy casualties. The Church had to wait for the 1917 Revolution to be able at last to convoke her first national or local council in over two hundred years.

order to expedite the election of the patriarch a council of bishops would be sufficient, but then the patriarch would have to convoke a full laity-clergy sobor for other church matters. See Aksakov, "Chto govoryat kanony o sostave sobora?" in *Tserkovnyi golos* (St. Petersburg, 1906) 29; Gilyarov-Platonov, *Voprosy very i tserkvi* (Moscow, 1905) 1:221-9; Mikhail, *Pochemu nam ne veryat?* (St. Petersburg, 1906) 53-63.

[14]Simon "Church, State and Society," 206-12. For conferences and other local activities of the Evangelical sectarians, see Ivan Prokhanov, *In the Cauldron of Russia, 1869-1933* (New York, 1933) 150-1. In 1906, the Third Congress of Moslems of All Russia met in Nizhni Novgorod; in 1909, the First All-Russian Sobor of the Priestless Old Believers convened, etc. See Bishop Aleksii (Dorodnitsyn), *Polnoe sobranie sochinenii* (Saratov, 1913-1914) 3:394; Pervyi vserossiiskii sobor khristian-pomortsev, priemlyushchikh brak, *Deyaniya* (Moscow, 1909).

[15]Nominally the head of the Synod was the Metropolitan of St. Petersburg, but it was the tsar who personally appointed bishops to that see, and consequently they were almost always either unprincipled bureaucrats or weak and pliable characters. Even the well-meaning Antony (Vadkovsky) belonged to the latter category. See Fr. Georgy Shavelsky, *Vospominaniya* (New York: Chekhov, 1954) 2:136.

[16]Among the Rasputinite bishops Shavelsky names the following: Makary, Metropolitan of Moscow; Pitirim, Metropolitan of Petrograd; the future Ukrainophile Aleksii (Dorodnitsyn); Seraphim (Chichagov); and Pallady. Ibid., 59.

CHAPTER 1

The Revolution and the Church

Lacking canonical administration (a patriarch) and the traditional conciliar system, which would have fed the center with information from the periphery, the Church as an institution entered the revolution divided and uninformed about the ideas and feelings of her own lower clergy and parishioners. She also lost her temporal head of two hundred years, once Nicholas II had abdicated. In short, at such a decisive moment of general collapse the Church lacked the organizational mechanism of a self-ruling institution. And it was common knowledge to every responsible churchman that the old monarchic establishment was to blame for this sorry state of affairs.

These moods were reflected in the Synod's refusal to satisfy the request of its overprocurator to appeal to the nation "to support the crumbling monarchy." Instead, on March 17, 1917, it gave full support to the Grand Duke Michael's decision to refuse the offer of the throne and to leave the question of the future form of government to the free decision of the future national Constituent Assembly. And on July 26 it acclaimed the events as "the hour of general freedom for Russia; the whole land . . . rejoiced over the bright new days of its life."[1]

The moods of the lower clergy and of some of the laity were generally rather radical immediately after the installation of the Provisional Government. In March 1917, "clerical and lay members of the Duma and certain other leaders of Russian society

[1]Simon, *Church, State,* 28; and Regelson, 26-7 and 202-7.

25

formed a Council for Affairs of the Orthodox Church; its existence however was brief. . . . a number of diocesan gatherings of clergy adopted liberal resolutions supporting the Provisional Government and favoring a sobor . . . the Ekaterinodar diocesan congress asked that bishops be elected by the clergy and laymen of the dioceses, from candidates from the married clergy as well as from the monastics." The same gathering asked for the distribution of large estates among needy peasants, except for church lands needed to support the clergy. Thus, contrary to the claims of Soviet propaganda, the laity did not view the village priest as a parasite. Similar assemblies with liberal and radical resolutions met in the dioceses of Petrograd, Kiev, Kishinev, Tver, etc. In Moscow, an All-Russian Congress of Clergy and Laity gathered in June 1917 and adopted resolutions calling for popular sovereignty in Church and state, the handing over of land to the cultivators and labor reforms for factory workers. On internal church affairs and issues dealing with the clergy, however, the resolutions were very moderate. "In several dioceses . . . stormy diocesan congresses . . . deposed their bishops. . . . A Moscow diocesan assembly [of clergy and laity] elected Tikhon as Metropolitan of Moscow and a Petrograd diocesan assembly elected . . . Venyamin as Metropolitan of Petrograd."[2]

Vladimir Lvov, the overprocurator of the reinstated Synod, purged that body of its most reactionary elements. The new Synod, under this pressure, adopted a regulation that henceforth bishops be elected by assemblies of clergy and laity of their dioceses, in accordance with the practice and canons of the early Church. A wave of such assemblies in most cases reelected the incumbents, and peace soon prevailed within the Church, after the removal of a few of the most reactionary bishops from their dioceses.

The Provisional Government granted permission to convoke an all-Russian sobor of bishops, lower clergy and laity. The preparatory work for the sobor was carried out by the First All-Russian Preparatory Conference of Clergy and Laity, which began its sessions on June 11/24 in Moscow. It was there that the two main opposing views on the future form of church administration became most prominent. One, represented by Professor Pokrovsky, was in favor of a complete separation between the Church and

[2]Curtiss, *Russian Church*, 15-7.

the state and wanted a synodal-conciliar structure of church administration. The other view, represented in particular by Prince E. Trubetskoi and Sergius Bulgakov, although equally in favor of religious freedom, wanted the retention of a special status for Orthodoxy as a national Church, *primus inter pares.* The Church, they argued, being organically intertwined with the nation, its culture and its state, cannot be wholly separated from the national organism, i.e., the national state.[3]

The only lasting conflict between the Church and the state under the Provisional Government was over parochial schools, which were confiscated and nationalized, contrary to the wishes of the Church. Complete religious freedom was granted by the Provisional Government to all confessions, but the Orthodox Church succeeded in retaining the title of the state religion. The special status of the Orthodox Church was reflected in the decree of the Provisional Government of August 5/18 abolishing the old Synod and replacing it by a state Department for Religious Affairs. The prerogatives of this department would be subject to change in accordance with the principles established by the forthcoming Orthodox sobor. The Minister and both of his deputies, one for the Orthodox Church and the other for all other faiths, would have to belong to the *Orthodox* Church.[4]

The All-Russian Preparatory Conference drafted detailed regulations on elections for and representation at the forthcoming sobor, and these were approved by the Synod on July 10/23. The date for the opening of the sobor was set at August 15/28, 1917. The sobor opened with 563 voting members and with the internal divisions well represented. The left wing, consisting of some theology professors, both lay and clerical, as well as many well-educated, ambitious, urban married priests, favored the weakening

[3] A.I. Vvedensky, *Tserkov' i gosudarstvo* (Moscow, 1923) 39-46. This Orthodox idea of *sobornost'*—i.e., of the spiritual responsibility of the Church for the whole collectivity of the national flock, not just for the individuals—was very well expressed by one of the most intelligent bishops of the Russian Orthodox Church, Andrei (Ukhtomsky), in a conversation with Kerensky in 1917: "To separate the Russian state from the Church would mean a separation of the nation from its conscience, its deprivation of moral foundations." Mark Popovsky, "Protopop Avvakum XX veka," *Russkaya mysl'* (August 27, 1981) 12.

[4] "Postanovlenie vremennogo pravitel'stva ob uchrezhdenii Ministerstva Ispovedanii," Svyashchennyi Sobor Pravoslavnoi Rossiiskoi Tserkvi, *Deyaniya* (Moscow, 1918) 1:52.

of the monastic-episcopal domination, preferring a synodal-plural-ist-democratic system of church administration where the voice of a delegate from the lower clergy would have equal weight with that of a bishop.[5] Before the revolution, some of these elements were in favor of restoring the patriarchal system as a means of greater independence of the Church from the tsar. But after the fall of the monarchy, their more radical representatives began to oppose the idea of a patriarch as monarchic, preferring a popularly elected synod made up of bishops, the lower clergy and laymen—all with equal voting rights.

Original documents do not bear out the later claims of Renovationist authors that at first the antipatriarch opinion had prevailed and "only the October coup d'etat forced the sobor center [i.e., the moderates] to swing to the right." This apparently was true of the atmosphere at the Preconciliar Commission where, according to the partisan testimony of the Renovationist Professor A.I. Pokrovsky, "even bishops, with the Archbishop [Stragorodsky] at their head, buried the idea,"[6] but at the sobor, at least seven days prior to the October Bolshevik coup, it was stated that the number of speakers in favor of restoration of the patriarchate exceeded that of its opponents. That the sobor majority favored a patriarch was confirmed by a passionate opponent of the patriarchate, Professor Titlinov, as early as October 21/November 3, 1917.[7]

The propatriarchal majority consisted of the conservatives, who wanted a strong patriarchal-episcopal system conceding only a consultative function to the lower clergy and laity; and the moderates, including many neophytic intellectuals (e.g., the professor, later priest, Sergius Bulgakov), who also favored restoration of the patriarchal system but with a strong conciliar representation of bishops, laity and priests, acting in a harmonious unity with

[5]Ibid., 3-51; also Alexander Bogolepov, *Church Reforms in Russia, 1905-1918* (Bridgeport, Conn.: Committee of the Metropolitan Council of the Russian Orthodox Church of America, 1966), 27 et passim.

[6]"O sobornosti, mitropolich'ikh okrugakh i patriarshestve," *VSS*, no. 2 (1925) 15. Archimandrite Illarion (Troitsky) also confirms that the Preconciliar Commission reached a negative decision regarding the patriarchate (*Deyaniya*, 2:382). Likewise, none of the documents announcing the forthcoming sobor (see note 5 above) mention the restoration of the patriarchate as its aim.

[7]Astrov's statement at the sobor on October 18/31; Fr. N.P. Dobronravov and Prof. B.V. Titlinov, on October 21/November 3. *Deyaniya*, 2A:339, 346 and 355.

each other rather than in divisive separate chambers, but still guaranteeing priority to the bishops. It was this line that prevailed in the whole organization of the Moscow Sobor, where all three categories of delegates deliberated jointly in a single chamber and voted as equal individuals. Subsequently, however, the bills went for final approval to a separate session of bishops, the same bishops, now sitting separately, who had earlier deliberated and voted on the same bill in the general assembly. If, nevertheless, the bishops' session were to reject the bill, it would repeat the journey to the general assembly and back to the bishops' session, and would be dropped altogether on the latter's second rejection.[8]

Among the arguments in favor of a patriarchate was the opinion of many that the Provisional Government, by virtue of its pluralist nature, would be at best alien to the interests of the Church; therefore the Church needed, particularly in this hour of uncertainty, a strong personal leadership of a patriarch working in full consultation with the whole body of the Church via an effective conciliar system with broad prerogatives.[9] This view clearly prevailed during the session of October 28/November 10, with 346 delegates present. The Renovationists later claimed that when the propatriarchal party had prevailed, the antipatriarchals left and did not participate in the elections. But their numbers could not have been very impressive and could not have accounted for the high absenteeism in relation to the nominal number of delegates, for even at the session of September 20/October 3, when there was no question of any protest departures, only 419 delegates were present. This fell to 304 on October 31/November 13, when the actual elections of the patriarch began. In the last stage of the election the numbers again increased to 364 (November 5/18), and the total number of radical antipatriarchals could not have been much more than sixty persons—i.e., about 11 percent of the total sobor membership. The other absences must have been caused by the material and other uncertainties of those

---

[8]Bogolepov, *Church Reforms*, 40-7; and "Ustav sobora," *Deyaniya*, 1:38-51.
[9]This relates in particular to the session of October 18/31. A certain D.I. Volkov spoke in these terms about the Provisional Government and received broad support from the participants. Most of the propatriarchals were also in favor of a strong conciliar representation. *Deyaniya*, 2A (sessions of October 18/31 to October 28/November 10, 1917).

troublesome days. Indeed, by February 1918 the number of participants would dwindle to about two hundred.[10]

Among the crucial speeches swinging the sobor definitely in favor of a patriarch were those of Archimandrite Illarion (Troitsky), the brilliant young theologian and future chief adviser to Patriarch Tikhon, and of Professor Bulgakov. Both were left-of-center, and this may have made their opinions particularly effective. Illarion argued from the point of view of historical and canonical theology, attacking Peter the Great in no uncertain terms and stressing that when the patriarchs ruled the Russian Church, they did so in close consultation with the sobors, and Peter the Great, in liquidating the patriarchate, also liquidated *sobornost'*.[11] The Christian-socialist and former Marxist Bulgakov stressed the particular necessity for a patriarch at the current "turning point, before an unknown future and the frightful present." He also pointed to the cumbersome, bureaucratic and inflexible synodal system, which lacked a head who could direct the Church more effectively, particularly in the times of opening vistas in interfaith relations—e.g., with the Anglicans and the Old Catholics.[12] But perhaps no less effective, reflecting the prevalent moods of the believing peasant masses, were the words of one peasant delegate who said: "We have a tsar no more; no father whom we love. It is impossible to love a synod; and therefore we, the peasants, want a patriarch."[13]

The electoral process itself consisted of two stages:

> Three candidates for the patriarchate were elected by the whole Sacred Council: bishops, clergy and laity. Then, following the example of the selection of the Apostle Matthias (Acts 1:23-26), lots were drawn to determine which of the three was to be patriarch.[14]

[10]See the relevant volumes of *Deyaniya*.

[11]Illarion made no secret of his condemnation of Peter the Great and of the tsar's interference in church affairs in general in his numerous oral and written statements long before the revolution. See S.A. Volkov, "Arkhiepiskop Illarion (Troitsky)," *VRKhD*, no. 134 (1981) 227-33.

[12]Ibid., 377-83; and appendix 1 to session 31, *Deyaniya*, 2:17-21.

[13]Prince Grigory N. Trubetskoi, *Krasnaya Rossiya i svyataya Rus'* (Paris, 1931) 42.

[14]Bogolepov, *Church Reforms*, 50.

Although, in the absence of the leftist delegates, Metropolitan Antony Khrapovitsky, the leader of the extreme right wing and staunch supporter of episcopal hegemony (who had lost his seat in the Synod under the Provisional Government), received the majority of the electoral votes, the draw favored Tikhon Belavin, Metropolitan of Moscow. A moderate and tolerant man by nature, Tikhon had spent a number of years prior to 1907 as the ruling bishop of the Russian Orthodox missionary archdiocese of North America, where he did much to cultivate the conciliar principle in church administration and practices.[15]

Right from the beginning Patriarch Tikhon faced passive opposition from the right and militant opposition from the left, soon to erupt into an open revolt.

The Sobor and Lenin's State

Consistent with the primitive Marxist doctrine according to which religion is but a part of the superstructure on the material base, Lenin had apparently thought at first that he would kill the Church by depriving her of all her real estate. His decree of November 8 nationalizing all land made the Church's and parish priests' landholdings illegal. This decree was further spelled out in all detail on February 19 to specifically deprive the Church of the right to own real estate. This was a logical consequence of Lenin's decree of January 23, which separated the Church from the state and nationalized all former church property (houses of prayer, schools, seminaries, monasteries, candle factories, charity institutions, etc.). It also deprived the Church of the status of a legal person and of the right to acquire property in the future, banning at the same time state subsidies for all religious bodies. Henceforth, property needed for religious use was to be leased by the local government bodies to individual religious associations free of charge, but only when and if the local government body found that it could dispose of vacant property for this purpose. Once leased, the property was subject to regular taxes levied on private enterprise. Some six thousand church and monastic buildings were further confiscated from the Orthodox Church on the

---

[15]*Orthodox America*, 83-101.

basis of this decree as having special historical and/or archeo-
logical-architectural value. A decree of January 28 nationalized all
bank accounts belonging to religious associations.

The decree of January 23 also banned the teaching of religion
in all general education schools, whether state or private, and
forbade the Church to open any schools of a general nature, or
even Sunday schools, to teach exclusively religious subjects. "Citizens may teach and be taught religion [only] privately." The term
"citizens" would henceforth always be interpreted as adults only.
All church and religious associations were declared subject to the
laws governing *private* associations, rather than those governing
social organizations, and were deprived of the right to impose any
obligatory dues, reprimands or punishments on their members.[16]
Since only groups of laymen were recognized as the contractual
party in the leasing of the church property, the clergy, including
bishops and the patriarch, became legally superfluous, retaining
authority with the faithful only as long as the latter agreed to
accept them and to fulfil their bishops' orders, which now became
more like petitions than orders. This situation obviously invited
all types of schisms, which were soon to appear.

A decree of June 13, 1921 declared only such sermons legal
which would be limited to purely religious subjects, without ever
defining these terms and thus opening another wide margin for
arbitrary acts against the clergy. Further decrees, of April 27 and
June 19, 1923, legalized the closure of churches and their confiscation from religious associations if the buildings were needed
"for other use," and dissolution of these associations by local
government bodies on the grounds of "political unreliability and
anti-Sovietism" on the part of their members. Many churches were
also closed in these years when the government authorities formally agreed to lease them to believers on certain days of the week,
but on others allowed them to be used as clubs and dancing
places. Believers refused to celebrate services in churches on such
conditions, viewing this as desecration of their churches. Thus, a
church would cease to function as if it had been closed voluntarily

---

[16]See the January decree in *Sistematicheskoe sobranie zakonov RSFSR, ukazov
prezidiuma Verkhovnogo Soveta RSFSR i reshenii Pravitel'stva RSFSR* (Moscow,
1968) 2:537-8.

by the believers—one of the legal gimmicks used by the official press.[17]

The sobor continued its sessions with occasional intervals until September 1918, when it had to close down for lack of funds, caused by the Bolshevik measures just mentioned. Thus, it could not complete all its legislative and reform plans, including a liturgical reform, but nevertheless it did pass the necessary legislation to give the Church once again her canonical conciliar structure, all the way from the local parish[18] (which received a model statute adopted from that of the Russian missionary parishes in the USA, implemented there by Tikhon during his tenure as the diocesan bishop) to the office of the patriarch. It declared the sobor of bishops, priests and laymen "the supreme legislative, administrative, judicial and auditing authority," to be convoked periodically by the patriarch. The latter, declared *"primus inter pares"* among the bishops, became the chairman of the sobors as well as of the Synod of Bishops and of the Higher Church Council. The Synod would consist of thirteen members: the Patriarch-Chairman and the Metropolitan of Kiev as permanent members, plus six bishops elected for three-year terms by the sobors (which were thus to meet at least once every three years), and five bishops chosen from the dioceses by the Synod by rota for twelve-month terms. The whole empire was to be divided into five autonomous metropolitan districts with a metropolitan at the head and numerous dioceses within each. The five rota bishops in the Synod were to represent the five metropolias. The Higher Church Council would consist of three bishops from the Synod, as elected by the Synod, and the following members elected by the national sobor for three-year terms: one monk representing the monasteries, five members of the lower clergy and six laymen. Questions relating to theology, religious discipline and ecclesiastical administration were to be the prerogative of the Synod. Secular-juridical, charity and other church-related social questions were to be the prerogative of the Higher Church Council. Both bodies would function between the convocations of the sobors.

[17]Bogolepov, *Tserkov'*, 10-5.
[18]*Prikhodskii ustav pravoslavnoi tserkvi,* the Parish Statute adopted by the Sobor of the Russian Orthodox Church on April 7/20, 1918 (Warsaw, 1922) 1-28.

The patriarch's prerogatives were effectively curbed by the powers of the two collective bodies. Provisions were made for the disciplining and even forced retirement of the patriarch by a full council of all bishops of the country convoked on the decision of a joint session of the Synod and the Higher Church Council.[19]

The sobor reintroduced the ancient Orthodox practice of election of bishops by diocesan councils of clergy and laity. Episcopal candidates were to be nominated by the Synod and/or by the given diocese subject to synodal approval on the basis of moral, religious and theological competence. The elected and consecrated bishop would remain in the diocese for life. Normally, only a higher ecclesiastical court would be able to remove and/or retire a bishop. Only in "exceptional circumstances, for the good of the Church, may a bishop be appointed or moved about from one diocese to another by the higher church authority." Bishops were to rule their dioceses together with elected diocesan councils on the patriarchal model.[20]

The other important purely ecclesiastical decrees of the sobor included those on preaching, monasticism and the activization of women in the Church. The one on preaching (December 1/14, 1917) stipulated that sermons be delivered at all liturgical services, not just on Sundays and great feasts—as had been the usual prerevolutionary practice. In addition to bishops and priests, deacons, psalmists and dedicated laymen were to be encouraged to deliver sermons and to preach the word of God to congregations. The institution of "gospel-messengers," or lay preachers, was to be developed, and the use of local dialects in place of a formal language was to be encouraged to reach the broad masses of believers. Special preachers' fraternities were to be set up at the diocesan headquarters. Similar fraternities were to be set up at monasteries and convents to enlighten pilgrims. Seminaries and other theological schools were encouraged to pay particular attention to the art of preaching and to organize special training programs for the clergy and laity for this purpose. The decree emphasized the im-

---

[19]Svyashchennyi Sobor Pravoslavnoi Rossiiskoi Tserkvi, *Sobranie opredelenii i postanovlenii: Prilozheniya k Deyaniyam* (Moscow, 1918) 1:7-16, 4:3-12.

[20]Ibid., 1:17-22, etc.

portance of an enlightened sermon in the conditions of a secular-atheistic state.[21]

The decree on monasticism restored autonomy and internal democracy to the monastic institutions and assigned a greater role in religious enlightenment and education to monasteries. It also called for such things as the establishment of monastic theological academies and other schools for a proper education of monks and nuns to carry on their mission to the world. For intermonastic cooperation and information, periodic conferences of monastic delegates were to take place each time on the eve of the all-Russian church sobors. Monastic scholars and other learned monks were to form an All-Russian Monastic Brotherhood of Church Enlightenment, with several monasteries especially designated for their residence and work. The decree made a conscientious effort to integrate academic monasticism into the regular monastic institution by obligating the so-called "learned monks" to observe all the monastic vows and spiritual discipline as strictly as possible and to reside in actual monasteries as much as their professional duties would permit.[22]

On the subject of women, the sobor adopted a resolution on September 7/20, 1918, "recognizing the usefulness of the active participation of women in serving the Church in all fields corresponding to their particular qualifications." These included participation in parish meetings and membership in parish councils, with such functions as those of church wardens; the right to participate in deanery and diocesan conferences; and the right to hold all offices in the educational, charitable, missionary and economic institutions of the Church. They are not, however, to hold offices in the deanery or diocesan councils, nor in the judicial and administrative institutions of the Church. Also, in exceptional situations women are to be allowed to serve as psalmists and readers on a par with men, but without the status of members

[21]Ibid., 2:9-12, 4:31-43 and 47. There were also the important decrees on those Old Believers who were in communion with the Orthodox Church but retained their ritual: their status was now fully equalized with that of the other Orthodox. A decree on clerics defrocked or otherwise banned before the revolution opened the way to and resulted in the reinstatement of those who had been under bans for political reasons—including, for instance, Fr. Grigory Petrov, one of the founders of the St. Petersburg group of reformers of 1905. See the relevant decrees in ibid., 2:3-5, 4:45.

[22]Ibid., 4:42-3.

of the clergy.[23] The reintroduction of the ancient institution of deaconesses was likewise discussed at the sobor in a positive context. Had not the sobor been forced to abruptly discontinue its sessions, owing to the shortage of funds caused by the nationalization of the Church's bank accounts, the reinstitution of deaconesses would most probably have been approved.

At the end of the sobor, two extraordinary decisions were adopted. One granted the patriarch unrestricted administrative powers in case the Soviet government made it impossible to convoke a sobor or for the Synod to function. The other instructed the patriarch to compose a will with the names of three persons to replace him as locum tenentes should he become incapacitated or die and should the Soviets prevent the convocation of a sobor.[24]

Along with these wise and constructive decrees, most of which could not be implemented in the ensuing conditions of chaos and persecutions, the sobor passed a number of decrees directly bearing on Church-state relationships that were quite unrealistic in the light of the new Soviet conditions and Lenin's aforementioned legislation. These reflected the widespread belief at the time in Russia that the Bolsheviks would not remain in power for any substantial length of time. Even the decree on monasticism, issued on August 31/September 13, 1918, demonstrated disregard for the Soviet law of January 23 inasmuch as it stipulated that all monastic possessions and real estate "are owned by the monastery and constitute the property of the whole Russian Orthodox Church," whereas Lenin had not only deprived the Church of property but denied her any right of acquiring it. On the other hand, a decree of August 30/September 12, 1918, "On the Protection of the Church's Sacred Objects against Blasphemous Seizure and Desecration," was a direct response both to the early Soviet decrees against the Church and to the still mostly haphazard persecutions and attacks on the churches. It prescribed no violence against the state, but, in cases of seizure of a church, instructed the parish communities not to disband but to keep the priest and

[23]Ibid., 4:27.

[24]Metropolitan Elevfery of Lithuania, *Moi otvet Mitr. Antoniyu* (Paris, 1935) 15 et passim. While inspecting the first nine of the eleven volumes of the full stenographic report of the Moscow Sobor (*Deyaniya*), I did not find the texts of these decisions.

hold services privately.[25] This decree obviously prepared the Orthodox people for the so-called catacomb existence and continuation of the Church during and after the holocausts of the 1930s and again in the 1960s.

But the decree that went totally against the new militantly atheistic social system was the one of December 2/15, 1917, "On the Legal Status of the Russian Orthodox Church." Indeed, it could even have provoked the particular harshness of the subsequent Soviet anti-Church laws. Not only did it continue to claim a legal precedence for the Orthodox Church as the national Church of Russia, but ruled that the state should issue no law relating to the Church without prior consultation with and approval by the Church. On the other hand, any decrees and by-laws issued by the Orthodox Church that did not directly contradict state laws were to be automatically recognized by the state as legally binding. Church holidays were to remain state holidays, blasphemy and attempts to lure members of the Church away from her were to remain illegal, and schools of all levels organized and run by the Church were to be recognized by the state on a par with the secular schools. But the most unrealistic stipulation, coming nearly six weeks after Lenin's coup d'etat, was: "The head of the Russian state, the ministers of religion and of education and their deputies must belong to the Orthodox Church."[26]

Although the conciliar system proved to be an impossibility under the new regime at the top, at the parish level the new responsibility granted to the parish councils and the security of priests' tenure, in the opinion of many church historians, saved the Church from disintegration in the years of the practically total collapse of the central church administration caused by the

[25]The first warning of the things to come was the report to the sobor given by a sobor commission, headed by Bishop Nestor of Kamchatka, which had just inspected the churches and monasteries in the Kremlin after its storming by the Red troops on November 15-16, 1917: "During only a few hours of Red control of the Kremlin the churches have been desecrated and icons shot at . . . ." These acts had nothing to do with the damages caused by the storming itself. The report was published by the patriarchate in Moscow in a run of ten thousand copies, almost all of which were destroyed by the Bolsheviks. A second edition was published in Tokyo in 1920. P. Kovalevsky, "Tserkov' v SSSR za sorok let," *Russkaya mysl'* (November 7, 1957) 6. The text of the decree is in *Sobranie opredelenii,* 4:28-30.
[26]Ibid., 2:6-8.

cited state legislation, by periodical arrests of bishops and by the proliferation of schismatic groups.[27] It also reintroduced the ancient Orthodox practice of electing candidates for episcopal ordination by local diocesan assemblies of clergy and laity. Historians have observed that in those dioceses where this practice came into use, and where, consequently, the ruling bishops were chosen by the believers, loyalty to the patriarch prevailed.[28] Resistance against the schismatic movements of the 1920s and against other government intrigues was much more consolidated and effective in such dioceses than in those where the old centralized system remained intact.

The sobor gave full support to Patriarch Tikhon's encyclical of January 19, 1918, which admonished the Soviet government for its anti-Church actions and for the persecutions and terror. The encyclical excommunicated all those "open and secret enemies of [Christ's] Truth" who are engaged in "persecutions . . . and in sowing the seeds of hatred and . . . fratricide." The response of the believers was that of full and enthusiastic support for their patriarch, demonstrated especially during his triumphant visit to Petrograd in May 1918: his whole route from the railway station to the cathedral was filled with kneeling crowds. This and similar demonstrations of support gave him the needed assurance for his extremely frank address to Lenin on the first anniversary of the October Revolution: after a recital of the crimes of the Bolshevik regime, he requested a cessation of bloodshed and of further persecution of the faith. The state retaliated: in the course of 1918-1920 at least twenty-eight bishops were murdered, thousands of clerics were imprisoned or killed, and twelve thousand laymen were reported to have been killed for religious activities alone. After internal debates on the subject, the Soviet government decided not to arrest the patriarch himself, who was protected by a round-the-clock unarmed volunteer guard of the faithful. The patriarch was deprived of ration cards as a "bourgeois parasite" and was fed by the donations of the faithful. Church printing

[27]Struve, 30-1.

[28]For instance, Stratonov, *Smuta*, 58-9. This is acknowledged in a roundabout way by some Soviet antireligious writers, e.g., those cited in Fletcher, *Church Underground*, 38-42.

establishments were confiscated and some churches and monasteries shut.[29]

The Soviet government issued two contradictory circulars. One, of December 1918, condemned the arbitrary closing of churches and other acts of suppression of religious practices. The other, of March 1, 1919, ordered the opening of the relics of the saints. This was followed by another order of August 1920 to proceed "to the complete liquidation of the cult of corpses and mummies" by transferring them to state museums.[30] The resistance of the faithful and the clergy resulted in further arrests, trials and deportations of thousands to prison camps or to prescribed areas of exile under surveillance.

The patriarch decided on a course of civil loyalty to the Soviet regime and issued an encyclical on September 25, 1919 ordering the clergy to stand aloof from politics of any kind and freeing the faithful from all political obligations on the grounds that the Church and the state had been separated by the Soviet Constitution of July 1918. This was the turning point in the Church's policy toward the new government. The faithful were to remain loyal to the new government as long as its orders did not contradict their religious conscience. As far as the Civil War was concerned, the freedom from political obligations allowed each cleric to choose his own political stance while releasing the Church from any institutional responsibility for those clerics who would support the White Armies. The patriarch categorically refused to send even secret blessings to the White Armies, for the Church could not bless fratricidal war.[31] (It goes without saying that the faithful would receive no blessings for fighting on the Red side after the above-cited act of excommunication, although the Soviet government was not mentioned in it by name.) At the same time, he did send his blessings to the imprisoned tsar and his family; but this was an act of Christian compassion for the suffering quite apart from the Civil War, although Soviet propaganda would deliberately confuse the two issues in its attacks against the patriarch in the course of the 1920s.

[29]Spinka, 19-24.
[30]Struve, 31-2.
[31]Ibid., 33.

The Status of Orthodoxy in Relation to Other Confessions

Describing these early years of Bolshevik administration, the leader of the Russian sectarian Christian-Evangelical movement, Ivan Prokhanov, says that they were marked by "an unprecedented persecution of the Greek Orthodox clergy and the Church."[32] The aim was apparently to destroy the *national* Church, as the spiritual backbone of the nation, first.

To facilitate this the Bolsheviks on the whole tried to gain the friendship or at least neutrality of the other religions. This policy of dividing believers in their attitudes to the new political system was implemented by presenting the attacks in official statements as not against religious beliefs but against the elements who had enjoyed privileges under the old regime and thus were allegedly guilty of counterrevolutionary activities. Two religious groups even had special representation in the top government and party echelons. In 1918, a Moslem Commissariat was set up under the chairmanship of a Moslem mullah, Nur Vakhitov. The other group, the Jews, had special Jewish sections formed within the Communist Party of the Soviet Union. To be sure, these were to represent the Jews as a nationality, not as a religion, and one of their purposes was to stamp out the Judaic faith and to secularize Jewish culture and education. But, as opposed to Russian Orthodoxy—or any other religion later on—whose churches were often forcibly shut by the decision of the local party, government or communist youth bodies, synagogues could be closed only by the Jewish sections of the local party bodies, which consisted of Jews alone.[33]

Some religious groups tried to make use of the new situation. Both the Evangelicals and the Roman Catholics (whether of Latin or Greek rite) at first rejoiced over the decree on the separation of Church and state. Although the Roman Catholics had valuable real estate, they at first thought that the confiscation of church property related only to the Orthodox, as the formerly ruling Church. But a frontal attack against the Roman Catholic Church

---

[32]*In the Cauldron*, 165.

[33]See this author's "Russian Nationalist Thought and the Jewish Question," *Soviet Jewish Affairs* 6:1 (1976) 8.

began in 1923, and by the end of the 1920s, lacking, in contrast to the Orthodox, a mass popular base, the Catholic Church virtually ceased to exist in the USSR, except for a handful of individual parishes in the largest cities.[34] The toleration of the Evangelicals and other sects lasted longer, most probably owing to their oppression under the old regime, the humble social origins of most of their clergy (although many came from wealthy merchant families) and the greater emphasis on social and economic egalitarianism in their doctrines. In 1919 the Evangelical peasants, with the permission of the Soviet government, began to set up collective farms with a sample statute drawn up by Prokhanov. Whereas all the petitions of Patriarch Tikhon and later of Metropolitan Sergii to permit the opening of Orthodox theological seminaries and the establishment of a regular religious press remained unheeded,[35] the Evangelicals published several religious periodicals, ran theological colleges and organized conferences and rallies up until the end of 1928.[36]

The first five-year plan, with its attack against the peasants, kulaks and private entrepreneurs, and with the destruction of religion as one of its undeclared aims, spared no religion: all faiths, temples and believers were henceforth persecuted more or less indiscriminately.

[34]James Zatko, *Descent into Hell: The Destruction of the Roman Catholic Church in Russia, 1917-1923* (Notre Dame, Ind.: University Press, 1965) 65 and 72-3.

[35]In 1918, after the confiscation of all ecclesiastic educational facilities by the state, several attempts were made in Moscow, Petrograd and some other cities to carry on with some form of regular theological education for adults, legally or clandestinely. In Moscow there began to function in 1918 a Theological People's Academy, which the civil authorities forced to shut down after the arrest of Patriarch Tikhon in 1922, whereupon it continued to function secretly under the leadership of Bishop Varfolomei (Remov) until 1936, when it was betrayed to the NKVD. All students and professors were arrested and the bishop executed. A theological institute functioned legally in Petrograd from 1919 to 1922, and then in secret for several years more. See Chrysostomus, 3:63-5 et passim; and Hegumen Georgy, "Dukhovnye uchebnye zavedeniya v SSSR," *Russkaya pravoslavnaya tserkov' v SSSR* (Munich, 1962) 196-7.

[36]Prokhanov, 137-9, 175-7, 187 and 252-8.

CHAPTER 2

Leftist Schisms within the Russian Orthodox Church

The Renovationist Schism:
Its Origins, Sources and Symptoms

There were at least two principal sources of internal conflict and frustration within the post-Petrine Orthodox Church in Russia. The most traumatic was the church reform of Peter the Great; the other was the introduction of learned monasticism.

Peter not only subordinated the Church to the imperial bureaucracy; he also separated the Church from the mainstream of Russia's cultural development. Declaring the vernacular dialect the official secular literary language and simplifying the alphabet for it, he at the same time forced the Church to continue to use Church Slavonic. Moreover, the language of instruction in the seminaries became Latin (and remained so until the 1840s). Thus, as the seminaries with time became schools exclusively reserved for clerical offspring, the clergy was turned into a self-enclosed social estate educated in one foreign language (Latin) to serve in another (Slavonic), so that with the growth and development of the Russian vernacular, the linguistic-cultural cleavage between religious and secular culture widened and deepened. (The clergy spoke the Russian vernacular with a peculiar accent and used many archaisms, which often made it the target of Russian jokes.) The educational standards of the clerical school network, which had proliferated in the eighteenth century, were high, but the

43

schools remained static after Catherine the Great had confiscated the Church's landholdings.

Once the seminaries had become the only schools accessible to priests' sons, including nonbelievers who would never become priests, the spirit of true divinity in the schools began to erode. Atheism, nihilism and revolutionary radicalism became rampant in schools that were supposed to prepare pastors for the nation. Of the 2,148 seminary graduates in 1911, only 574 were ordained by 1913. At the 1906 Preconciliar Commission the vast majority of the bishops were in favor of an immediate and drastic reform of theological education that would abolish the clerical-estate character of the seminaries. Some bishops even favored the closing of all seminaries and their replacement by genuine liturgically oriented divinity schools, to be established in monasteries and suitable rural districts.[1]

The other source of internal frustration was the system of academic or "learned" monasticism, which had nothing to do with the genuine Orthodox monastic traditions of contemplation, prayer, otherworldliness and piety. Academic monasticism was borrowed by the Kiev Theological Academy in the seventeenth century from the Roman Catholics. As theological schools based on the Latin model spread to the rest of Russia, so did the institution. "There was nothing in common between this 'learned monasticism' and the monastery monasticism, and the conflict between them sometimes reached a tragic acuteness."[2] These "monks" were for the most part students of the graduate academies who took the tonsure in order to pursue episcopal careers in the world—motivated by pride, power and ambition, in direct opposition to the real purpose of monastic tonsure. Although none of the ecumenical canons of the Church had prescribed monasticism as a condition for episcopal consecration, and some canons in fact emphasized the incompatibility of the episcopal and monastic functions,[3] the practice in both the Western and Eastern Churches, established by the end of the eighth century, was to consecrate as bishops only monks, widowed priests or at

[1]Florovsky, *Puti*, 478-9, et passim. Clergy statistics are in John S. Curtiss, *Church and State in Russia, 1900-1917* (New York: Octagon, 1940) 310-7.

[2]Florovsky, *Puti*, 340-1.

[3]See the explicit statement to this effect in Gruppa peterburgskikh svyashchennikov, *K tserkovnomu soboru* (St. Petersburg, 1906) 136-45.

least unmarried individuals who would give an oath of celibacy. This tradition doomed the married priest to remaining forever a bishop's subordinate. Yet, the dissatisfaction among the married clergy and among those theologians who refused to accept tonsure was directed not so much against genuine monasticism as against the abovementioned academic monasticism. The learned who refused tonsure remained subordinated to the less scrupulous from among their ranks, who had become bishops by means that often cast into doubt their alleged piety and moral superiority.

No sooner did the greater freedom of the Great Reforms of the 1860s permit hopes and discussions of church reforms than this antimonastic bias came to the fore. Such authors as Dmitry I. Rostislavov, a former lay theology professor, the married priest I.S. Bellyustin and lay theologians like V.I. Askochensky passionately attacked monasticism and the monastic episcopacy per se, thereby setting a precedent for the antimonastic bias of the Group of Thirty-two St. Petersburg Priests of 1905. These in their turn were among the precursors of the postrevolutionary Renovationist schism. Fr. G. Florovsky calls this antimonasticism "Protestantism of the Eastern Rite."[4]

The Church's most dedicated clergy and laity never came to terms with the uncanonical structure of the Church established by Peter the Great, and they took every opportunity to appeal to the monarch to reconstruct the Church as an autonomous institution headed by a patriarch.[5] The renewed hopes aroused by the secular reforms of Alexander II were, however, squashed by the appointment of Count Dmitry A. Tolstoi as overprocurator in 1865. Florovsky views him as a religiously indifferent person, actively hostile toward the Church and engaged in minimizing her influence in society and curbing her activities to the greatest possible extent. In the ten years of his administration, over two thousand Orthodox parishes were liquidated. He imposed an almost total control by laymen over the Church, from the lay overprocurator to the local lay officials of the Spiritual Department. The famous

---

[4]*Puti*, 340.

[5]A. Molchanovsky, "Dva proekta vosstanovleniya patriarshestva v Rossii v XVIII veke," *ZhMP*, no. 12 (December 1944) 52-7. Also, Robert Nichols and Theofanis Stavrou, eds., *Russian Orthodoxy under the Old Regime* (Minneapolis: University of Minnesota Press, 1978), particularly the articles by Donald Treadgold, Nichols and Gregory Freeze.

church historian Golubinsky wrote that the "Enslavement of the Synod by the overprocurator is a domination of an aristocrat over the seminarians. Had the members of the Synod been aristocrats, had they any contacts at the court, the procurator would not have had that power over them."[6]

If Tolstoi was full of a secular reforming zeal for the Church, Konstantin Pobedonostsev, who inherited from him fulness of control over the Church, used that control to stop all reform trends, whether secularist, in the Tolstoian style, or religious and desired by the concerned clergy and ecclesiastically minded laity. The ferment within the Church and society nevertheless continued. Growing numbers of the intelligentsia returned to the Church in the early twentieth century, mostly via Marxism and disillusionment with it, but retaining their activism and reform zeal of a Christian-socialist orientation. For instance, Ern and Sventsitsky (the latter became a priest in the postrevolutionary Patriarchal Church) founded in Moscow in 1905 a "Christian Fraternity of Struggle," aimed at "breaking the reactionary connection between Orthodoxy and autocracy" and at involving the Church in the struggle of Russian society for a constitutional-democratic order.[7]

In general, the voice of the neophytic intelligentsia (owing to its continuing ties with the liberal and left-of-liberal press) began to be heard in society to a much greater degree than its proportion in the Church would suggest. Florovsky is rather skeptical about its positive contribution: "the intelligentsia was returning to the Church full of anticipation of reforms . . . it is here that 'the new religious consciousness' failed. It was but a new form of the same old and typical [in the ranks of the intelligentsia] utopian temptation, insensitivity to history."[8] But if we remember that genealogically the *raznochintsy* intelligentsia largely came from the clerical estate, then kinship of thought patterns and frustrations between the reformism of the re-Christianized intelligentsia, on the one hand, and of the academy-educated married clergy as well as of some lay theology professors, on the other, was to be expected. It was these ambitious urban priests and lay theologians

⁶Cited in Florovsky, *Puti*, 342-4.
⁷Jutta Scherer, *Die Petersburger Religioes-Philosophischen Vereinigungen* (Berlin, 1973) 144-5.
⁸*Puti*, 470-5.

who felt particularly bitter about the limits on their advancement opportunities within the ecclesiastical structure imposed by their marital status.

The already mentioned Group of Thirty-two, which later, on amalgamation with some lay Christian-socialist intellectuals, renamed itself the Union for Church Renovation, is, owing to their memorandum presented in 1905 to Metropolitan Antony (Vadkovsky), one of the best-known expressions of this radical-reformist trend within the Church. The very name it adopted foreshadowed the Renovationist schism of the 1920s. Inter alia, the memorandum demanded the separation of Church and state, a democratic-conciliar form of administration for the Church, the introduction of the Gregorian calendar, services in spoken Russian instead of Slavonic, the reintroduction of married bishops and the abolition of the monopoly of monastic bishops. They argued that the monastic episcopate was not only contrary to the canons but went against the very heart of the monastic vocation—which was contemplation, silence and obedience. Bishops, in contrast, had to administer, preach, instruct and command. Likewise, the Union was against the restoration of the patriarchate on the grounds that it would weaken both the conciliar principle and the concept of Christ as the real Head of the Church.[9] A little later they declared that it was the duty of the Church to protect the workers from exploitation by the capitalists. One of their supporters, Archimandrite Mikhail Semenov, a professor at the Petersburg Theological Academy, even produced a *Program of Russian Christian Socialists.*[10] In this respect, the group was close to Professor (later Priest) Sergius Bulgakov, who planned to found a League of Christian Politics, and to Nicholas Berdyaev.

Christian radicalism and Christian socialism of different brands were not isolated phenomena in Russian Orthodoxy of the time. Orthodox Christian agricultural communes existed before the revolution; the most famous one was founded by the very wealthy

[9]*K tserkovnomu soboru,* 61 and 149-81. The same arguments were continued in the central Renovationist periodical, *VSS,* particularly by Prof. B.V. Titlinov in his "Prikhodskie zadachi obnovlencheskogo tserkovnogo dvizheniya," no. 12-13 (1926) 16-20.

[10]Simon, *Church, State,* 22-3. See also Mikhail (Semenov), *Kak ya stal narodnym sotsialistom,* an undated brochure in the Lieb Archive (Hc 335), and the same author's *Khristos v vek mashin* (St. Petersburg, 1907).

landed aristocrat N. Nepluev out of his own resources in the
1870s. It flourished economically and in all other respects, grew
and had other similar communes develop on its model well until
the Bolshevik coup d'etat.[11]

The Orthodox Church, alas, even had her "Nechaev" in the
paradoxical person of Archimandrite Serapion (Mashkin), a naval
officer who, following early retirement, attended Moscow University as an auditor, then went to Mt. Athos for four years, and
on return to Russia graduated from a theological (graduate)
academy and took the tonsure. He praised social democracy, but
reproached Marx for his historical determinism, which, allegedly,
led to a passive attitude to historical processes. He held that
physical revolution was necessary for the achievement of a just
socialist order. All means were justified in this struggle, including
"espionage, reporting on each other and even secret murder." But
unlike Nechaev, in private life he was morally irreproachable: he
distributed his whole inheritance of 200,000 rubles to the poor.
Living as a recluse in the Optina Monastery, he used to give all
his food, money and even the clothes he wore (often remaining
in underwear) to poor pilgrims. The justification for murder in
the struggle for justice he found, characteristically, in the Old
Testament.[12]

The radicalism of the Unionists and their predecessors like
Fr. Serapion, however, differed from that of Sventsitsky or Bulgakov in that for the latter the goals did not justify the means and
that, as Bulgakov would later put it: "Socialism for a Christian
has only an applied meaning, . . . not a question of *Weltanschauung* but only of practical ethics." He then points out that
the Gospels do not indicate any connection between Christianity
and any particular sociopolitical system—the Church is above
them all. In his view, the social justice aims of socialism are irreproachable from the point of view of applicability in practical
terms, which the Church should not ignore either.[13] In the same

[11]On Nepluev's communes see, inter alia, N. Nepluev, *Trudovye bratstva*
(Leipzig, 1893), a brochure; I. Abramov, a former member of the commune and
its critic, *Khristianskaya kommuna* (St. Petersburg, 1914); and *Kratkiya svedeniya
o pravoslavnom Kresto-vozdvizhenskom trudovom bratstve* (Chernigov, 1905).

[12]Mikhail Morozov, *Pred litsom smerti* (St. Petersburg, 1908) 5-7.

[13]"Pravolsavie i sotsializm," *Put'*, no. 20 (February 1930) 93-5. See also
Bulgakov's *Avtobiograficheskie zapiski* (Paris, 1946) 76-92; and George Putnam,

Laity. It supported the political and social program of the Socialist Revolutionaries, condemning the monarchy and stating that
even in the event of its restoration it would never deal with it;
choosing the republic as the best form of government; professing
struggle against capitalism and the granting of all land to peasants and factories to workers; and favoring church reform
and the separation of the teaching of religion from other school
subjects. Among its adherents was Professor Titlinov of the
Petrograd Theological Academy, who was editor of its popular-
theological journal, *The Church and Social Messenger* (*Tserkovno-
obshchestvennyi vestnik*), which thereupon became the organ of
the future Renovationists. This radical organization failed to gain
any significant following in Moscow. However, in June 1917
there appeared a Social-Christian Workers Party, with a political
program similar to that of the Socialist Revolutionaries but not
aiming at any structural or canonical church reforms. After 1919
it renamed itself the "Christian-Socialists."[18] Although none of
these Christian-socialist groups condoned the use of force and
terror, their support or sympathy for the Socialist Revolutionaries,
who practiced individual terror as a basic instrument of policy,
illustrates the deterioration in the understanding of Christ's basic
message among some Russian church circles of the time. It also
shows an affinity with the confused thinking and actions of some
Protestant and Roman Catholic Christian radical groups with
Marxist leanings of the second half of this century, and the
whole so-called theology of liberation.

There were many things in common between the aims of the
"Thirty-two," the Christian socialism of Sergius Bulgakov and
other intelligentsia Orthodox neophytes of socialist background,
the post-1917 socialist-Christian leagues just enumerated and the
eventual Renovationist Church schism, which was to come into
the open in 1922.[19] The former Marxists Bulgakov and Nicholas

---

[18]Simon, *Church, State,* 24; and Levitin-Shavrov, 1:4-6 et passim. Details on
the Petrograd league are in Alexander Vvedensky (who was one of its founding
members), *Tserkov' i gosudarstvo,* 32-5.

[19]Simon, *Church, State,* 22-5; Bulgakov, *Avtobiograficheskie zapiski,* 75-92;
Levitin-Shavrov, 1:4-6 et passim. It may be noted that the "Thirty-two" called
themselves "Union of Church Renovation" (*K tserkovnomu soboru,* vii), while
Bulgakov, even as a priest, toward the end of his life still maintained that the
monasticism of Orthodox bishops contradicted both the aims of monasticism and
the canons of the ecumenical councils and has corrupted the historical Church

vein Bulgakov criticized the intelligentsia as people who on join
the Church simply reoriented their revolutionary anger from t
secular sphere to the ecclesiastic one: "Such a Christianizin
intelligent . . . feels himself most at home as a Martin Luther o
. . . as a prophetic carrier of a new religious consciousness, called
upon not only to renovate the church life, but even to create its
new forms, almost a new religion."[14]

Although the post-1907 reaction led to the defrocking of a
number of the most prominent members of the "Thirty-two,"[15]
the church socialists were by no means silenced, as the Eighth
Orthodox Missionary Congress which met in Kiev in 1909 would
show. There, some prominent clerics vehemently defended Christian socialism, elements of which they found in the personalistic
concepts of Mikhailovsky and the Socialist Revolutionaries (ignoring their practical program of terrorism). They attacked in particular Archbishop Antony Khrapovitsky, the future head of the
émigré Church Synod, as a revolutionary-from-the-right radical-
izing the Church in the wrong direction.[16] But whereas these
speakers at least criticized Marx for his materialism and militant
atheism, a former professor at the Kiev Theological Academy,
Vasily Ekzemplyarsky, who had been expelled from his teaching
position for defending Leo Tolstoy after his excommunication,
openly praised Marxist Social Democrats as practicing real, active
love for man—a principle that the historical Church often betrayed.[17]

But organizationally, the leanings of the "Thirty-two" would
come up into the open again only after the February Revolution,
when a group with similar ideas and containing many of the
original members of the "Thirty-two" now adopted the name of
the All-Russian League of Democratic Orthodox Clergy and

Russian Alternatives to Marxism (Knoxville: University of Tennessee Press, 1977)
93-121 and 152-76.

[14]Cited by Florovsky, *Puti*, 475. It may be of interest that toward the end of
his life the last Renovationist leader, commenting on the fact that he had been
abandoned by all his former followers, remarked: "Luther did not appear suddenly. He had predecessors." Did he see himself as a predecessor of a Russian
Luther? See Levitin-Shavrov, 3:411-2.

[15]Simon, *Church, State*, 22-3.

[16]I.G. Aivazov, *Obnovlentsy i starotserkovniki* (Moscow, 1909) 3-4 and 56-62.

[17]"Evangelie i obshchestvennaya zhizn'," a public lecture delivered at a session
of the Kiev Religious-Philosophic Society (Kiev, 1913).

Berdyaev "criticized the state Church for her lack of responsibility and action." Bulgakov argued that the proper form of social organization for Christians was the early Christian commune, which rejected private property; Christianity must lead to "political liberation and religious renewal." The aforementioned Archimandrite Mikhail, in his *Program*, although rejecting the use of force, advocated abolition of private property, as if this could be peaceably achieved. Instead of class struggle, he proposed to form Christian-socialist fraternities attached to parishes which would gradually reeducate the masses and promote socialism. Deprived of his teaching post and clerical titles, he joined the Old Believers and became one of their bishops. This, apparently, would have some effect later on the pro-Renovationist sympathies of at least some Old Believer groups. In fact, some of their clergy later joined the Renovationist schism.[20]

However, the Renovationists differed radically from the Christian-socialists of the Bulgakov orientation in their attitude to the Bolshevik victory and to Lenin's dictatorship. The difference logically follows from Bulgakov's above-cited assessment of socialism as having only an applied meaning, and from his emphasis that no Christian could accept socialism's militant atheism. For the Renovationists, apparently, socialism had an a priori value, and if they were sincere in their admiration for Lenin, then they were typical sectarian social utopians. Then again, it may have been a case of plain opportunism—which appears more likely in view of their unscrupulous behavior.[21]

Although the anti-Patriarchal putsch of the Renovationists was

by leading ambitious people to monastic vows in hope of becoming bishops. *Avtobiograficheskie zapiski,* 50-5.

[20]On Semenov in particular, see M.M. Sheinman, *Khristianskii sotsializm,* a biased Marxist book, but with most of its factual data reliable (Moscow, 1969) 137-9. For a discussion on the Old Believer attitudes to the Renovationists, see below and notes 66 to 69.

[21]On the official Renovationist attitude to Lenin, the case in point was the latter's death, when the Renovationists, in contrast to the Patriarchal Church, served requiems for him. This set a precedent that would be followed by the Patriarchal Church in the case of Stalin's death. But what was more, and what would never be repeated even by the cowed post-World War II Russian Church, was that Renovationist leaders in their requiem orations called Lenin "a Christian by nature." Other epithets likewise surpassed anything bestowed on Stalin by the Church twenty-nine years later. See "Otkliki na smert V.I. Lenina," *Khristianin,* no. 1 (June 1924) 6.

conspicuously timed to take place immediately upon the arrest of Patriarch Tikhon on May 12, 1922, the action had been prepared to some extent by the talks in 1919 between Fr. Alexander Vvedensky and the Petrograd party chief Grigory Zinoviev. In conclusion of the talks, Zinoviev told Vvedensky that his group would be the appropriate one for an eventual concordat between the state and the Church.[22] The importance that the Soviet regime assigned to the struggle against the Church is demonstrated by the fact that the Soviet agency in charge of church affairs was a department of the GPU, the secret police, and this department was headed by one of its senior officials, Evgeny Tuchkov. Vvedensky admitted later that it was there that the Renovationist strategy and tactics were planned.[23]

We now come to the third, and in terms of immediacy and decisiveness probably the most important, factor leading to the appearance of the Renovationist schism: a communist attempt to subvert the Church. The totalitarian character of the Marxist-Leninist ideology, its soteriological and quasi-ecclesiastical claim to having the total answers to all social, existential and essential problems, makes its coexistence with religion logically and practically impossible. Both aim at the transfiguration of man, at creating a new man. Religion aims at a spiritual transfiguration by the reorientation of man's values and his inner and voluntary moral reformation, while Marxism aims at achieving this by a revolutionary (i.e., enforced) change of society and of its economic structure, which, once enacted, would change the nature of the individual.

Marx formulated his hostility toward religion and a directive for its abolition in the following words:

> *Religious* poverty is . . . an *expression* of the reality of poverty and a protest against real poverty. Religion is a sign of the oppressed creature, the soul of a heartless world, the spirit of soulless timelessness. It is the *opiate* of the people.

---

[22]Levitin-Shavrov, 1:54-5.
[23]Ibid., 77-8.

Abolition of religion as an *illusory* happiness of the people is necessary for the *creation of its real* happiness.[24]

Lenin then "refined" Marx's formula by calling religion "a moonshine"; he categorically ruled out "any flirtation with . . . a god." For the purpose of compromising religion the communists should tolerate "a priest who violates young girls" rather than morally attractive and well-educated clerics, because it would then be easier to undermine the Church.[25] On another occasion, he stipulates that "the Party must carry on a most active struggle against religion."

Once religion had failed to disappear despite the removal of its "economic base," the regime decided to use more devious tactics, and the Renovationist project was one of them. Genuine grievances, socioreligious misconceptions and confusions, unfulfilled ambitions and the unscrupulousness of some of the main actors could all be manipulated to coalesce into a seemingly united organization that in reality owed its existence solely to the support given it by the regime. Indeed, the motley character of the movement is clearly seen in a profile of its leadership. Only six leading personalities had any connection with the original "Thirty-two." Other well-known prerevolutionary church radicals were Bishop Antonin Granovsky, who in a sermon in 1907 had declared that autocracy was satanic, and Archbishop Evdokim, formerly of North America, who was a progressive and socially conscious church reformer, but hardly a radical.[26] Alexander Vvedensky, who would soon become the intellectual, and eventually also the official, leader of the schism, was a controversial figure, an unstable intellectual, morally and politically unscrupulous, but a

[24]"Critique of the Hegelian Philosophy of Right," cited in *Sputnik antireligioznika* (Moscow, 1939) 7-8.

[25]Lenin's letter to Gorky of November 1913, in Collected Works, 35 (Moscow, 1964) 122-3. This argument explains why the regime has persecuted popular priests and bishops in particular.

[26]In an open letter to Evdokim, Metropolitan Antony (Khrapovitsky) claims that Evdokim has led a licentious life with numerous "lovers [and has] illegitimate children," and that because of this he has been blackmailed by the Bolsheviks into the schism. If this is true—and there is no reason to doubt either Antony's knowledge of Evdokim's private life or the former's honesty—then it becomes clearer why, of all Renovationist leaders, Tikhon will later categorically refuse to have any dealings with Evdokim. *TsV*, no. 19-20 (October 1923) 4-5.

brilliant orator and apologist for the faith and a sincere believer, in a somewhat romantic style.[27] Several other leading personalities in this schism were former Black Hundred activists. One of its founders and leaders, the Archpriest Vladimir Krasnitsky, had even written a paper on "Socialism as a Product of Satan" and had been the St. Petersburg chaplain to the anti-Semitic, radical-rightist and protofascist Union of Russian People.[28] In the case of convinced Black Hundreders going over to the Bolsheviks there may have been, besides pure opportunism and fear of reprisals (overcompensation to appease the new civil authorities and to prevent a vendetta on their part), the reverse of the processes in fascist Italy or Hitler's Germany, where many a former Marxist radical became a fascist or a National Socialist. Besides, the Russian radical right did have a form of syndicalist concept in Lev Tikhomirov's ideas of corporativist, self-ruling, professional and social "estates"—not unlike those of future fascism—and even in Sergei Zubatov's ideas of a monarchist "Progressing Socialism" and loyal trade unionism.[29] The opportunistic and careerist character of many Renovationist leaders was stressed by no lesser leading personalities of the movement than Antonin Granovsky and Professor Titlinov, who said that the antiepiscopal Living Church branch of the schism was a revolt of power-hungry, married priests pursuing their petty class interests against the bishops and monks.[30]

Liberal and radical social ideas were not uncommon among the lower clergy, both before and after the revolutions. Yet despite (or, perhaps, because of) the support given the Renovationists by the Soviet government in order to weaken the traditional national Church, the three major branches of the Renovationist schism—

[27]Levitin-Shavrov, 1:64, 19-21, 56-61, 145-56, 175-8; 3:185-342; Simon, Church, State, 25.

[28]Levitin-Shavrov, 1:66. Among the other former "Black Hundreders" in the ranks of the Renovationist leadership were the priest, later metropolitan, Nikolai Platonov, Hieromonk Iliodor, archpriests Kalinovsky and Diakonov, etc. Ibid., 1:51-3 and 125-35; 2:76-7, 108-9 et passim.

[29]Hans Rogger, "Was There a Russian Fascism? The Union of Russian People," in Henry A. Turner, Jr., ed., Reappraisal of Fascism (New York: New Viewpoints, 1975) 170-93; D. Pospielovsky, Russian Police Trade Unionism (London: Weidenfeld & Nicolson, 1971) 70-83.

[30]Levitin-Shavrov, 3:192; Titlinov, Novaya tserkov' (Petrograd-Moscow, 1923) 12-3.

the Living Church, the Union of Communities of Ancient Apostolic Churches, and the Union for Church Renovation—failed to direct the bulk of the laity from the Patriarchal Church.[31] By 1923, the majority of the bishops still at large had been induced into formally accepting the Renovationist administration, and the majority of functioning church buildings were then handed over by the Soviets to the Renovationists. Yet this had little effect on the believers' behavior.[32] It was probably mainly due to insufficient support from the scores of millions of the faithful that the Renovationists began to use various devious means and to appeal more and more to the Soviet government for support in their attempts to accomplish their purposes.

These methods marred the very first steps of the movement. Patriarch Tikhon was placed under house arrest on May 6, 1922, accused of resisting the confiscation of church valuables ordered by the state, allegedly to help the famine-stricken (see below in the next chapter). The Renovationists used this pretext for their revolt, accusing the patriarch and his associates of selfishness and heartlessness. Six days after the arrest, a group of church rebels from Petrograd, including the married priests Vvedensky, Krasnitsky and Kalinovsky, arrived at the patriarch's residence, where the GPU guard had been instructed by their superiors to let the priests through. On the way they had assured themselves of support from a single canonical bishop, Antonin Granovsky. On the pretext that the patriarch's arrest would be a long one and that he would not be able to administer the Church, they secured from him permission to run his chancery temporarily, until the arrival

[31]According to Levitin, it was the Renovationists' active collaboration with the regime that destroyed their reputation in the Russian public eye the most. In particular, he cites their press articles and their statements in court during the trial of the most popular and saintly Metropolitan Venyamin of Petrograd, which resulted in his execution and the condemnation to death of nine other leading Petrograd church personalities. The gravity of the sentences was caused by the fraudulent attacks against the defendants by such Renovationist leaders as Vvedensky and Krasnitsky. Even Archbishop Granovsky called the Renovationists "a sewer of the Orthodox Church" (Levitin-Shavrov, 1:111-6). Venyamin's defense counsel, Gurovich, a Jew, said about him: "There went a saint." Struve, 37.

[32]Only four of the over four hundred functioning Orthodox churches in Moscow of the time were still held by the "Tikhonites," but they were packed while the ones held by the Renovationists were empty. Levitin-Shavrov, 2:61-3, 86-7, 138-232; see also the revealing *samizdat* novel from the life of a Volga priest, *Ostraya Luka* (ms. in Keston College Archives) 370 et passim.

of Metropolitan Agafangel of Yaroslavl, who, according to the patriarch's decree, was to take charge of the Church. While Agafangel hesitated, wondering whether to believe the oral message transmitted to him by Krasnitsky, the GPU issued an order forbidding him to leave the city. In the meanwhile, the rebels declared themselves the Supreme Church Administration, concealing the limitations on their prerogatives set by the patriarch. Agafangel responded by issuing a decree declaring them an uncanonical body. He further advised dioceses to establish themselves as temporarily independent, owing to the breakdown of the true central church administration—they were not to recognize the "Supreme Church Administration." The latter body then deposed eighty bishops still loyal to the patriarch.[83]

The Renovationists' greatest internal problem was lack of unity. At their conference in August 1922 they tried to achieve it by electing Bishop Antonin Granovsky (elevating him to the title of Metropolitan of Moscow and All Russia) as the nominal head of a loose federation of schismatic groupings. Titlinov, their historian and a sympathizer of the Granovsky group of "Church Renovation," explains their failure to achieve real unity by "the prevalence of class interests [i.e., the antiepiscopal and antimonastic feelings of the married clergy] over the idea of the Church . . . the tendency toward the use of force in the struggle for reforms. . . . But the most salient characteristic, which became apparent at the conference, was the original sin of the Renovationist movement: its isolation from the church masses."[34]

While Patriarch Tikhon was under arrest and awaiting trial, the Renovationists called a sobor (on April 29, 1923). The sobor sang in corpore "Many Years" to the Soviet government and passed resolutions in support of the Soviet socialist social system. They condemned counterrevolutionary clerics, sent greetings to Lenin—calling him a fighter "for the great social truth"—and eventually staged an illegal trial in absentia of the patriarch, whom they "stripped" not only of his clerical titles but even of monastic status. Tikhon's anathema against the Bolsheviks was declared null and void.[35]

[83]Levitin-Shavrov, 1:116-24.
[34]Titlinov, 20 et passim.
[35]Spinka, 29-34; Levitin-Shavrov, 2:103-15.

Later, the Renovationists would justify their rebellion against the patriarch by accusing him of violating the statutes of both canon law and of the Moscow Sobor on conciliarity: the three-year term of the Synod expired in 1921, and yet, nothing allegedly was being done by the patriarch to convoke a new sobor and to elect new members for the Synod and the Higher Church Council. Metropolitan Sergii (Stragorodsky), a senior Synod member, reminded the patriarch in March 1922 that the central church administration could be saved only by instituting the Synod and the Higher Church Council. To his surprise, the patriarch replied that there was no need for a Synod at the time and that, instead, he used the advice of bishops who happened to be in Moscow at the time. What this passage from Sergii's report ignores is the fact that bishops were then being arrested and exiled all over the country. In all probability the patriarch saw no practical possibility of running a regular collective office in these conditions and was afraid that bishops sitting in a central administrative body would be the first ones to be persecuted. Apparently, Sergii himself soon realized the incredibly difficult position of the patriarch—he was one of the first bishops to return with repentance from the schism to the patriarch in 1923, immediately upon Tikhon's release from prison.[36] As to the convocation of the sobor, Sergii was soon to experience himself the Soviets' intransigence on this score; despite his repeated petitions to permit the convocation, that permission was not to be granted until 1943.

But whatever the formal excuses, they did not warrant Tikhon's unfrocking, let alone the deprivation of monastic status, which can be applied only on the grounds of very serious moral transgressions. Moreover, the "sobor" officially condemned the patriarch not for canonical irregularities, but for allegedly reactionary policies and (somewhat ironically) for interfering in political matters. But did not the Renovationists engage in politics when they praised the Bolshevik coup d'etat, Lenin and Marxism? Demonstrating their own politicization, in place of the communists, who had been excommunicated for their persecution of the Church, the "sobor" excommunicated all Russian émigré clerics and laymen who had participated in the 1921 Church Council in

---

[36]See Evdokim's "Sobornyi razum ili edinovlastie?" *Khristianin*, 1:2-3 (1924) 2-3.

Karlovci, Yugoslavia (which shall be discussed in chapter 4).

The other resolutions of the "sobor" recognized married bishops and the right of widowed priests to remarry. It also granted more control of the dioceses to the parish clergy. Monasteries were to be tolerated only as working communes in areas distant from the cities.[37]

The formally unified but in reality factionally split Renovationist church organization was now to be administered by a Higher Church Council (VTsS) of eighteen members, headed by the aged Metropolitan Antonin. Its other members included four bishops—at least two of them married—eleven priests, one deacon and one layman. Ten of these men represented Krasnitsky's Living Church; six, Vvedensky's Union of Communities of Ancient Apostolic Churches (SODATs in its Russian acronym); and two, Antonin's Union for Church Renovation.[38]

The sobor was hardly representative of the real Church. Of its 476 delegates, only 66 represented what the Soviet press at the time called "moderate Tikhonites." (Staunch and active Tikhonites presumably did not participate at all.) Most sources indicate that many Tikhonites "had boycotted the sobor . . . many others were either arrested . . . (and replaced by clerics of the 'Living Church' persuasion), or denied transportation to attend the Sobor." Many propatriarchal delegates were simply prevented from taking the floor: "of 20 to 30 persons who put down their names to speak, only two or three would be allotted time to do so." This may be the answer to the puzzle why only one or two timid disagreements with the resolution condemning and defrocking the arrested patriarch were heard at the sobor.[39]

It is interesting that although the Renovationists claimed that

[37]A concession to Antonin Granovsky, a passionate advocate of monasticism, for his reluctant acceptance of married bishops and of the remarriage of widowed priests. According to Levitin-Shavrov, this license soon degenerated into general promiscuity among the Renovationist clergy (2:119).

[38]Ibid., 119-33.

[39]Fletcher, *Church Underground*, 26; Levitin-Shavrov, 2:86-7 and 118; *Ostraya Luka*, 281-2. Metropolitan Manuil (Lemeshevsky), in his catalogue of Russian bishops, mentions under the letter "A" (which is the extent of vol. 1) thirty-eight bishops active in the USSR in 1923. Of these, twelve joined the Renovationists, six are described as active fighters against Renovationism and the remaining twenty appear as loyal Patriarchals, presumably either in prison or in forced retirement at the time. See the West German reprint of Manuil's *samizdat* ms., *Die russischen orthodoxen Bischoefe von 1893 bis 1965* (Erlangen, 1979) passim.

their "sobor" was canonically valid, their leading theologian, Professor Titlinov, conceded that it could not be considered an all-Russian sobor, because "it has not been accepted by the ecclesiastical consciousness and its decisions have been rejected by a considerable proportion of the faithful."[40]

The unrepresentative sobor also failed to gain support from foreign church bodies, including even those Eastern Orthodox patriarchates that had at first expressed sympathy with the Renovationists as the legitimate Orthodox Church of Russia. None of these churches sent observers, although they were all cordially invited to do so. The arrest of the patriarch, the press campaign against him in the Soviet Union and the unconcealed participation of the Renovationists in this campaign, as well as in the persecution of clerics, became too widely known abroad. Indeed, a number of protests were submitted by western churches and governments, including the government of Great Britain, which in a formal note threatened to withdraw its para-diplomatic mission from Moscow if the regime did not release the patriarch.[41]

Tikhon's sudden release from prison barely a month after the sessions of the sobor had closed upset all the plans and hopes of the Renovationists, for the clergy (including bishops) and laity began to flock back to the patriarch.

Even in prison, when presented with the defrocking verdict by a "sobor" delegation, he daringly wrote over it that the gathering was unrepresentative and hence its verdict invalid. He reiterated this on June 28, 1923, in his first encyclical after his release.[42] There, as well as in his encyclical of July 15, the patriarch assured the Soviet government of his civic loyalty, apologized for his former anti-Soviet stand and maintained that he had adopted a loyal stance since 1919. As evidence of this he cited his disagreement with the Karlovci émigré Church Synod's political and monarchist resolutions, and his decree of 1922 that the above church organization be dissolved.[43] The first Bolshevik assault on

---

[40]"Kak vosstanovit' edinstvo tserkvi?" *Khristianin* 1:2-3 (1924) 5-8.

[41]Fletcher, *Study in Survival,* 19-20. For Vvedensky's promise to Tuchkov to have delegations from the eastern patriarchs at the sobor, see Levitin-Shavrov, 2:91-2.

[42]Tikhon's original repudiation occurred on May 4, 1923. Ibid., 122 and 154-8.

[43]Ibid., 148, 152-8 and 162-4.

the Church had been only a partial success. Confusion had been caused, but the Renovationists had hardly triumphed.

The Renovationists soon showed their continued disunity when, through the intrigues of Krasnitsky, Antonin Granovsky was forcefully retired, on June 25, 1923, from the chairmanship of the Higher Church Council and replaced by Bishop (soon to be Metropolitan) Evdokim Meshchersky, formerly the head of the North American mission of the Russian Orthodox Church. Seeing the disarray in the schism after the patriarch's release, its desertion by thousands of the clergy and its empty churches, Metropolitan Evdokim, in collusion with the GPU church overseer Tuchkov, decided to regain some respectability for the Renovationists by bringing their organization closer in line with traditional Orthodoxy. A hurriedly assembled conference in August 1923 annulled most of the radical decisions of the sobor of only three months earlier—retaining, however, the institution of married bishops. It also renamed itself the "Russian Orthodox Church" and installed a traditional Synod at the top.

In one of its last attempts to regain popular support, the Renovationist leadership appealed to the Patriarch of Constantinople, misinforming him of the real situation. Constantinople, contrary to Orthodox canons forbidding the interference of one ruling bishop in the internal affairs of another, appealed to Tikhon to retire "for the sake of the schismatics," and gave recognition to the Renovationists as the Orthodox Church of Russia.[44] Yet this did not weaken Tikhon's prestige and popularity in Russia.

A number of participants in a conference of clergy of the Moscow Renovationist diocese in June 1923 called on the leadership to return to the patriarch. Its final resolution, however, accused the patriarch of having caused dissension, civil war and bloodshed in the Church and approved his "defrocking" by the Renovationist sobor.[45] The debate showed that many members of the diocese did not regard Tikhon as a layman but as a spiritual leader, retaining his former charisma, and they were numerous and important enough to force the Renovationist leaders to begin

[44]Stratonov, *Smuta*, 84-6 and 162-4.

[45]See the text of the resolution in *VSS*, no. 1 (September 18, 1923): "Blagochinnye nastoyateli prikhodskikh tserkvei o pokayanii"; and the even more vicious statement by Metropolitan Evdokim: "Mitropolit Evdokim o Tikhone."

reconciliation talks with the very patriarch whom they had "defrocked." Thus, the act of "defrocking" was reduced to a comedy. Paradoxically, it was one of the initiators of the comedy and of the schism itself, Archpriest Krasnitsky, who now appealed to the Renovationists to return to the patriarch's fold. The GPU official Tuchkov, their putative ally, threatened Tikhon with rearrest if he did not agree to enter into negotiations with Evdokim, now head of the Renovationists. Tikhon flatly refused to deal with Evdokim, but reluctantly agreed to negotiate with Krasnitsky. Negotiations lasted several months, in the course of which Krasnitsky was accepted into the patriarchal Higher Church Council, a body which, in Tikhon's own words, remained a dead letter simply for lack of funds and space to function. The reaction of the faithful and clergy to Krasnitsky was so negative that on June 26, 1924 the patriarch was forced to formally revoke his May agreement with Krasnitsky.[46] All Tuchkov's efforts to force the patriarch's hand failed. Krasnitsky, now of no more use to the GPU, was dropped from membership in the reformed Renovationist Synod and fell into the obscurity of the deanship of a Renovationist church in Leningrad.

The actions of Tuchkov or the GPU suggest a change of tactics that at first appears hard to explain. Why were the Soviet authorities, who in 1922 were fomenting a split in the Church in order to weaken it, interested in church reunification two years later? The answer lies in the dismal failure of the subservient Renovationists to attract and keep the masses of Orthodox believers.

At the end of 1922, the Soviet government handed over to Renovationists of all kinds nearly two-thirds of all functioning churches in the RSFSR and Central Asia—close to twenty thousand churches. Churches in the Ukraine and Belorussia, where the situation was more complicated owing to the existence of additional nationalist church jurisdictions (a tiny one in Belorussia, but a large one in the Ukraine), are not included in that figure. By November 1924 these churches had been reduced to 10,016 in Russia, Siberia and Central Asia, plus some 3,000 in the Ukraine, 500 in Belorussia and 400 in the Far Eastern District. By the end of 1926 the total figure for all 84 dioceses of the

[46]Levitin-Shavrov, 2:255-74.

Renovationist Church, including the Ukraine and some 30 Renovationist parishes in North America, was 6,245 parishes served by 10,815 priests and deacons.[47] This may be compared with some 30,000 parishes across the whole Soviet Union in the Patriarchal Church claimed by Metropolitan Sergii in 1930.[48] Since the latter figure was given two years after the beginning of mass closures of churches by the state, the 1926 total would have been higher. On the other hand, the following two documents indicate that the reduction in the number of Renovationist churches could hardly have been attributed to GPU actions. One document is a secret internal party directive of 1929:

> . . . the most reactionary current of the Tikhonites is growing in strength, . . . while the Renovationist current is decreasing and shows cases of desertions back to the Tikhonites. . . . therefore, the internecine church struggle, which disintegrates the Church from within and contributes to a decrease of religiosity, has reached a very low ebb.[49]

In the Aesopian language found even in internal party documents (whose aim is to convince the party membership, or at least to present the appearance, that the Party is always victorious, the Church is dying out whatever may occur in the short term, and there can only be slowdowns, not reversals, in the process) this means that the Party has been counting on schism and splits within the Church and therefore, by implication, was supporting the schismatics.

The other document is a letter from Russia which says that because Soviet law recognizes only the lay church group of "twenty,"

[47]Curtiss, *Russian Church*, 190-1; "Obzor sovremennogo polozheniya R.P.Ts.," *VSS*, no. 1 (1925) 15-6; "Sostoyanie eparkhii," *VSS*, no. 2 (1927) 17.

[48]Sergii's interview with foreign correspondents, February 18, 1930, in Regelson, 477.

[49]"Dopolnitel'nye direktivy . . . 'O sostoyanii religioznykh organizatsii v Zapadnoi oblasti i borbe s nimi,'" supplement 2 to the West Obkom Protocol no. 26, of the All-Union CP, 10:12, 1929. Smolensk Archives, XT 47 (460). This may be compared with the 1925 data for one of the counties of the same province: for a population of 175,000, there were fifty-seven functioning Orthodox churches, of which only eighteen were controlled by the Patriarchal Church, the rest being still Renovationist of one kind or another. See the report on the activities of the Society of Friends of the *Bezbozhnik* Newspaper in ibid., file 459.

the priest's influence depends entirely on his [moral] authority in the parish. The "twenty" decide whether to entrust the given church to the "Living Church" or to the Patriarchal . . . the lay majority opinion is almost invariably conservative, and if a priest decides to join the . . . Renovationists, he is almost always forced to request from the Soviet authorities that they dissolve the existing "twenty" and permit the election of a new one. But such action usually leads to the falling apart of the parish and to the emptying of the church.[50]

It was this failure of the Renovationists that forced the Soviet government to modify the earlier policy of "divide and rule" and insist on reunification in order to achieve full control over the Patriarchal Church by infiltrating its administration with GPU collaborators from the Renovationist Church such as Krasnitsky and Evdokim. The failure of this plan annoyed Tuchkov. It also makes one wonder if the GPU did not have a hand in Tikhon's death in 1925.[51] Metropolitan Peter, who replaced the deceased patriarch as his locum tenens, had applied considerable pressure on Patriarch Tikhon to induce him to follow a policy of maximum reconciliation and accommodation with the Soviet government.[52] The latter, as well as the Renovationists, apparently mistook this for a sign that, once in power, Peter would be more pliable and willing to come to a reconciliation with the Renovationists and the Soviet state. This was a miscalculation. Peter proved even more uncompromising on the issue of the Renovationists than the late patriarch. In fact, he considered them a greater threat to the Church than the Soviet government's physical persecutions. He

[50]N., "Pis'mo iz Rossii," *Put'*, no. 2 (January 1926) 8.

[51]The opinion that the patriarch had been killed by the GPU was held by the late Alexander Tolgsky, a respectable Moscow priest who had heard the confession of one of the doctors of the Botkin Hospital, where the patriarch had died. See Levitin-Shavrov, 3:351-65. He cites from personal experience the Renovationist Metropolitan of Leningrad Nikolai Platonov's service to the GPU as their secret informer. In 1938 Platonov openly broke with religion and became a professional propagandist of atheism, only to repent and return to the regular Orthodox Church in 1942, shortly before death from dystrophy. Ibid., 347-69.

[52]A case in point is the patriarch's testament, composed apparently by Peter or under his direction. Its declarations of loyalty and of reconciliation with the Soviet regime went apparently too far in Tikhon's eyes, and he reluctantly agreed to sign it only after Peter had threatened to resign and to retire. Ibid., 7-9.

only hoped that by proving the complete civic loyalty of his Church to the Soviet government he could win the necessary freedom to deal with the Renovationists.[53] This policy made GPU infiltration a bit more difficult, just as it offered fewer reasons to intervene in ecclesiastical matters.

During 1925, the Renovationists were preparing for their second sobor, to which they hoped to bring Metropolitan Peter and delegates from his dioceses. They aimed at achieving some form of reunification, or at least a show of unity that would win them some respect among the laity and continued state support. But just as they failed to impress Russian believers, their sobor did not convince the Soviets of the Renovationists' international usefulness, since it failed to induce important foreign churches to send their delegates. The Ecumenical Patriarch, Grigorios VII, insecure in postwar Turkey and eager to win some support from the Soviet state, had urged Tikhon to step down in favor of the Renovationists, and had extended his recognition to the latter. Yet, in response to the Archbishop of Canterbury's protest, whose support he also needed, Grigorios VII assured him that he recognized Tikhon alone as the legitimate head of the Russian Church.[54] The new Patriarch of Constantinople, Vasilios III, continued the ambivalent policies of his predecessor: while extending recognition to Metropolitan Sergii (the acting locum tenens of the Russian Patriarchal Church after the arrest of Metropolitan Peter) after the "legalization" of his Synod by the Soviet government, the ecumenical see continued its fraternal relations with the Renovationists until 1939, even though it had avoided sending a delegation to the Renovationist sobor of 1925.[55]

[53]Ibid., 8-16, 30-1 and 124-66; and *VSS*, no. 5 (1925) 23; no. 8-9 (1926) 3 and 9-10—documents and statements related to the 1925 Sobor's attitude to a pan-Orthodox council.

[54]S.V. Troitsky, *Chto takoe Zhivaya tserkov'?* (Warsaw, 1928) 36-8.

[55]Levitin-Shavrov, 3:183-4. On December 7, 1972, Vasilios III sent out two telegrams: one to Sergii, recognizing him as the temporary head of the "one and unified" Orthodox Church of Russia, and the other to the Renovationist Synod, urging reconciliation with Sergii. This followed the recognition of Sergii by the Patriarchs of Jerusalem and Alexandria some two months earlier. Regelson, 414-22 and 483-4.

Levitin points out that the terms used by the Renovationists in their message of invitation to the Ecumenical Patriarch were so servile as to amount to an abdication of autocephaly. But this may have been an attempt to play up to the flamboyant style of oriental diplomacy to which the eastern patriarchs were so used.

The failure of all the attempts to bring Metropolitan Peter to the sobor, as well as the sobor's fiasco in the international Orthodox arena, obviously caused the GPU to begin a slander campaign against Metropolitan Peter. At the sobor, Metropolitan Alexander Vvedensky (who had replaced Antonin Granovsky as the intellectual leader of the schism after the latter had broken with the Renovationists in late 1923 following his removal from the leadership by the Renovationist Synod), read a letter from the Renovationist Bishop Nikolai Solovei, who had been sent abroad two years earlier with the aim of winning over at least a few of the émigré churches for the Renovationists. Solovei had at first publicly denounced the Soviet persecutions of the Church and tried to join émigré churches.[56] Having failed in his bid for acceptance into the émigré churches in Europe, he found his way to Uruguay, whence he begged the Soviets to forgive him and to

In fact, Sergii argued as early as September 1925 that the relations between the eastern patriarchs and the Renovationists amounted to not much more than diplomatic maneuvers so long as the patriarchs had not partaken of the sacraments together with the Renovationists—which never took place. See Sergii's letter to an unnamed Renovationist bishop, in *TsV*, no. 9-10 (May 14-28, 1927) 1-3.

[56]In the Archives of the Orthodox Church in America there are two undated letters that Bishop Nikolai Solovei sent from Berlin (addressee unnamed) just before his departure for South America. In both he condemns the Soviet system, calling it "bloody hell," and claims that he had played the role of a loyal Soviet citizen and a Renovationist activist in order to win the regime's trust and so be able to leave the USSR to tell the truth to the world. He complains that he is not trusted by émigré Russian Church circles either, and he then condemns the Renovationist schism, calling Metropolitan Evdokim, who had supported Solovei's episcopal candidacy and his assignment abroad, "a criminal." According to Levitin-Shavrov (3:154), Evdokim was forcefully retired after having undergone physical harassment in a GPU cell for several days after Solovei's desertion. Indeed, *VSS* (no. 12-13 [1926] 14) lists the fifty-seven-year-old former chairman of the Renovationist Synod as retired.

The Karlovcian *Tserkovnye vedomosti* at first responded enthusiastically to Solovei's denunciation of the Renovationists on his arrival in Riga and to his appeal to Metropolitan Antony (Khrapovitsky) to accept him as a bishop in the émigré Church, and commented that the information that Patriarch Tikhon, in response to Solovei's letter of repentance from Riga, refused to reaccept Solovei into the Orthodox Church may have been a deliberate Bolshevik hoax. (E. Makharoblidze, "Golos vopiyushchego v pustyne," no. 13-14 [July 1924] 5-6). But nine months later it was condemning him for at first accepting and then rejecting the decision of the Karlovci Synod that his episcopal consecration was invalid and that he could be accepted into the Church only as a layman; and for establishing an illegal Renovationist "Synod" for South America in Montevideo, Uruguay. It also says that originally Solovei was aiming at San Francisco as his episcopal seat-to-be. Makharoblidze, "Zhivotserkovnyi sinod v Yu. Amerike," no. 7-8 (April 1925) 17-8.

allow him to return to the USSR. Apparently, the Soviets requested a pound of flesh from him in return. This came in the form of the above-cited letter, in which he claimed to have acted as a messenger of the late Patriarch Tikhon and Metropolitan Peter to some monarchist émigré groups. The letter implicated Peter as a leader in a monarchist plot.[57] The whole thing seems an obvious fabrication. Had there been such a plot, the patriarch and Metropolitan Peter would hardly have confided it to Solovei, who was not trusted even by the Renovationists, partly because his episcopal consecration had been forced upon them by the GPU. Moreover, the subsequent arrest of Metropolitan Peter, which stemmed from this letter, was done administratively, and he was not brought to trial. Had there been such a plot there certainly would have been a trial and a formal sentence. Yet despite the transparency of the whole affair, Vvedensky pretended to believe Solovei's letter, publishing it later in the Renovationists' official organ. There he also condemned Peter as an enemy of the Soviet state, giving the Soviets a pretext to arrest and exile him for life.[58]

The Soviet government continued to recognize the Renovationist schism as the legal Orthodox Church of Russia, still denying this status to the Patriarchal Church. It was also looking for a church faction that would appear totally Orthodox to the believers and be able to attract a lay following and yet be politically under GPU control. As will be discussed below, such a group was soon found and came down in history under the name of the "Grigorians," after their leader, Grigory, Archbishop of Ekaterinburg (Sverdlovsk).[59]

Sergii was now under attack from both sides. The main thrust

[57]Levitin-Shavrov 3:151-3.

[58]Ibid., 151-9; *VSS*, no. 6 (1925) 10.

[59]Emulating the Renovationists' action vis-à-vis the incarcerated Patriarch Tikhon, Archbishop Grigory likewise gained permission from the GPU to visit the arrested Metropolitan Peter in prison, taking advantage of his lack of information and gaining a written approval for Grigory's initiative. Peter later retracted his approval on being informed of the real situation by Sergii. Regelson, 104-6 and 390-414; Stratonov, *Smuta*, 150-71. The Renovationists immediately showed their sympathy for the Grigorians. See, for example, "Perevorot v Tikhonovshchine," *VSS*, no. 8-9 (1926) 8-9; no. 10 (1926) 24-5. At the time of the extension of Soviet legalization to Grigory's group, Tuchkov said: "We need another schism among the Tikhonites." Levitin-Shavrov, 3:30; Spinka, 64.

of the Renovationist attack was Sergii's alleged disloyalty to the Soviet state and his "counterrevolutionary" contacts with Russian émigré churchmen; the Grigorians, passing for Orthodox traditionalists, attacked Sergii for having been a Renovationist in 1923 and for alleged equivocations in relation to Rasputin and to the highly unpopular Synod procurator under the Provisional Government, Vladimir Lvov. Although Sergii held out steadfastly against both attacks, they were accompanied by the arrest of 117 of some 160 Patriarchal bishops between 1925 and 1927, and with GPU threats to shoot all of the arrested clerics unless Sergii complied with the GPU policy demands. Beyond a doubt, it was these combined pressures that eventually forced Sergii to issue his infamous Declaration of Loyalty in June 1927.[60] The major splits from the right in reaction to Sergii's 1927 declaration[61] made it only easier for the Soviets to annihilate one-by-one the whole garland of individual church jurisdictions and schisms, including the Renovationists, who were no longer needed once Sergii had shown complete subservience.

The Renovationists' miscalculations really sealed their fate. But why did the nation not follow them? First, those who had embraced the atheistic revolution either did not return to any church or, if they later did, it was to the traditional Orthodox Church via a process of disillusionment with the Soviet experiment. This experience precluded acceptance of a church that had tried to collaborate with that regime or that had adapted to it. Second, those laymen of the lower classes who had remained faithful to the Church rejected the atheistic regime per se and, lacking training in Hegelian dialectics, could not justify any active collaboration with or praise of a regime that was visibly and cruelly persecuting their bishops, priests and lay religious activists. Because the laity was less educated, it was also more conservative than the clergy.[62] Third, while the size of nominal church member-

[60]Chrysostomus, 2:276.

[61]In some dioceses as many as 90 percent of the parishes returned the declaration to Sergii unsigned, and refused to pray for the Soviet government.

[62]For example, according to Levitin-Shavrov, the Patriarchal Church, owing to the persecutions, "was a mass without organization; the Renovationists, an organization without masses" (2:284). And even in those churches that remained formally Renovationist the priests often could not cope with the laymen. In the city of Klin, for instance, in a Renovationist church every liturgy ended with the choir and the congregation singing "Many Years" to Patriarch Tikhon and his

ship decreased after the revolution, there was a large influx from the intelligentsia and masses of nationalist traditionalists of different social backgrounds who abhorred the rootless internationalism of communist doctrine, which they held responsible for the destruction of the national culture.[63] If the prerevolutionary neophytes from the ranks of the intelligentsia had retained strong socialist leanings, most of them and the majority of the post-revolutionary intelligentsia Christian recruits now inclined in the opposite direction, in reaction to the Soviet reality.

As already noted, in the thirties (1929-1930, 1932-1934 and 1936-1938) there began a general offensive against all religions, including Renovationism. By the end of the decade so few open churches remained that people no longer paid any attention to which church recognized which administration—they were happy for any church at all still open in their district. When the revival began in 1943, it was a revival of the Patriarchal Church. Only in Central Asia, the northern Caucasus and the Don areas were there some signs of attempted survival and renewal of the Renovationists. In the Central Asian area the Soviet government, which was now interested in a church that had the support of the lay masses for the sake of a consolidated national war effort, took care of the question: it simply blocked (confiscated or destroyed) all letters from those communities to Alexander Vvedensky, by that time head of the Renovationist schism. Hearing nothing from him, they returned to the fold of the Patriarchal Church.[64] In other areas, several Renovationist clergymen tried to revive the movement under the German occupation, but it failed either to regain the masses or to win the support of the occupier, being former collaborationists with the Soviet regime.[65]

As mentioned before, these three areas, and for a while parts of southern Siberia, were the only territories where the Renovationists had a major lay following. It is worth noting that these

local bishop Gavriil—and the Renovationist clergy could do nothing to stop it (3:56). These, as well as other examples cited elsewhere in this work, show a spontaneous negative response of the masses to a Church that was collaborating with the atheist state.

[63]Mikhail Agursky, "Russkii natsionalizm i evreiskii vopros," *Sion*, no. 13 (1976) 86.

[64]Levitin-Shavrov, 3:399-400.

[65]See W. Alexeev and Th. Stavrou, *The Great Revival* (Minneapolis: Burgess Publishing Co., 1976).

areas have historically had the highest concentrations of followers of the Old Believer schism and of popular Russian sects, most of which were an extreme development of the priestless wing of the Old Believers. In fact, surprisingly enough, Old Believers showed considerable sympathy for the Renovationists, and at least one Old Believer bishop and several priests joined them.[66] Why? Traditionally, Old Believers were known or thought to be extremely conservative. But there is some inner logic in this, just as in the fact that one of the founding fathers of the "Thirty-two," Archimandrite Mikhail (Semenov), joined the Old Believers and became one of their bishops.[67] Being persecuted and/or oppressed in one way or another until 1905, the Old Believers, in order to survive and prosper, had developed a tradition of close communal life and internal social solidarity. Along with the development of Old Believers' capitalism and industrial entrepreneurship, which was also a by-product of this internal solidarity and mutual support,[68] there were such socialistic and almost communistic communities as the one at Vyg.[69] Moreover, sectarians such as the Dukhobors, the Molokans and their like practiced a real communal-socialistic organization in their life and economy, rejecting private property, etc. At the same time, two centuries of persecutions made them enemies of much that had to do with the past establishment, including the official Church. These factors combined led many of them to sympathize with the socialistic and anti-old-establishment church movement—however ironical it may appear that a seventeenth-century schism which condemned the official Church and the tsars of the time as satanic should in the twentieth century be tempted by an openly anti-Christian social system.

The Renovationist Church has died, but not without trace. Alas, only the ugliest legacy of Renovationism survived in the

[66]See, for instance, the letter of Nifont Bocharov, a former Old Believer priest and later a Renovationist clergyman, in *ZhMP*, no. 7 (July 1946) 31; and A.A. Shishkin, *Sushchnost' i kriticheskaya otsenka obnovlencheskogo raskola v russkoi pravoslavnoi tserkvi* (Kazan, 1970) 288 et passim.

[67]M.M. Sheinman, *Khristianskii sotsializm* (Moscow, 1969) 137-9, and elsewhere.

[68]See William Blackwell, *The Beginnings of Russian Industrialization, 1800-1860* (Princeton, N.J.: University Press, 1968).

[69]Florovsky, *Puti*, 70-2; and Robert Crummey, *The Old Believers and the World of Antichrist* (Madison: University of Wisconsin Press, 1970) passim.

postwar Patriarchal Orthodox Church: that which some critics have called "adaptation to atheism."[70]

Other Schisms of the Left

There were three other major schisms that could conditionally be called "leftist." Two of them occurred in the Ukraine—the Ukrainian "Self-consecrated" Autocephalous Church and the Ukrainian version of the Renovationist Schism, which received autocephalous status from the 1925 Sobor of the Renovationists; and one in Russia—the so-called "Grigorianism," named after its founding bishop, Grigory. While the Ukrainian issue deserves separate treatment, the Grigorian schism, potentially very dangerous for the fragile unity of the Patriarchal Church after the death of Tikhon, but in practice rather short-lived, can be briefly treated in this section.

Having realized the failure of the Renovationist schism, and having equally failed in his attempt to infiltrate the Patriarchal administration with his collaborators from the Living Church group, Tuchkov now went on record with the statement: "We need another schism among the Tikhonites."[71] The following scenario fits these words perfectly: Metropolitan Peter is in prison; isolated from the outside world, he is not aware of the comings and goings in the Church. His locum tenens, Metropolitan Sergii, whom Peter had named as his first choice of three bishops mentioned in his secret will as his replacements in case of arrest, is prevented by the Soviets from moving from the provincial city of Gorky to Moscow to assume effective administration over the Church. On December 22, 1925, a group of nine bishops, with Archbishop Grigory (Yakovetsky) at their head, gathers at the Moscow Donskoi Monastery, which has served as the Patriarchal headquarters since 1922, and issues a declaration stating that since Metropolitan Peter has been arrested for counterrevolution[72] he

---

[70]Boris Talantov, "Sergievshchina ili prisposoblenie k ateizmu," AS 745 (Kirov, USSR, *samizdat*, 1967-1968).

[71]Levitin-Shavrov, 3:30; Spinka, 64.

[72]On the eve of Peter's arrest (December 10, 1925), Grigory, with two other bishops, visited Peter and requested that he deny in print Soviet accusations of disloyalty and call a sobor of all the bishops present in Moscow. It was, apparently,

cannot administer the Church, and that the above group of bishops assumes temporary responsibility over the Tikhonite Church by electing a Provisional Supreme Church Council (VVTsS) with five members. The declaration assures the Soviet government of the council's total civic loyalty. Then, on January 2, 1926, the VVTsS receives formal legalization from the Soviet government, which no other previous leader of the Tikhonite Church had managed to achieve. On February 1, 1926, Grigory visits the un-initiated Peter in prison with a report on the church situation that states that Sergii cannot assume administration over the Church, while both of the other candidates for the locum tenens position named by Peter, Metropolitans Mikhail and Yosif, have refused to do so. What is concealed from Peter is that the other two metro-politans had recognized the supreme authority of Sergii as the deputy locum tenens in Peter's absence. Unaware of the fraud (he was not even informed that two of the five bishops making up the VVTsS were in prison) Peter, not unlike Patriarch Tikhon in May 1922, gives his written agreement on the spot to hand over the administration of the Church to Grigory and his group.[73]

Shortly afterward, on being informed of the real situation by Metropolitan Sergii, Peter revoked his recognition of Grigory's VVTsS and condemned it, but Sergii's situation did become very difficult for a while, because, in contrast to the Renovationists, the Grigorians were regular Orthodox traditionalists. They recognized the authority of the deceased patriarch and of the imprisoned Peter (who suited them precisely as long as he was in prison) and promised to relinquish all claims to power as soon as a sobor could assemble and elect a new patriarch. Moreover, the years of a precarious illegal existence were beginning to tell on the Patriarchal clergy, and some bishops were pressing Metropolitan

on the grounds of the metropolitan's refusal of both that the Grigorians accused Peter of counterrevolutionism after his arrest. See the relevant articles in *Vozrozh-denie,* no. 410 (July 17, 1926).

[73]The text of Peter's resolution read: "if in order to pacify believers and help the Church it is necessary to . . . change the current order of church administra-tion, then, in the interest of peace and church unity, we recognize the usefulness of temporarily transferring our prerogatives . . . to the VVTsS until our case is cleared." *APV,* no. 3-5 (March-May 1926) 34-5. On the whole issue see Regelson, 104-6 and 390-414; and Stratonov, *Smuta,* 150-71. Fletcher (*Church Underground,* 46-9) erroneously calls the Grigorian group "a schism on the right" and Grigory Archbishop "of Ekaterinoslav" instead of Ekaterinburg.

Sergii to come to terms with Grigory. Although they agreed that his methods and prerogatives were doubtful, he alone had managed to achieve legalization for the regular Orthodox Church, and therefore they hoped the VVTsS would be able to restore canonical order to the life of the Church. But Sergii did not budge. He issued a declaration stating that Grigory had gained Peter's approval by misinforming him and that the VVTsS college was not a reality because half its members could not come to Moscow for sessions anyhow. Metropolitan Peter's subsequent revocation of recognition left the VVTsS with no authoritative personalities. Although at its peak it was supported by twenty-six bishops, not one of them had the prestige and stature necessary to induce overwhelming support for the schism in the Church. The GPU appreciated this and was in pains to convince some of the leading bishops to join the Grigorian group. A case in point was Archbishop Illarion (Troitsky), one of the most learned theologians and an influential, dynamic young bishop in Patriarch Tikhon's immediate entourage prior to his arrest in 1924. At that time he was even ready, in the name of church unity, to advise the patriarch to retire. This, apparently, the GPU took for a sign of compromise in his character; for suddenly in late 1925 he was whisked from the Solovki concentration camps to Yaroslavl prison, where he was kept under exceptionally privileged conditions. There Tuchkov personally visited him and tried to convince him to join the Grigorians, promising freedom in exchange. Illarion refused, although he did write a letter to Sergii from prison begging him not to be too harsh on the Grigorians and not to impose church bans on them, which Sergii had done. For his refusal to join the Grigorians, Illarion was returned to Solovki. He died in prison in 1929 at the "ripe" age of forty-four.[74]

Unable to gain any significant personalities and lacking any program that could attract some reform-seeking elements, the Grigorian group became doomed to extinction after the granting of official legalization to Metropolitan Sergii's Synod in 1927. Grigorianism disappeared without trace in the general holocaust of the 1930s.

[74]Mikhail Polsky, *Novye mucheniki rossiiskie* (Jordanville, N.Y.: Holy Trinity Monastery, 1949-1957) 1:130-9. The Renovationists showed sympathy with the Grigorians. See *VSS*, no. 8-9 (1926) 8-9, and no. 10 (1926) 24-5.

The Ukrainian Church Schisms

The appearance of various nationalist governments in the Ukraine during the Civil War was accompanied by autonomist and separatist church movements. The right-wing Hetman Skoropadsky's administration recognized the regular Orthodox Church in Russia: Metropolitan Antony Khrapovitsky, the future head of the émigré Church Synod of Karlovci, was appointed Metropolitan of Kiev, and through him the hetman was in close touch with Patriarch Tikhon.[75] In response to a request from a group of Ukrainian nationalists, the Moscow Sobor granted the Church in the Ukraine the status of an autonomous exarchate with the right to use the Ukrainian vernacular in sermons and in some parts of the service, but autocephaly was ruled out by Patriarch Tikhon.

It was the nationalist-socialist government of Petlyura, which had replaced the hetman, that, in its first directive of January 1, 1919, "laid guidelines for the establishment of a national Ukrainian Church." But Petlyura's regime was short-lived, and the Autocephalous Church was created already under the Bolsheviks in 1921. The Bolsheviks readily extended it their support for three reasons: (1) this was the era of Ukrainification[76] policies in the Soviet Ukraine; (2) any schism within the Orthodox Church, weakening the latter, suited the Bolsheviks; and (3) "the new Church was infected with that same enthusiasm for reform that the Living Church groups were soon to display . . . introducing . . . married episcopate, lay preachers and the transformation of monasteries into working collectives . . . In its attitude toward the Soviet government the Ukrainian Church displayed enthusiasm similar to that of . . . the Living Church . . . seeking to demonstrate loyalty to the Soviet government and a willingness to cooperate in return for what legal status might be granted."[77]

The main problem of the 1921 Ukrainian Sobor was that not one canonical bishop of the Ukraine (most of them ethnic Ukrainians)

[75]Curtiss, *Russian Church*, 54.

[76]We use the term "Ukrainification" to mean an artificial and enforced policy, in contrast to "Ukrainization," which denotes a natural, voluntary process of assimilation. The same etymological differentiation will be applied in the case of "Russification" versus "Russianization," etc.

[77]Fletcher, *Church Underground*, 165-6.

agreed to participate. In the words of Vasyl Lypkivsky, the head of this Church, as long as the subject was some form of local Ukrainian church autonomy within the all-Russian Patriarchal body, several Ukrainian bishops sympathized with the movement; but as soon as the group started to act against the patriarch's will, the bishops refused to have anything to do with it.[78] Neither would any bishop agree to consecrate new episcopal candidates, and any other form of consecration of episcopal candidates would place them outside the apostolic succession—i.e., it would be uncanonical and invalid. Nevertheless, the Ukrainian Church Sobor of October 1921 carried out an unprecedented kind of consecration: laymen laid hands on the shoulders of priests and priests on the head of their first candidate, a widowed priest Lypkivsky. The latter thereupon "consecrated" additional bishops, some from among widowed priests, others from among married ones who, following the consecration, continued to live with their wives. Henceforth, all Orthodox churches in all countries would ban all sacramental relations with this schismatic Church, and the ban remains valid to the present day.

The other decisions of the sobor were similar to those of the Living Church: permitting clergy to divorce and remarry, legalizing married bishops and structuring the Church along a pattern similar to that of the Renovationists in Russia. Although, just as in most other parts of the Soviet Union, the vast majority of ordinary believers remained faithful to the Patriarchal Church, the Autocephalists in the Ukraine commanded by the mid-1920s an organization of "34 bishops, over 2,000 priests and deacons, and about 1,500 parishes," with most of the nationalistically inclined part of the Ukrainian intelligentsia in their fold.[79]

At first, the Soviet government extended its full support to the Autocephalists. The latter took advantage of the Soviet legislation removing church structures from under the control of bishops and passing them on to groups of twenty. Such nationalistic groups of twenty went about confiscating churches from the Patriarchal Church, including the famous St. Sophia Cathedral in Kiev. Soviet

[78]Metropolitan Vasyl Lypkivsky, *Vidrodzhennya tserkvy v Ukraini* (Toronto, 1959) 15.
[79]Bohdan R. Bociurkiw, "The Renovationist Church in the Soviet Ukraine, 1922-1939," *Annals of the Ukrainian Academy of Arts and Sciences in the U.S.* 9:1-2 (1961) 41-2 and nn.

government bodies readily obliged by legalizing such confiscations. As early as May 1920, a meeting of the temporary administration of this schismatic body condemned Patriarch Tikhon and bishops loyal to him as "servants of darkness" and representatives "of the old regime and a prince of this world."[80] But the Autocephalists themselves closely collaborated with the Soviet regime:

> taking literally the early Leninist doctrine of national independence within a community of nations . . . the adepts of the Ukrainian Autocephalous Church saw themselves as the vanguard of the free Ukraine. By proclaiming independence from the Moscow Patriarchate, this Church felt that it was working in line with the Party doctrine concerning national independence, and therefore welcomed the advent of Soviet power as the harbinger of a new . . . freedom.[81]

In 1929, however, the Soviet nationality policy changed, and a campaign, accompanied by purges, was launched against bourgeois nationalism. In 1930, in the context of this campaign, the Autocephalous Church was attacked, but the arrests of its clergy had begun as early as 1923. The degree of artificiality of much of its strength was shown by the fact that as soon as it lost the support of the civil authorities, most of its parishes transferred their allegiance to the Patriarchal Church. In 1930 the Autocephalists held a hurried sobor, which decreed self-dissolution of the Church and urged parish priests to continue their ecclesiastic functions without any guidance from a central church body.[82]

Its seeds proved much more long-lasting in the Ukrainian diaspora in the West. When Ukrainian Americans, mostly ex-Uniates from the former Austro-Hungarian empire, learned that an independent Church had been created in the Ukraine, without knowing the details they appealed to Kiev to send them a bishop to organize its branch in North America. A Lypkivsky-consecrated bishop, Ioann Teodorovich, was thus sent to the US from the

---

[80]K.V. Fotiev, *Popytki ukrainskoi tserkovnoi avtokefalii v XX veke* (Munich, n.d.) 29.

[81]Fletcher, *Church Underground*, 166-70.

[82]Fotiev, 47-9; Curtiss, *Russian Church*, 235; Fletcher, *Church Underground*, 168-70.

USSR in 1924. Although Teodorovich would be reconsecrated by a Greek archbishop in 1954, priests ordained by him prior to that date—and therefore uncanonical—continue to officiate in his Ukrainian Autocephalous Church without reconsecration. Instead of recognizing the 1921 self-consecrations as wrong and invalid, the Church proclaimed special days of remembrance of Lypkivsky and his associates as church heroes and martyrs, thus making it impossible for the rest of the Orthodox *oikoumene* to recognize it and to concelebrate with it.[83]

The Renovationists in the Ukraine

Renovationism also spread rapidly in the Ukraine soon after the appearance of the schism in Moscow and Petrograd. And just like the Self-consecrationists, they gained support and recognition from the Soviet authorities. At the 1923 Renovationist Sobor the Ukrainian delegation requested autonomy in order to struggle more effectively against the Self-consecrated Autocephalists and their rabid nationalist propaganda. The sobor recognized the right of autonomy in principle, but decided to relegate the formal decision on the matter to the next sobor.

Indeed, the 1925 Sobor of the Renovationists in Moscow did proclaim the Ukrainian branch of the Renovationist Schism an autocephalous Church, but "the terms of this 'autocephaly' only slightly extended the 'autonomy' granted to the Ukraine by the Moscow [Patriarchal] Sobor in 1918 . . . the Moscow [Renovationist] Holy Synod . . . retained the right to . . . confirm the metropolitan (to be elected at an All-Ukrainian Local Sobor) and to serve as the appellate instance for the Ukrainian Church. The latter was to send its delegates to the All-Russian Sobors and to be represented on the All-Russian Holy Synod."[84]

[83]Fotiev, 60-2.

[84]Bociurkiw, 55. For a comprehensive survey of this and numerous other Ukrainian church schisms in the 1920s, see the cited article and Bociurkiw's paper "Ukrainization Movements within the Russian Orthodox Church and the Ukrainian Autocephalous Orthodox Church," delivered at the June 2-4, 1977 Symposium on the Ukrainian Religious Experience, Harvard Divinity School and the Harvard Ukrainian Research Institute. A briefer story of the Ukrainian Renovationist autocephaly appears in Levitin-Shavrov, esp. 3:173-4.

Characteristically, in its opening message to the Renovationist "All-Russian

The story of Ukrainian Renovationism closely paralleled the story of the Renovationist Church in the rest of the country, except that in the Ukraine it was mending its way between the Patriarchal Autonomous Orthodox Church of the Ukraine and the Self-consecrationist nationalist autocephaly. The evidence of the poor success of the nationalists among the Ukrainian religious masses is exemplified in a Renovationist statement that they should court the Tikhonites, for "Tikhonites are more important to us than the Lypkivtsi."[85] Just as in the RSFSR, so also in the Ukraine the Soviet regime showed its preference for the Renovationists. They alone had a published journal and a theological institute in Kiev. But after Metropolitan Sergii's declaration the Soviet regime lost interest in the schism, and by 1936 Metropolitan Pimen, the head of the Ukrainian Renovationists, was apparently compelled to resign. A year later he was arrested and disappeared.[86] His fate thus followed that of the Lypkivtsi and paralleled that of the Patriarchal and other churches being destroyed at that time.

The difference between the fate of the Ukrainian Renovationists and that of the schismatic Orthodox nationalists of Lypkivsky's brand, however, was that whereas the former died never to reappear again, the latter did experience considerable revival under the German occupation (not without support from both the Germans and the Ukrainian nationalist partisans). This indicates that the nationalists had at least some natural propensity for existence in the Ukraine, while the Renovationists had no real roots in the population.[87]

Sobor" of 1925, the Ukrainian Renovationist Church calls it "her," i.e., Russia's, "national [*pomestnyi*] sobor." Stating that their delegation will participate in the sobor, the message concludes: "let the light of Christ's truth shine in the relations of the independent and free separate autocephalous Orthodox Churches . . ." In contrast, the Belorussian message speaks about one and indivisible all-Russian Church within which the Belorussians remain. The Ukrainian message appeared in Ukrainian, the Belorussian in Russian. *VSS*, no. 6 (1925) 7-8.

[85]Bociurkiw, "The Renovationist Church," 58.

[86]Ibid., 70-2.

[87]See the appendix: "The Ukrainian Autocephalous Orthodox Church," in ibid., 191-2. For an eyewitness recollection, see appendix 1 in volume 2, below (pp. 473ff).

The Lubny Schism

There was still another nationalistic schism in the Ukraine, centered in the Poltava diocese city of Lubny. According to Friedrich Heyer, the Lypkivsky schism left those Ukrainian nationalists who were at the same time dedicated Orthodox churchmen unhappy because of its uncanonicity. It was they who prevailed upon the Tikhonite Bishop Grigory (Lisovsky) of Lubny, on his appointment to Poltava, to consecrate a certain widowed priest, Feofil (Buldovsky), as his vicar for Lubny. The consecration occurred in Poltava on January 1, 1923. This was followed by the consecration of another nationalist, Sergii (Labuntsev), in the same diocese. In 1925 the two vicar-bishops decided to declare themselves an autocephalous Church of the Ukraine, differing from the "Self-consecrators" in that Feofil and his bishops had been properly consecrated. A bishop from the diocese of Podolia and two from the Chernigov diocese joined Buldovsky, and the government readily permitted them to hold a "church sobor" in Lubny in May 1925. The "sobor" declared the formation of a "Council of Bishops of the Whole Ukraine," separate and wholly independent from Moscow. Their claim to canonical legitimacy, however, remained unfounded, as not a single diocesan bishop joined the movement, while vicar-bishops, according to the canons, have no independent administrative powers whatsoever; they can only act as delegates of their diocesan superiors when empowered by the latter.

Patriarch Tikhon and his Synod responded by excommunicating these new schismatics. Several parishes in the Lubny district and in the dioceses of Kharkov, Dnepropetrovsk and Chernigov joined Buldovsky, but the dissemination of the schism was so limited that even in Poltava it failed to win a single parish. Thereupon Buldovsky tried his luck in Kharkov and Lugansk. After the closing of the last church in Lugansk, which apparently had belonged to Buldovsky, by the Soviets in 1937, he returned to Kharkov again, where apparently he had no adherents, because he lived there as a private citizen.[88] He resurfaced again under the

[88]Heyer, 90-2.

Nazi occupation in Kharkov, joining the renewed Ukrainian Autocephalous Church, according to a source of that Church.[89]

Were there Sincere Theological Seekings in Renovationism?

The most common complaint from the provincial Renovationist press after 1923, and one of the most prominent themes at the 1925 Sobor, was the terrible poverty of the faithful provincial clergy of this movement.

> Boycotted by the local population, carrying the burden of "income" taxes exceeding their earnings, some Renovationist priests were leading a pitiful, semi-starved existence. They served in unheated, half-ruined churches and were constantly insulted by the traditionalist fanatics as well as by those of the atheist camp.
>
> They presented a striking contrast to the well-fed, prosperous priests in the Renovationist administrative posts who were mostly OGPU collaborators. But the latter . . . were a tiny minority that was not representative of the mass of the Renovationist priesthood. Even Vvedensky recognized that:
>
> "I am drawn to tears by your sight, because I know in what conditions you are functioning . . ." said Vvedensky in his closing speech at the 1925 Sobor. "I know that many bishops have a hot meal once in three days, that priests have to live on 10 rubles a month . . . when I see [them] and the laymen who have grasped the value of renovation of the Church, I bow low to them all." (He kneels and bows to the ground.)[90]

What was this "renovation," then, for the sake of which *honest*

[89]Dublyansky, 39. Characteristic of a sense of canonical insecurity, the Autocephalist author stresses that "Metropolitan Feofil" recognized "the canonical situation of our Church." The author conceals the more than shaky canonicity of the "Metropolitan of Kharkov," as Buldovsky named himself.

[90]Levitin-Shavrov, 3:48 and 163. See also *VSS*, no. 10 (1926) 25-6; and no. 11 (1926) 20-2.

people were ready to sacrifice so much, for which they were even willing to be associated knowingly with a Church led by OGPU collaborators?

The most sincere and theologically oriented faction was that of Antonin Granovsky. Breaking with the rest of the Renovationists and declaring his autocephaly on June 29, 1923, he stated his opposition to the "autocratic principle" of the Patriarchal Church and to "the priestly oligarchy" of the Renovationists. This was followed a few months later by the abolition of all clerical titles, decorations, miters, etc., and the retention of only the three basic ranks: deacons, priests and bishops. He then gave up his title of metropolitan and modified his vestments, thence distinguished from those of regular priests only by an omophoron, the pectoral episcopal medallion of the Virgin and the episcopal staff. Further modernizing his Church, he replaced Church Slavonic with Russian and adopted the Gregorian calendar; but his modernism did not prejudice him against monasticism, which he admired as the ultimate expression of man's search for asceticism, solitude, prayer and humility. He saw these also as a necessary spiritual preparation for the episcopacy and opposed the idea of married bishops as too much concerned with family matters to fully dedicate themselves to the Church. He moved the altar from behind the icon screen to the center of the church in order to celebrate the eucharist in direct communion with the faithful. He composed two beautiful liturgies in the Russian idiom by drawing upon the theologically most meaningful parts in the ancient liturgies commonly used by the Orthodox Church. In his liturgies he placed the whole emphasis on the eucharistic prayers, which he expanded at the cost of cutting down most of the other parts. He also insisted on frequent communion, in which he administered the body and blood separately, deviating from the Orthodox tradition of mixing the two in one chalice. He was a great preacher, sometimes delivering sermons of two hours in duration. Assessments differ, however, on the effect of his sermons. His admirer Levitin, who had never attended his services, claims that he preached to full audiences and was very popular among his flock. Other eyewitness reports by both Russians and foreigners claim that his listeners never exceeded "one or two hundred people." According to them, his sermons were very crude and relied upon name-calling, cynical jokes and exchanges with the audience to build rapport and to gain effects. Evoking similarly rude and vocal comments from the audience, he would then respond in the same vein. Soon after breaking with the Renovationists, whose nominal leader he had been, he was cursing them in his sermons, calling them "a pot of refuse by the smell of which the believers can accurately conclude what it is worth."

Politically, Granovsky had been a consistent enemy of monarchism since at least 1906. He embraced the idea of Christian socialism, which he apparently believed the Soviet system would help to bring about. In some of his sermons he even thanked the Soviets for having shaken up the country, claiming that it was his own duty "to revolutionize the Church."[91] He also enthusiastically welcomed the separation of Church and state and claimed that Christianity had suffered more from church establishments than from regimes like that of the Soviets. His attacks on Tikhon and his Church as sclerotic, monarchist and counterrevolutionary seem to indicate that he believed that the persecutions of religion by the Soviets were caused by Soviet fears of reaction and counter-revolution, not by the regime's intrinsic hatred of Christianity.

Antonin and his small group of dedicated priests preached and practiced material poverty. In 1921-1922 he was an enthusiastic supporter of the Soviet campaign to confiscate church valuables. Antonin apparently had no doubts about the government's sincerity, and he actively participated in the campaign to help the famine-stricken. All these points were contained in the resolution of their only sobor, held in Moscow on June 30, 1924 and attended by two bishops, three priests and 120 laymen. His constant emphasis, as well as that of other speeches at the sobor, was on the inseparability of clergy from the laity and upon the former's dedication and service to the latter.[92] Despite its socialism, mod-

---

[91]See the letter from Russia in *APV*, no. 18 (October 31, 1923) 142-3. A similar negative opinion is expressed by d'Herbigny, who attended Granovsky's church and a conference of his group, probably the 1924 "Sobor." See his *Tserkovnaya zhizn' v Moskve* (Paris, 1926) 45-51.

[92]The factual information on the Granovsky group and on his reforms is from Levitin-Shavrov, 3:235-96. Titlinov, whose sincerity is not in question, also argues that Patriarch Tikhon's objection to the confiscation of sacramental objects was contrary to the ancient church canons, which state that " 'the church estate is the estate of the paupers and beggars . . .' so much more then is it the property of the famine-stricken starving people." *Novaya tserkov'*, 6.

ernism and theological and liturgical good sense, however, this movement fell apart very soon after Antonin's death in 1927. This seems to indicate that the source of its vitality lay not in its ideas or reforms, but in the charismatic properties of its leader and the enthusiasm he generated while he lived.

Vvedensky's Union of Communities of Ancient Apostolic Churches (SODATs) was the second largest branch of Renovationism, after Krasnitsky's Living Church. Its social policies and ideas and some of its original aims of theological reform were not unlike those of Antonin Granovsky's movement, but Vvedensky never went that far in liturgical experiments.

Vvedensky first came into prominence in 1910 as the author of a survey of the religious notions and convictions of the Russian intelligentsia, conducted through a liberal secular periodical. From the analysis of this survey he concluded that 90 percent of the Russian intelligentsia were either atheists or religiously indifferent, and that a radical reform of the Church was needed to reconvert the intelligentsia. This did not make him politically radical, however. As an army chaplain during World War I, according to one source, he attacked socialism in his sermons until the fall of the Provisional Government. Even "in 1918 and until the abolition of army chaplains . . . he attacked Bolshevism in his sermons to the soldiers."[93] But after the Bolshevik victory he would soon proclaim Marxism "the Gospel printed in the atheistic language."[94]

An unstable romantic-neurotic product of Russia's "decadent" Silver Age, he chanted the liturgy as if reciting poetry, working himself up into an almost hysterical frenzy. This frequently brought him into conflict with his ecclesiastic superiors when he was still a member of the regular Orthodox Church. His religiosity was sincere, yet he lacked moral scruples and engaged in such sexual promiscuity during his Renovationist career (divorcing, remarrying and having lovers "on the side") that had he

---

[93]Shishkin, 260. On his own Shishkin would not have been a reliable source, but on Vvedensky he quotes the Karlovci Synod's *Tserkovnye vedomosti* (no. 1-2 [1924]), which was quite well informed on such matters in those years. Vvedensky conceals such facts from his autobiography and presents himself as invariably progressive and prosocialist. However, he is not a reliable source—as witnessed by his false claim that the idea of a patriarch was unpoular among the religious masses, whereas the opposite was true. See his *Tserkov' i gosudarstvo,* 30 and 225-7.

[94]Simon, *Church State,* 25.

remained in the regular Orthodox Church he would have been defrocked for this alone. As a married priest and a very ambitious man, he differed radically from Granovsky on the question of monasticism. Vvedensky hated monks and wanted to see married priests consecrated as bishops. On this Vvedensky's views coincided with those of Krasnitsky, the leader of the most numerous faction in Renovationism. This branch, calling itself the Living Church, most perfectly fitted Granovsky's description of Renovationism as a "greed-for-power" rebellion of the married priests, at least as far as its leadership was concerned. Otherwise, it had no independent intellectual and theological value and was in these respects a pale reflection of Vvedensky's ideas. It does not warrant an independent discussion in this brief survey.

Despite its lack of originality and distinction, it was the Living Church and Vvedensky's SODATs which commanded the most clerical allegiance. Both were also most intensively hated by the bulk of the laity.[85] All the original factions shared the aim of simplifying and modernizing the service. All translated it into Russian to render it more comprehensible to the laity. (Vvedensky, however, was more preoccupied with philosophical sophistication in sermons, in order to attract the intelligentsia.) All sought to prevent a "monarchic"-patriarchal system of administration, and to increase the active participation of the laity and the lower clergy in the Church and their role in church administration. On this point they stood not too far from the official platform of the Patriarchal Church, whose 1917-1918 Sobor laid the groundwork for a conciliar-federal church administration where the role of the patriarch was to be limited to that of a primus-inter-pares chairman of elected conciliar bodies of both upper and lower clergy and laity.

As far as liturgical and ritual reforms were concerned, the council left the door open and the patriarch took a liberal attitude by not interfering with Granovsky's experiments, and only in 1924 banned him as a clergyman for denouncing the Patriarchal Church and for declaring his autocephaly.[96] The patri-

---

[85]Vvedensky himself was several times physically attacked by Orthodox laymen, and once required two months in a hospital to recuperate from a head injury caused by a rock hurled at him. Levitin-Shavrov, 1:111-5 et passim.

[96]Ibid., 3:205.

arch also expressed sympathy for services in Russian and for the adoption of the Gregorian calendar. Both, however, met with stubborn resistance from the laity, which now associated them with the hated Renovationists.[97] Such changes had to be dropped not only by the Patriarchal but eventually even by the Renovationist churches. Indeed, after 1924, practically all innovations except married bishops and divorced and remarried priests were dropped by the Renovationists. Even provisions for broad participation by laity and lower clergy in the administration had to be replaced by a traditional synod of bishops. Another distinction separating the Renovationists from the Patriarchal Church was their unquestioning loyalty to the Soviet government and its socialist ideals. They attempted to collaborate with it, and this left them open to OGPU infiltration and manipulation. Ironically, by the second half of the 1920s, the "revolutionary" Renovationists came much more closely to resemble the prerevolutionary "reactionary" synodal Church, in the form of its organization as well as in its spirit of subordination to the state, than did the Patriarchal Church, which insisted on separation and independence from the state.

Since complete subordination to the state remained the most unchangeable and persistent trait of the Renovationist schism, it is here that one should search for the reasons why, even by the late 1920s, nearly ten thousand clerics remained faithful despite great material and moral suffering and a genuine awareness of the political and personal immorality of many of their leaders. Moreover, as Levitin writes, in the late 1920s and early 1930s there "began to appear in the Renovationist Church young priests who were not contaminated by the spirit of subservience to the GPU to the same extent as the 'Old Renovationists.' " This was highly disquieting to Tuchkov, who looked upon Renovationism only as a "figure on the chessboard of the struggle against the Church." In 1934 arrests of the Renovationists began with the rounding up of the Renovationist youth in Leningrad, alleged to be members of

[97]Tikhon even issued a decree in support of these reforms in 1923 but had to revoke it because of the laity's opposition. In *Ostraya Luka* the protagonist, Fr. Sergii, laments the use of Russian and the Gregorian calendar by the Renovationists, because this will delay for many years the psychological possibility of their use in the Orthodox Church (281-2).

the fictitious "Brotherhood of Sts. Zachariah and Elizabeth."[98] While the movement repelled the believing lay masses, it continued to attract some young priests and candidates for the priesthood. Why?

Vvedensky's writings and speeches reveal a dedicated, if somewhat perverse, Hegelian who speaks about the *Zeitgeist* and the danger that those clerics and religious laymen who fail "to embrace the contemporary spirit of life . . . will not be able to keep pace with the victorious run of the chariot of life . . . will be crushed by this triumphal chariot."[99] This type of reasoning in simplistic Hegelianism can lead to the rationalization and full acceptance of any victorious political power, for "everything that is real is rational." This Hegelianism and related theories of general progress dominated the nineteenth-century philosophical thinking on which the generations of seminarians who were serving as priests in the 1920s and 1930s had been raised. True, Nietzscheanism began to penetrate and influence Russian intellectuals in the late nineteenth and early twentieth centuries, but a misreading of its concepts could have easily been used to supplement Hegelianism and to justify the Soviet "reality" of a victorious political party, historically justified, and led by revolutionary "supermen" to whom ordinary morality and laws, according to Nietzsche, did not apply.[100]

These Hegelian and Nietzschean rationalizations were grafted onto other intellectual and emotional layers. One was what Fr. Florovsky calls a tradition of "social Christianity" in Orthodoxy coming down from the great eastern fathers of the Church, particularly St. John Chrysostom, who viewed wealth as invariably unjust, individualism as selfish, and had called for a simple life of communal sharing. Dostoevsky called it "our Russian socialism." This was emphasized by the Slavophile patristic revival and its emphasis on communality and by the traditional poverty of the Russian rural clergy and its compassionate appreciation of peasant poverty—an attitude that often made the nineteenth-century semi-

[98]A. Levitin-Krasnov, *Vospominaniya*, vol. 1: *Likhie gody* (Paris, 1977) 256-7.
[99]Levitin-Shavrov, 1:118-20.
[100]On the destructive effect of Nietzscheanism on the Russian intelligentsia of the time, see Nadezhda Mandelshtam, *Vtoraya kniga* (Paris: YMCA Press, 1972) 51-3 et passim.

naries hotbeds of social radicalism.[101] It was apparently these
members of the Christian intelligentsia, who had retained radical
traditions and preserved some elements of the religion of progress
even despite the shock of the revolution and its horrors, who
continued to be attracted to Renovationism. Indeed, there is much
emphasis on social Christianity in the Renovationist periodicals
of the time, as well as on apologetics in a modern social context
and on mission toward the atheists.[102] This prominence of the
Renovationist thrust was, of course, helped by the fact that the
Patriarchal Church was denied publishing rights. Likewise, the
Renovationists were much more prominent in public disputes with
propagandists of atheism. This again could have been explained
by the semi-underground status of the Patriarchal Church, but the
fact remained that the Renovationists were definitely visible and
trying very hard to appear "modern" and "progressive." Thus,
the programs of their theology schools emphasized such subjects as
Christian ethics, public speaking and homiletics, apologetics and
the "philosophical justification of the Christian Weltanschauung,"
but totally lacked courses in liturgics, biblical studies and canonical, dogmatic, patristic and pastoral theology.[103] They were also
the first theological colleges in Russia to accept both sexes as
students. All this was very modern and must have appealed to
some, but what sort of priests would they prepare without any
knowledge of basic subjects in theology?

But why did the most prominent prerevolutionary social-
Christians not side with the Renovationists? Primarily because for
them, as has already been mentioned, social doctrines were of
secondary value and could not take precedence over the fact of
the militant atheism of the socialist state. They could not serve
God and an anti-God regime at the same time. Apparently, they

---

[101]The first Russian hospitals, orphanages and old peoples' homes were organized by the Church, as early as the fifteenth century. The state engaged in these
activities directly only from the end of the eighteenth century. Georges Florovsky,
Christianity and Culture, Collected Works, 2 (Belmont, Mass.: Nordland, 1974)
134-9. On the seminaries' radicalism, see Evlogy, *Put',* 15-27.

[102]This observation is based on the scrutiny of most issues of the official *VSS*
and two issues of *Khristianin* (nos. 1 and 2-3 for 1924). They contain such
articles as "The Social Teaching of Christ," a section of basic theology and
apologetics for the adult layman, etc.

[103]Bishop Georgy Dobronravov, "Moskovskaya bogoslovskaya akademiya,"
Khristianin, no. 1 (June 1924) 25-7.

took the view that in the conditions of persecution the Church could not afford the luxury of reforms and experimentation. Let her preserve the main treasure intact. The mass lay support that the Patriarchal Church enjoyed was proof that this attitude was generally shared by the Russian Christians, particularly by the less sophisticated who were unable to find dialectical excuses for the regime and its attacks on the Church, as the intellectuals with their Hegelian legacy were prone to do. We must remember that this was the era of the relatively liberal New Economic Policy and later of the beginnings of the first five-year plan, when illusions about the great social future were quite rampant among the intelligentsia and must have affected also the social-Christians among them.

This illusion merged with the traditional Byzantine idea of church symphony with a Christian state, which in post-seventeenth-century Russia had been replaced by the almost total subordination of the Church to the state—and to a much more secular state at that. When this semi-Christian state collapsed, the victory of the most militantly atheistic ideology and party was thought by many to have been providential. In a nation that had adopted the idea of Holy Russia as its national dream, this collapse had a truly traumatically confusing effect on many. It was clear to everybody that if a large section of the population, perhaps even a majority, had not become either violently atheist or at least indifferent to religion, the terror and persecution of religion could not have reached such proportions as they did. This led to the recognition by many Christians of a major failure of the historical Church as well as of the historical Russian state.[104]

In the context of Hegelian thinking, this could and did lead to the recognition of the Bolshevik victory and of the Soviet state as a historical necessity. The failure of the Bolshevik attempts to export the revolution and the subsequent reduction of Bolshevism to the re-creation of the Russian state allowed the Hegelian mind to see in this a dialectical transformation of internationalism into

[104]"What the western churches are going through now we experienced in the 1920s, and we are just beginning to recover from their effects," said one contemporary leading Soviet Russian priest and theologian to this author, adding that many serious studies had been written at the time by leading churchmen in Russia on the effect of the theomachistic revolution on the Russian mentality. These manuscripts remain mostly unpublished.

a national state. Add to this Nietzschean amoralism, and the result is cases like that of Bishop Vladimir Putyata, who, as early as 1919, declared the formation of a Church of the Toiling People (*Narodnaya trudovaya Tserkov'*), "which would cooperate with the Bolsheviks." This case could be viewed with suspicion, as Putyata was in serious moral trouble and Tikhon had defrocked him. But there were other similar trends among the clergy and the hierarchy that cannot be as easily dismissed—for instance, the so-called "Movement of Church Bolshevism," which appeared very soon after the February Revolution but which, however, would fall apart after the Bolshevik victory and its attack on the Church. The claim that its head was Georgy Shavelsky, the Chaplain-in-Chief of the Imperial Armed Forces, a very influential church leader and a close acquaintance of Nicholas II, is highly questionable. The other leading members are alleged to have been the priests Vvedensky and Boyarsky, all (except Shavelsky, who would emigrate with the Whites) future leading Renovationists.[105]

[105]Mikhail Agursky, *Ideologiya natsional-bol'shevizma* (Paris: YMCA Press, 1980) 107. The author gives no source for this information, although he adds to this other unsubstantiated labels for Shavelsky: "an opportunist" and "a participant in the Union of Russian People." All three claims are in doubt, in view of (a) Shavelsky's tremendous popularity in the armed forces—in early 1917 he was elected by secret balloting of all army chaplains as Chief Chaplain for life; and (b) at the 1917-1918 Sobor the right-winger Antony (Khrapovitsky) begged him to accept episcopal consecration and the title of metropolitan, while the moderate Platon and the liberal Arseny (who himself would become the runner-up for the patriarchal throne) nominated him as their choice for patriarch. Shavelsky declined, and remained a priest, which does not speak for his opportunism. The fact that such politically divergent bishops favored him suggests that the motives must have been purely pastoral and that Shavelsky was free from either left or right extremism. In fact, he became the deputy chairman of the Stavropol Sobor of 1919, which formed the Provisional Higher Church Administration for the territories under the Whites. After the victory of the extreme right-wingers in the Karlovci Synod's administration, Shavelsky was forced to "retire" in 1924 from active clerical-administrative duties among the Russian émigrés in Sofia (Bulgaria), remaining, however, active in the Bulgarian Church until his death after World War II. See Fedor Bokach, "Protopresviter G.I. Shavel'skii," an obituary; and Prof. N.N. Glubokovsky, *Protopresviter o. G.I. Shavel'skii*, a brochure on the occasion of Shavelsky's thirty-five years as a priest (Sofia, March 21, 1930)—all in the Shavelsky Collection, the Bakhmeteff Archives (box 6, file mss.).

There is some confusion as to the title of Putyata's "Church." Agursky calls it *Narodnaya tserkov'*, Levitin, *Trudovaya tserkov'*. Otherwise, Agursky's information appears to be factually correct on Putyata, except that according to other sources, he had never had such a mass following as Agursky claims. Eventually,

The birth and development of the Renovationist movement itself coincided with the "Change of Signposts" movement among the Russian intelligentsia, who believed that with the introduction of the New Economic Policy the Bolshevik regime was evolving from Marxist internationalism to a Russian nationalist and strongly authoritarian state. Levitin rightly concludes: "The Living Church ambitions to become a part of the Soviet state apparatus made sense only in terms of the ideas of the Change-of-Signposts ideologists."[106] Since the latter movement was strongly *etatist* and nationalistic, it is no wonder that so many former members of the Union of Russian People and other pro-tsarist, right-wing clerics found their way to the Renovationist movement. They could rationalize close and active collaboration with the Soviet regime, even with the GPU, in Hegelian terms or by employing a Nietzscheanism superimposed upon national-messianic concepts. It is in these terms that the following statements should be understood: "Every honest Christian must . . . become a fighter for the human truth and do his utmost to materialize the great ideas of the October Revolution."[107] "Not in vain did Dostoevsky prophesy that the East, Russia, would give the new word to the world."[108]

In other words, while some Renovationists, such as Vvedensky and Granovsky, sympathized with the new regime because it was socialist, others did so for nationalistic reasons. Both, however, were using Hegelian and Nietzschean arguments to justify the regime's legitimacy and to rationalize its dictatorial policies. The fact that the Renovationist movement entered into a particularly rapid decline with the abandonment of the New Economic Policy (i.e., with the death blow to the intelligentsia's illusions that the Marxist-Leninist ideology was being abolished and a Russian national state was replacing it) is an indication that the non-Marxist nationalistic motives were more typical among the rank-and-file Renovationists than were socialist, Hegelian or Nie-

left without any following, he returned to the Orthodox Church as an ordinary monk through repentance. In 1934 he was finally defrocked for joining the Grigorians. See Sergii's decree no. 58, *ZhMP*, no. 22 (1934) 2: Levitin-Shavrov, 1:51-2 et passim.

[106]Ibid., 1:138.

[107]See the message of the 1923 Renovationist Sobor to the Soviet government in ibid., 2:93.

[108]Ibid., 102, Vvedensky's speech at the above sobor. In it he also amply cites Nietzsche with great reverence, as an authority and "prophet."

tzschean ones. At any rate, the most ideologically socialist and theologically creative branch of Renovationism was also the smallest. In other words, the socialist, Hegelian and Nietzschean rationalizations may have been characteristic only of the Renovationist leaders. The mass of their clerical followers might have been guided by some *etatist* Soviet-Russian nationalism under the influence of their leaders, but probably more typically by concern for their families' safety. The Soviet attacks on the Patriarchal Church in the 1920s evoked domestic pressure from priests' wives on their husbands to join the politically safer factions.[109] Another motive was the traditional antiepiscopal (or more correctly, antimonastic) strain in Renovationism. This trend commanded the support not only of ambitious and "learned" lower clerics, but of many a sincere priest and lay theologian. The traditional populism of the rural clergy must also have led it to hope that by modernizing and adapting to the new realities the Church would be able to return to her fold that part of the nation which had fallen away. This led thousands of the clergy to side with a Church that accepted and even welcomed the Soviet system. Hegelian rationalization, combined with the post-seventeenth-century historical *etatist* mentality of the clergy, justified cooperation with any government, particularly one that had been swept into power by the revolution—one that could claim legitimacy in terms of Hegel's historicism.

All these justifications became untenable with the general onslaught against all religions by the end of the 1920s. The crisis of the Christian-socialist consciousness expressed itself for those who continued to cling to some of the original illusions in suicides and desertions to the camp of active atheists.[110]

The Renovationists' degeneration from sincere Christian-radicals or reformists to unscrupulous agents of the OGPU was the

---

[109]Mikhail Polsky, *Polozhenie tserkvi v sovetskoi Rossii* (Jerusalem, 1931), as cited in *Deyaniya vtorogo vsezarubezhnogo sobora russkoi pravoslavnoi tserkvi zagranitsei* (Belgrade, 1939) 68.

[110]According to the Soviet historian Sheinman (see note 67) Bishop Mikhail (Semenov) committed suicide in a state of mental breakdown, and the Renovationist Metropolitan Nikolai Platonov and Fr. Kalinovsky became antireligious propagandists. Irinarkh Stratonov, *Krizis tserkovnoi smuty v Rossii i dal'neishii ee rost za rubezhom* (Berlin, 1929), an offprint from an unnamed journal, in the Lieb Archive, Hd, no. 21. According to Levitin, Platonov returned to the *Orthodox* Church on his death bed.

result of their isolation. Having found themselves alone, without
the support and protection of any reliable and dedicated lay following, they had to search for alternative support and protection.
The only option was the overtly theomachistic Soviet state. To
accept this option they had to rationalize their collaboration by
claiming affinity of socialist ideas, and by pretending that the
regime's violent atheism was not an integral property of the
ideology but a legacy of the historical circumstances of the recent
past in which the Church had been an organ of the ruling and
exploiting classes. In this process the Renovationists shifted the
burden of guilt from the executioner to the victim, closing their
eyes to the official Soviet leaders' own public admissions that any
Church at any time was their enemy and would be fought unto
destruction.[111] Temporarily the state would oblige the Renovationists, but only at the price of full submission to *its* church policies;
the Renovationists were to fulfil the functions of a church branch
of the GPU. The above rationalizations made it psychologically
possible for the Renovationist leaders, with the help of some
Hegelian and Nietzschean juggling, to accept this role, hopelessly
compromising themselves in the eyes of the believers and thus
losing the flock on the way.

The Renovationist legacy of Church-state cooperation, of using
the Church for the regime's political aims, had a long-lasting effect
on the Orthodox Church, which was allowed to revive during
World War II, but only under the conditions of complete political
submission to the atheistic state. A Soviet atheist historian sums
this up in the following words:

> The Tikhonites were forced to adopt the positions of
> the Renovationists . . . although under a Tikhonite flag. . . .
> The masses of believers could not forgive the Renovation-
> ists . . . their attempt to "corrupt the faith" . . . by their
> reforms. The Tikhonites vocally announced that they were
> the guardians of the "old faith" . . . winning the believers.

---

[111]I.I. Skvortsov-Stepanov, a Central Committee member and a leading party
ideologist, openly stated in a published lecture in 1922 that for the while the
splits in the Church were in the communist interest, but that in principle the
Party remained an enemy of all religions and would eventually struggle against all
of them. Quotation in Levitin-Shavrov, 1:186-8.

> The Patriarchal Church has taken the position prepared
> by the Renovationists. . . . This was not voluntary . . . the
> Church had to adapt herself to new conditions and thus
> to win a right to exist. This road . . . was built by the
> Renovationists.[112]

Whatever the oversimplifications of the above statement, the truth is that the regenerated Patriarchal Orthodox Church was forced to inherit the worst traits of both "worlds": the extreme conservatism of the prerevolutionary official Orthodoxy, and the sycophancy (at least as far as the leadership of the Church is concerned) of Renovationism.

---

[112]Shishkin, 355-7.

CHAPTER 3

Eradication of the Best:
Trials of the Church in the 1920s

In the course of the Civil War, the grain storages in the eastern grain districts, exposed to periodic droughts, were used up, and the droughts of 1920-1921 consequently resulted in an unprecedented famine across the country lasting from the summer of 1921 to the summer of 1922. In August 1921, Patriarch Tikhon appealed for aid to the heads of various Christian churches outside Russia. Simultaneously, "a national ecclesiastical committee was set up to succor the starving, and collections were taken at every church." The government ordered this committee closed, and the collected money was handed over to the government Famine Relief Committee. On February 19, 1922, the patriarch appealed to the parochial councils to surrender all articles of value belonging to the churches, except those used in sacraments, for the benefit of the starving. The government at first authorized the publication of this patriarchal order in state newspapers, but then changed its mind and issued a decree of February 28 ordering the confiscation of all objects of value by state agents, *including* those used for the sacraments. On the same day, the patriarch responded with another pastoral letter banning the handing over of sacramental objects, but urging the believers once again to be generous in their aid to the famine-stricken.[1]

It was precisely this response that the government was hoping for, in order to begin a propaganda and terror campaign against the

[1]Struve, 34-5.

Church, deliberately misrepresenting her as a heartless institution indifferent to human suffering. A case in point is a secret internal order of February 22, 1922, never made public to the present day. *Samizdat* sources, distributing the document over Lenin's signature, attribute it to him.

> The incident in Shuya must be correlated to . . . resistance to the confiscation of church valuables . . . here our enemy is committing a great error, trying to involve us in a decisive struggle precisely when it would be particularly hopeless and unprofitable for them. Contrarywise, for us this is not only exceptionally beneficial but the only moment when we are given 99 out of 100 chances to gain a full and crushing victory over our enemy and assure for ourselves the necessary positions for decades ahead. It is precisely now and only now, when there is cannibalism in the famine-stricken areas and hundreds if not thousands of corpses are lying along the roads, that we can (and therefore must) carry out the confiscation of valuables with fanatical and merciless energy and not hesitate to suppress any form of resistance. It is precisely now and only now that the vast majority of the peasant masses will either support us or at least will be unable to give any decisive support to those . . . who might and would want to try to resist the Soviet decree.

> We must confiscate in the shortest possible time as much as possible to create for ourselves a fund of several hundred million rubles . . . Without this fund, government work . . . and the defense of our positions in Genoa are absolutely unthinkable . . . With success we can do this only now . . . for no other opportunity but the current terrible famine will give us a mood of the wide masses such as would provide us with their sympathies or at least neutrality . . . during the operation of confiscating the valuables . . .

> Now our victory over the reactionary clergy is guaranteed. Moreover, the main part of our enemies among the Russian

émigrés, i.e., the SRs and the Milyukovites, will find it very hard to carry on their struggle against us . . . precisely because of the famine . . .

Therefore . . . it is precisely now that we must wage a merciless battle against the reactionary clergy and suppress its resistance with such cruelty that it will remember it for several decades . . .

One of the most efficient members of the VTsIK should be sent to Shuya . . . with an oral instruction given him by a Politburo member. The instruction should be that he arrest in Shuya as many people as possible, and by no means less than several dozen local priests, craftsmen and members of the bourgeoisie on suspicion of direct or indirect participation in active resistance to the VTsIK decree on confiscations. Immediately on his return, he makes an oral report to the Politburo. On the basis of this the Politburo also gives an oral instruction to the judicial authorities that the trial of the Shuya rioters, for resisting aid to the hungry, be conducted in as short a time as possible, concluding in the maximum possible number of executions in the ranks of the most influential local reactionaries in Shuya. If possible, similar executions should be carried out in Moscow and other spiritual centers of the country.

At the next party congress a secret session should be organized jointly with leading members of the GPU, the Commissariat of Justice and the Revolutionary Tribunal. A secret decision of the congress should approve a mercilessly decisive confiscation of church valuables. The more members of the reactionary bourgeoisie we manage to shoot, the better. It is precisely now that we must give such a lesson to these characters that they would not dare to think of any resistance for at least the next few decades. . . . Lenin. (TOP SECRET. NO COPIES TO BE MADE.)[2]

The style of the document, particularly in the original Russian,

[2]Reprinted in *VRSKbD*, no. 98/iv (1970) 54-60.

is unmistakably Lenin's (though this in itself is no guarantee against a forgery by a talented imitator). The reference to Shuya likewise tends to confirm its authenticity. Particular resistance to the confiscation of church valuables took place in this industrial town not far from Moscow in March-April 1922. After a detachment of soldiers with machine guns had to be called in to suppress the believers, four civilians were killed and ten wounded. Fifty-four clerics and believers were tried. Eight priests, two laymen and one laywoman were executed and twenty-six imprisoned. The fifth and most complete edition of Lenin's works only mentions "a Lenin letter of March 19 to the Politburo members requesting immediate suppression of the resistance of clergy to the decree of February 23 on the confiscation of church valuables," but the text of the letter is nowhere to be found in this fifty-five-volume edition. The cited letter is probably the one. The only puzzling thing is the difference in dates. The error between March and February, i.e., between month 3 and month 2, can easily be explained by a *samizdat* copyist's typing error. Less easily explainable is the discrepancy between day 22 and day 19, unless the former could be the date of a copy of the letter made for one of its addressees; or again it could be a typing error committed in *samizdat.*[3]

An indirect indicator of the authenticity of the above document is the following evidence that Lenin's administration was trying to do the utmost to make capital for itself out of the famine. On September 8, 1921, the nongovernmental public All-Russian Famine Relief Committee was arrested. According to the *Cheka,* its members were underground members of the Central Committee of the prerevolutionary Constitutional-Democratic Party and had cooperated with the Antonov anti-Bolshevik peasant rebellion. Oliver Radkey, one of the most thorough and authoritative western specialists on the Antonovites, is convinced, however, that the *Cheka* allegation has no factual foundation whatsoever.[4]

But, to return to the Lenin letter, it should be stated that its

[3]Polnoe sobranie sochinenii, 45 (Moscow, 1964) 666-7. The error in dating on the *samizdat* copy may in fact be an indirect pointer to its authenticity: had this been a conscious forgery, the forgers would have been much more careful in giving accurate circumstantial details, e.g., dating.

[4]*The Unknown Civil War in Soviet Russia* (Stanford: Hoover Institution Press, 1976) 84 and n. 41.

essential recommendation corresponded to the Soviet treatment of the Church in connection with the church valuables issue. A total of 1,414 incidents involving bloodshed between believers and government representatives were reported by the Soviet press. The fate of Metropolitan Venyamin of Petrograd is another excellent illustration that it was not the feeding of the hungry that was the primary aim of the regime in its confrontation with the Church. An enlightened young bishop of rural clergy background, elected to his see by one of the revolutionary laity-clergy assemblies of 1917, Venyamin enjoyed too much popularity with the city working class and youth to be tolerated by the "proletarian dictatorship." On the issue of the church valuables he proved also "inconveniently" flexible. In Petrograd, the confiscations affair proceeded in the following manner. On March 24, 1922, the *Petrograd Pravda* published a letter signed by future Renovationist leaders—including Vvedensky, Krasnitsky, Belkov and Boyarsky —and some wavering elements—a total of twelve signatures. The letter attacked the position of the church majority as counter-revolutionary and requested the immediate and total surrender of all church valuables for the antifamine campaign. The letter granted, "however, that believers' representatives should partici-pate in the supervision over the process." At a diocesan clergy conference that followed, Venyamin pacified both sides by stating that the main thing was to avoid bloodshed. He delegated Vvedensky and Boyarsky for further negotiations with the Soviet government of Petrograd. An agreement between Venyamin and the city soviet followed, according to which all valuables were subject to confiscation, but believers would have the option of making collections and giving the famine-relief teams the equiva-lent of the value of the precious sacramental objects in money or jewelry. Moreover, Venyamin issued an appeal along these lines, also begging the believers not to offer any resistance to the Soviet teams and to avoid all forms of violence. Consequently, the Petrograd church valuables confiscation campaign went so smoothly that the head of the city militia complimented the metropolitan on this account in his official report.

However, the Vvedensky-Belkov-Krasnitsky-Kalinovsky May putsch (the taking over of the patriarch's chancery) Venyamin refused to recognize, even temporarily excommunicating Vvedensky "until his repentance." The link between the Vvedensky-Living Church-Renovationist putsch and the GPU is further illustrated by the reaction of the Soviet government: "A couple of days after his 'excommunication,' Vvedensky arrived at the metropolitan's residence accompanied by the ex-chairman of the Petrograd *Cheka,* . . . Bakaev . . . an 'overprocurator' of sorts for Petrograd church affairs . . . and presented the metropolitan with an ultimatum . . . to either revoke his edict of 'excommunication' or to face trial on the church valuables . . . which will result in death sentences for him and those nearest to him."

The metropolitan did not budge. Several days later he was arrested, along with the leading personalities of the Orthodox Church of the Petrograd diocese. In lieu of Vvedensky, who was in the hospital with a bad head injury from a rock hurled at him by Venyamin's faithful, the main prosecution witness had to be the Living Church priest Krasnitsky. The brilliant defense counsel Gurovich exposed the total inadequacy of the prosecution as well as Krasnitsky's former record of active anti-Semitism and anti-Bolshevism, whereupon he said: "I am happy that in this deeply tragic moment for the Russian clergy I, as a Jew, can witness to the whole world that feeling of sincere gratitude which the whole Jewish people owes to the Russian Orthodox clergy for the attitude to the Beilis case at its time." Moreover, he characterizes his client as a morally beautiful individual full of love, humility and compassion and concludes: "You can murder the metropolitan, but it is not in your power to deprive him of his courage and of the lofty nobility of his thoughts and actions."[5]

Nevertheless, the metropolitan and nine other leading Petrograd Orthodox clergymen and scholars were condemned to death. The metropolitan and three others were actually shot; the remaining six, including the future Metropolitan Grigory (Chukov) of Leningrad, had their sentences commuted to long prison terms. This was part of the new wave of terror, launched against the Church in connection with the famine and the church valuables

[5]M. Polsky, *Novye mucheniki rossiiskie,* 1:32-57. Note that the death sentence preceded any formal proceedings or trial. This tells a tale on the comedy of Soviet political trials. The Beilis trial (Kiev, 1913) resulted in the acquittal of a Jewish worker named Beilis, who was accused of a ritual murder of a Christian child. The Russian Orthodox Church played a prominent part in defending Beilis, presenting theological expertise proving the absence of ritual murders in the Judaic faith.

issue. But this issue, in Petrograd at least, was just an excuse. The real reason for his persecution lay in the fact that the metropolitan was an obstacle on the way to the subjugation of the Church via Vvedensky and his group. Apparently, at that early stage, the regime still believed that the operation could be carried out quickly through a simple eradication of the most authoritative, popular and intransigent clergy. Venyamin had been on the government's "bad books" ever since 1918, when on January 10 he had sent a letter to the Council of People's Commissars warning them not to issue a blatantly anti-Church decree (namely, the forthcoming January 23 one), for it would cause "spontaneous rebellions." A Soviet author calls this letter an attempt by the church people "to blackmail the Council of Commissars."[6] The prophetic character of this warning demonstrated the intelligence and leadership qualities of the bishop, and such qualities were intolerable to the totalitarian mentality of the communists.

The general state of the Church as an institution was not promising. The patriarch had been under arrest since May 10, 1922. Purges and imprisonments were rampant across the country, mostly under the pretext of the Church's resistance to the confiscation of valuables, in connection with which 2,691 married priests, 1,962 monks, 3,447 nuns and an unknown number of laymen loyal to the patriarch were physically liquidated in the course of 1921-1923.[7] As will be shown in the next chapter, the monarchist and militantly anti-Soviet resolutions of the émigré Church in Yugoslavia did not help the Church in Russia either.

When the patriarch died in April 1925 the Church was just recovering from the terror. But the physical persecutions could not stop the internal spiritual recovery of the Church, freed from all secular-governmental obligations for the first time in over four hundred years. In the words of a witness:

Sisterhoods appeared at all parish churches. They preoccupied themselves with charity, especially for the imprisoned

[6]F. Megruzhan's article in *XX-letie otdeleniya tserkvi ot gosudarstva* (Moscow, 1938) 45.

[7]Struve, 35-8. The original source of the figures appears to be the already mentioned Renovationist bishop Nikolai Solovei. See *TsV*, no. 19-20 (October 1924) 15. See also appendix 2 below, pp. 477ff.

clergy. Strong parish councils defended their churches. Charity collections for prisoners of conscience, concerts of religious music, popular theological lectures . . . were a regular occurrence. Churches . . . were always packed-full. . . . The faithful would always find the necessary funds out of their meager possessions . . . to support theological schools had these only been permitted. The Church was becoming a state within the state . . . The prestige and authority of the imprisoned and persecuted clergy was immeasurably higher than that of the clergy under the tsars.[8]

Religious lectures were even conducted, semiofficially, in some measure—e.g., at the Kropotkin Museum, where two public lectures per month were conducted from 1923 to 1928 on themes of social Christianity, each attracting sixty to seventy young people of Communist Youth League (Komsomol) age. These lectures were always copied in shorthand, then retyped in many copies and circulated in what we would now call *samizdat.* Even Soviet authors recognized that "at least since 1923 there was felt a rise in religiosity across the whole country," and another author gives some figures for the period from January 1 to November 1, 1925, when the following religious communities increased: "the Orthodox by 9 percent, Old Believer by 10 percent, the Moslem ones by 19 percent, Jewish by 10 percent, Evangelical Christian communities by 13 percent." The figures are for twenty-nine provinces in the Russian Republic.[9] The 1927-1928 dynamics of all function-

[8]E.L., *Episkopy ispovedniki* (San Francisco, 1971) 68-70.

[9]M. Artemev, "Zhiva li Rossiya?" *Put'*, no. 25 (December 1930); a lecture delivered (in Moscow?) in 1927 on the Transfiguration, *Put'*, no. 39 (July 1933) 41-2; V.D. Kobetsky, "Issledovanie dinamiki religioznosti naseleniya SSSR," in *Ateizm, religiya, sovremennost'*, a symposium published by the USSR Academy of Sciences (Leningrad, 1973) 116-27; A. Veshchikov, "Vekhi bol'shogo puti," *Nauka i religiya*, no. 11 (1962).

A contemporary correspondent from Russia wrote that while the urban churches were fuller than before the revolution—with a higher proportion of intelligentsia, particularly young intelligentsia, of whom very many reconverted to Christianity after the revolution—this revival did not affect the rural areas, where the fruits of antireligious materialistic "enlightenment" were just beginning to take effect. Hence, rural churches remained empty in many places. Many factory workers were likewise filling the churches (although some were joining the sects) in a process of reawakening from the revolutionary intoxication. On the whole, it is difficult to reassess whether the total number of urban believers exceeded the prerevolu-

TABLE 3-1

| | 1927 | | 1928 | |
	urban	rural	urban	rural
total number of religious communities	4,345	31,678	4,266	32,539
percent of communities belonging to:				
Orthodox	59.0%	71.5%	60.0%	72.0%
Renovationists	10.8	8.8	10.2	9.0
Jews	5.7	0.0	5.7	0.0
Moslems	2.8	6.3	2.9	6.2
Old Believers of all factions	2.6	5.5	2.5	5.5
Protestants (Evangelical, Baptist, etc.)	7.6	4.1	7.0	3.9[10]

ing religious communities of all confessions in the whole RFSFR, according to a Soviet source, can be seen in table 3-1.

Very significant in this table are the figures for the Orthodox Church in relation to the Protestant sectarians and the Old Believers. The modest growth of the Orthodox indicates a much more significant increase in prestige and popularity than the above indicators would warrant, in view of all the attempts by the Soviet state to undermine and split the Orthodox Church and in view of the continuing Soviet support for the Renovationists and the sectarians. The stagnation of the indicators for the Old Believers and Protestants indicates that their popularity was short-lived (hardly aided by the better deal the latter continued to receive from the state until 1929), while the sufferings of the national Church won for her an unprecedented degree of national support. The slight decrease of the total urban churches simply reflected this persecution and the enforced closures and confiscations of

tionary total because many churches were in the hands of the Renovationists, and these remained quite empty. See the anonymous article in *Put'*, no. 2 (January 1926) 6-7.

[10]A.P. Mariinsky, *Protiv popov i sektantov* (Moscow-Leningrad, 1929) 75. He adds that "according to some data the total number of religious congregations has doubled since 1922/1923" across the country. F. Oleshchuk is concerned with the impressive number of Orthodox churches being built by worker and peasant groups of believers by means of voluntary collections. For example, in the Vladimir province alone seven new churches were being constructed in 1928. *Kto stroit tserkvi v SSSR* (Moscow-Leningrad, n.d.) 76.

churches by the communists.[11] The massive return to religion in the 1920s must have been at least partly caused by the growing loss of faith in the promised materialist utopia in connection with the failure of the world revolution and the decline in the quality of life.[12]

The success of the Church in the relatively free competition with the official ideology in the conditions of freedom "of religious and antireligious propaganda" proclaimed by the 1918 Constitution, and the failure of the League of Militant Godless and all their endeavors,[13] forced the regime to turn to purely administrative measures as well as to amending its laws on religion. The most notorious and comprehensive of these was the 1929 legislation (which shall be discussed in more detail in a subsequent chapter, because it would serve as a rationalization for the holocaust of the 1930s and for all the Soviet church policies to the present day). The most immediate effect of the 1929 legislation was the prohibition of all church-related activities outside church walls under the ban on religious propaganda. The 1924 Constitution was amended: the original equal propaganda rights granted to atheists and believers were replaced by a formula permitting antireligious propaganda but banning the propagation of religion and limiting the rights of believers to the performance of the "religious cult" in buildings designated for this purpose. This was preceded by a number of decrees in the 1920s. One of them, in 1925, banned any religious processions or special services outside the churches, unless special written permission had been obtained from the local Soviet authorities for each particular case.

[11]Mass enforced closures of churches began at least from 1929. In the RSFSR alone 500 churches of all confessions were liquidated in 1928 and 1,100 in 1929. In the Ukraine in 1929, 364 congregations were shut. S. Troitsky, "Pochemu zakryvayutsya tserkvi v Rossii?" *Put'*, no. 23 (August 1930) 70. Data from official Soviet publications.

[12]See note 9 above. The situation in 1923 could thus be compared with the rises of religiosity by the mid-1930s after the terror of collectivization, during the cataclysm of World War II, and again with the withering away of the last traces of ideological illusions after Stalin's death.

[13]Oleshchuk, *Kto stroit,* 72-88. As early as 1925 an attempt was also made to counter the influence of religion by devising "revolutionary rituals" and rites to enact in a church-like manner the symbolism of communism. See the theses on antireligious struggle adopted by a branch of the Society of Friends of the *Bezbozhnik* Newspaper (the earlier name for the League of Militant Godless), in the Smolensk Archives, XT 47/459.

On August 26, 1929, a continuous work week, without breaks for Sunday, was introduced, resulting in rotating days of rest and depriving workers of the opportunity to attend Sunday services regularly.[14]

The Communist Party and Komsomol-supported and financed League of Militant Godless was finally formally launched in 1925 on an all-union scale, after three years of attempts to run organized antireligious campaigns on a local and sporadic basis. Its membership expanded from 87,000 in 1926 to 500,000 in 1929. Reaching 5,670,000 members in 1932, short of the goal of over 7 million, it nevertheless proclaimed a target of 17 million for 1933 and 22 million for 1941. Instead, despite the help it received in almost forcing people to join it in conditions of the growing terror of the 1930s and the physical annihilation of the Church, despite the 1929 legislation, and despite the publication and distribution of the league's periodical and other propaganda literature in tens of millions of copies; the league's membership began to fall, dropping to its lowest figure of under two million by 1938, then rising somewhat with the help of the terror of that year to 3.5 million in 1941. But even these figures were largely on paper only. The general tenor of the published complaints of the leaders of the league throughout the 1930s was that no more than a fraction of the nominal members paid their dues, not to mention participation in any real activities.[15] This is another indication that, had the regime not deprived the Church of the right of wider activities and had it not subjected her to physical liquidation, the "antireligious front" would not have been able to compete with her.

In the sphere of administrative attacks on the Church, the regime tried to prevent, and quite successfully at that, a regular administration of the Church by continuous arrests and administrative deportations of diocesan bishops as well as of the locum tenentes who took over administration of the patriarchal offices after Tikhon's death. The three interim administrators, designated by the patriarch in his will, were imprisoned one after the other.

[14]Curtiss, *Russian Church,* 192-213 and 241-2.

[15]Ibid., 205-80; Spinka, 73-87. In the twelve years between 1928 and 1940, for instance, 1,832 titles of antireligious literature were printed, with a total circulation of some 140 million copies.

The last of these, Metropolitan Peter (Polyansky), designated Metropolitan Sergii of Nizhny Novgorod (now Gorky) as his deputy locum tenens in case of his arrest. As Peter never returned from exile and died there in 1936, Sergii had become at first de facto and since 1936 de jure patriarchal locum tenens, and in 1943 was elected patriarch.

Sergii's first and most intensive objective was to achieve the legalization of the Church with the Soviet authorities, and thus to gain the right to reopen seminaries, have a regular canonical administration and a church press, at least on a par with the Renovationists, although according to the Soviet law of 1918 no hierarchical church organization was legal. Only independent groups of twenty laymen, leasing the parish church from the state, were legitimate in the official view.

The question of legalization in this context amounted to registration rather than legalization properly understood, because the Church as a hierarchical institution has never to the present day gained the full status of a legal person in Soviet law. A decree of the Soviet government on June 12, 1922 stipulated that the function of certain religious societies would be legal only if they were "registered" with the local government organs. This allowed direct persecution of all "unregistered" religious bodies and their lay and clerical servants, and also allowed the government to set any arbitrary conditions for registration and hence toleration. A convenient lever for the periodic elimination of unwanted clerics, particularly ruling bishops, was another decree, of July 10, 1922, permitting the People's Commissariat of Internal Affairs (NKVD) to administer exile without trial of "individuals whose residence in the given area . . . may be deemed dangerous from the point of view of defense of the revolutionary social order" for a period of up to three years. Registration included the registration of all individuals serving the given church, parish or diocese—thus permitting the government to control the appointments of clerics by agreeing to register, i.e., to give a working permit to, one bishop or priest while denying it to another. These conditions of registration the Patriarchal Church refused to accept, while the government refused to grant the Church any other form of legal recognition.

Shortly before his death, Patriarch Tikhon applied, in Feb-

ruary 1925, to the NKVD for the legalization/registration of his
Synod, meaning by this apparently something quite different from
the government's interpretation of the term. A response came
already when Metropolitan Peter was in charge. The NKVD
was offering him legalization on the following terms: (1) publication of a declaration of a certain character; (2) exclusion
from official position of those bishops whom the government did
not like . . .; (3) condemnation of émigré bishops; and (4)
henceforth, a certain permanent business contact between the
Church and the government as personified by Tuchkov.

Metropolitan Peter, according to the source, refused these
conditions.[16] By the end of 1925 the metropolitan himself disappeared behind bars and the deputy locum tenens, realizing the
impossibility of running the Church in conditions of alegality
and terror, applied for registration once again, in June 1926. But
instead, Sergii was arrested, in the autumn of the same year,
for participating in an attempt to elect a patriarch by a secret
poll of all bishops of the Church (over seventy votes had thus
been collected before the authorities found out and arrested most
of the participants—almost all of whom voted for Metropolitan
Kirill of Kazan, then completing his term of exile). This does not
mean that the authorities were unwilling to grant registration to
the Patriarchal Church. Having realized that the Renovationists
were in irreversible decline, they preferred a tamed Patriarchal
Orthodox Church to an untamed one. The Church, on her part,
wanted legalization and made advanced declarations of secular
loyalty to the regime (but not to its communist ideology), but at
the same time wanted to retain internal freedom of worship and
of pastoral appointments. It seems that the most that the ruling
bishops were willing to coordinate with the Soviet government
was the appointment of administrative officers of the central
church bodies—hence the repeated attempts to begin legalization.
A case in point was Tuchkov's attempt to convince Metropolitan
Kirill, the obvious candidate for the patriarchal see, to accept the
conditions of registration. In the spring of 1927, while Sergii was

---

[16]Polsky, *Novye mucheniki*, 137, citing a priest who escaped from the USSR
in 1930. Although of pro-Karlovcian orientation Polsky is quite reliable in reporting facts. Peter would probably have agreed to point 3 of the Soviet request—as
is reflected in the patriarch's testament of 1925, largely authored by Peter.

still in jail, he offered these conditions of legalization to three senior bishops in a row, culminating with Kirill, explaining that the agreement would mean that when the Soviet authorities deemed it necessary to remove a bishop from his see, the church administration should oblige. Metropolitan Kirill responded:

> "If the bishop is guilty of an ecclesiastic offense, I shall do so. But otherwise I would call him and tell him: 'Brother, I've nothing against you, but the civil authorities want to retire you, and I am forced to do so.'" "No," said Tuchkov, "you must pretend the initiative is yours, and find some accusation." To this the metropolitan replied: ". . . You are not a cannon, and I am not a shell with which you want to destroy the Church from within." The same day the seventy-three-year-old metropolitan was sent back into his Arctic exile, from which he never returned, dying there in 1944.[17]

To return to Metropolitan Sergii's appeal for legalization in 1926, its exact text remains unknown, but it could be guessed to some extent from his circular letter of June 10, 1926 to the bishops, priests and faithful of the Orthodox Church both at home and abroad. In return for legalization it promised complete civil loyalty to the state and the noninterference of the Church in any politics. However, it also stated that the Church " 'cannot enter into any special involvement to prove our loyalty' or accept responsibility for the political views of the clergy, whether at home or abroad . . . the Revolution itself had freed the Church from all political involvements and 'we assuredly cannot surrender that advantage.'" Sergii admitted that some of the émigré clergy had engaged in anti-Soviet political activity, but disclaimed, on behalf of the Church, "all connection with them and all responsibility for their acts." Moreover, in this letter and in another addressed especially to the émigré churches (October 12, 1926), he suggested that they break with Moscow and place themselves under the jurisdictions of local national Orthodox

---

[17]Regelson, 89-91, 412-3 et passim; Levitin-Shavrov, 3:41. An apparently reliable source from Russia writes that Sergii "refrained from direct participation, but gave his blessing" to this form of patriarchal election. N. Shemetov, "Arkhiepiskop Pavlin Kroshechkin," *VRKhD*, no. 132 (1980) 157.

churches or form local Orthodox church units with a nationally mixed membership in non-Orthodox countries.[18]

But the five commissars heading church affairs (Trotsky, Smidovich, Krasikov, the Renovationist priest Galkin and the GPU official Tuchkov) were not satisfied with such a spiritually independent stand of the Church. Her backbone had to be broken before she would be recognized by Stalin in 1943. The response of the government was the arrest of Sergii in December 1926, along with an estimated total of 117 bishops. Thus, writes Spinka: "the GPU in the end succeeded in purging the Church of all who possessed moral courage to oppose the policies of the state. This . . . was the process of 'eradication of the best.' "[19]

Having realized that the Renovationist schism had failed, Tuchkov now decided to support the Patriarchal Church, which first of all had to be further weakened as an institution—as he put it, "we need a new schism among the Tikhonites."[20] Such was the motivation behind his hasty legalization of the Grigorians and the game with releasing and rearresting such heirs to the title of locum tenens, chosen by Patriarch Tikhon and Metropolitan Peter, as Agafangel, Kirill, Serafim and Sergii. With difficulty Sergii managed to convince Agafangel and Kirill to withdraw their candidacies, and the imprisoned Peter to continue to support him as the sole deputy locum tenens.[21] Both the Renovationists and the Grigorians were legalized by the state, while Sergii, along with the whole national Church, remained completely outside any legal recognition, and that in as totalitarian a police state as was the Soviet Union of the late 1920s. The Grigorians were potentially more formidable than the Renovationists because they retained the fulness and order of the regular Orthodox Church and even recognized the authority of the late patriarch and of the imprisoned Metropolitan Peter, who was convenient to them and the GPU precisely *because* he was imprisoned. The Grigorians claimed legitimacy since they recognized Peter as their leader, and yet they could act independently because he had no physical means of controlling them. In his condemnations of the Grigor-

[18]Rahr, 22-3.
[19]Spinka, 62-3.
[20]Levitin-Shavrov, 3:30; Spinka, 64.
[21]Regelson, 109-20 et passim.

ians—with Peter's approval—Sergii rather stretched the point by arguing that their Supreme Church Council was a collegial body, while the 1917 Sobor had legislated that all collegial administrative bodies would function only in conjunction with and under the chairmanship of the patriarch or his locum tenens—i.e., it recognized the unitary principle of supreme church administration.[22]

Stratonov, a leading émigré church historian and an apologist for Sergii, argues that it was in view of Sergii's impossible legal position that he had to bow to Soviet demands and to issue the July 20, 1927 Declaration of Loyalty, which went far beyond his preimprisonment 1926 statements and even contradicted them. He had to do it, argues Stratonov, to gain the minimum necessary ground to struggle against the Grigorians and the Renovationists, and to put an end to the leapfrogging game with the locum tenentes staged by the GPU. As has been mentioned, Patriarch Tikhon had appointed, in case of the impossibility of electing a new patriarch, three locum tenentes in the following order: Kirill (Smirnov) of Kazan, Agafangel (Preobrazhensky) of Yaroslavl and Peter (Polyansky) of Krutitsy. Peter, in his turn fearing arrest, named the following three candidates: Sergii (Stragorodsky) of Nizhni Novgorod, Mikhail (Ermakov), Exarch of the Ukraine, and Iosif (Petrovykh) of Rostov-the-Great. When Sergii was rearrested in 1926 and Iosif briefly took over, he named four locum tenentes candidates, including Archbishop Serafim (Samoilovich), who would very briefly take over the administration of the Church, only to be arrested on the eve of Sergii's release in 1927. In addition, as mentioned before, there is circumstantial evidence of a GPU threat to liquidate all imprisoned bishops unless Sergii complied.[23]

Sergii was unexpectedly released on March 30, 1927, while other clerics were being imprisoned and exiled merely for recognizing Sergii as their leader.[24] Three months later the notorious declaration appeared. In it, Sergii blamed the anti-Soviet senti-

[22]Ibid., 104-6.

[23]Ibid., 98-115; Chrysostomus, 2:276; and Stratonov, *Smuta,* 160-1.

[24]Bishop Afanasy (Sakharov), for instance. At the same time that Afanasy received his three-year concentration camp sentence for belonging to "Sergii's faction," forty other bishops were given various sentences of detention for the same "crime." Regelson, 413.

ments of some Russian church people and the anti-Soviet declarations and activities of the Karlovci churchmen for the delay in the normalization of Church-state relations. He even thanked the Soviet government for permitting him to organize a provisional church Synod and for granting it "legalization." He then expressed hope that this legalization would soon extend down to the dioceses and parishes and that soon a true sobor of the Russian Orthodox Church could be assembled to elect a patriarch and regularly functioning bodies of church administration. His aim, he wrote, was to convince the Soviet government that it was possible to be a dedicated Orthodox Christian and simultaneously to "recognize the Soviet Union as one's civic motherland; her happiness and successes being our happiness and successes, and her misfortunes our misfortunes." It is this sentence that caused the greatest uproar of protests among very large sections of clergy and faithful both in Russia and among the émigrés. Somehow, no one seemed to notice that he was using the feminine after "motherland," while "Soviet Union" is a masculine expression in Russian. Metropolitan Sergii himself later pointed out to a visiting émigré bishop that he had deliberately made this semantic distinction in the text, which unfortunately so few people managed to notice.[25] In the same document, he stated that he had requested the émigré clergy to pledge loyalty to the Soviet government, and that those for whom this was unacceptable would be deleted from the lists of Patriarchal clergy.

In all fairness, it should be noted that there remained a great distance between even this capitulation by Sergii and the position of the Renovationists and the Grigorians. Nowhere did Sergii praise the Soviet ideological or social system. He only stated that

[25]Metropolitan Elevfery, *Nedelya v Patriarkhii* (Paris, 1933) 55-6. The author cites his conversation with Metropolitan Sergii on this subject, where Sergii explains that this relates only to the country, not to its regime, and points out the words about common grief or sadness: "Obviously . . . if the Church will be subjected to persecutions, we shall not be happy about it, as stated in my letter of March 14, 1929." The only letter of that date traced by Regelson relates to Sergii's arguments in favor of his rights to administer the Church with the prerogatives of a locum tenens as long as Peter is in prison (455-6). Either there was another letter of the same date or Elevfery misquoted the date.

A characteristic illustration of the common attitude to Metropolitan Sergii's declaration is that even such a knowledgeable (but highly emotional) author as Levitin-Krasnov misinterprets precisely this point. See his memoirs, *Likhie gody*, 95.

it should be accepted as a reality and that "for a Christian there can be no accidents [in history]"—hence, the regime exists by the will of God and it would be "a madness" to struggle against the regime or to try to hide in a corner and live as if it did not exist. He did not order the faithful to love the Soviet social system, but to accept the Soviet government as a reality, as the government of their country, and meekly suggested that those who could not reconcile themselves to this reality should at least temporarily retire from active church affairs. Those who were able to accept this platform were being asked "to leave their political sympathies at home, and bring only their [religious] faith into the Church and to work with us only in the name of faith."[26]

Some authors, in their criticism of this action by Sergii, argue that even from the tactical point of view this was a miscalculation. The Soviets fulfilled very few of the hopes Sergii placed in them in the declaration, and even that only temporarily. An Orthodox theological institute was permitted to reopen in 1927, but was forced to close down two years later.[27] The *Journal of the Moscow Patriarchate* began to appear legally, though erratically, in 1931, only to be closed down in 1935. Practically none of the exiled bishops were reinstated; on the contrary, arrests of the clergy and forced liquidations of churches continued and would soon rise to catastrophic proportions. As to the legalization, in the words of another Metropolitan Sergii (Voskresensky), who found himself under the German occupation in World War II, "The existence of the patriarchal administration was recognized by the Soviet government de facto, not de jure by any means . . . there existed nothing close to a legalized church

---

[26]Regelson, 430-4. The weakest point of the declaration was, of course, the threat of expulsion from the ranks of the Patriarchal clergy of all those émigré clerics who would refuse to pledge civic loyalty to the Soviet communist government—which of course the vast majority would refuse to do, thus further precipitating the émigré church splits. Thus, Sergii's request was political, and the punitive action was based entirely on political criteria—i.e., the very thing for which he criticized the Karlovci group: that they engaged in politics, from which the Church must keep aloof. See also appendix 3 below, pp. 483ff.

[27]Ibid., 187-93; Levitin, *Likhie gody*, 97-8. The Moscow Theological Academy had been shut in 1922, the one in Kazan around the same time, and the one in Kiev in 1924. Leonty, 86-9. See also Manuil, *Die russischen orthodoxen Bischoefe*, who cites, however, 1919 as the date of the closing of the Kiev Academy (223 and 246).

statute. The Church as a whole, individual dioceses and individual parishes, were neither institutions nor corporations. They were not legal persons of any kind, and no organ represented them juridically. They existed only in fact, but not in law."[28]

Sergii's apologists, however, argue that there was no other way to gain at least some modicum of legal survival in the era of rising Stalinism, and that, without such toleration, the GPU would have been successful with the Grigory experiment, if not with the by then completely compromised Renovationists. They point out that Sergii could not have foreseen that his other requests would not be fulfilled and that the 1930s would bring such a holocaust within the Church.[29] In any case, the preservation of at least a nucleus of a regular church administration at the top by Sergii allowed the Church to revive after 1943 under the aegis of canonical and definitely church-minded leaders. Perhaps, had there been no Sergii with his Synod or rather its remnants in 1943, Stalin, requiring a Church for his struggle against Hitler, would have entrusted the work to some sycophantic adventurers of the Renovationist category (although now observing all the necessary conservative appearances of the regular Orthodox Church). On the other hand, it could also be argued that had all bishops been imprisoned, Stalin would have had to rely on bishops straight out of jail for the reconstruction of the Church, which would then have been much less obliging than the Sergii-Aleksii-Pimen institution. However, the latter argument is not

[28] See his report to the Germans of November 12, 1941. The same was confirmed by the US Roman Catholic Moscow Embassy chaplain, Leopold Brown. Georgy Grabbe, *Pravda o russkoi tserkvi na rodine i za rubezhom* (Jordanville, N.Y.: Holy Trinity Monastery, 1961) 78-9.

[29] Levitin-Krasnov, "Slovo ob umershem," a *samizdat* obituary for Metropolitan Manuil dated June 2, 1969, pp. 4-6. Metropolitan Manuil, apparently, had also held hopes that Sergii's declaration would normalize Church-state relations, for he fully endorsed it and remained a Sergiite. He could not have been accused of cowardice, for he had been in and out of prisons all the way up to 1956, spending a total of 22 years in them. In 1930, however, he refused to cosign Sergii's statement on the freedom of the Church and the absence of persecutions in the USSR, and retired from any active diocesan position until the election of Aleksii as patriarch. Still, he never joined any of the shisms. See also note 25 above on Sergii's belief in the declaration serving to normalize Church-state relations. Metropolitan Elevfery held the same opinion, and claimed that Metropolitan Peter likewise approved of Sergii's 1927 declaration, according to a bishop he met in Moscow who had just returned from exile and had discussed the subject there with Peter. *Nedelya v Patriarkhii*, 97-118.

necessarily valid. The present Patriarch Pimen spent at least five years in prison and two years in enforced exile, and yet, in the words of one Soviet-Russian cleric, "his only fault is that he panically fears the civil authorities."[30]

Be it as it may, the point is that the terror liquidated the best, the most stalwart churchmen, while frightening others into obedience. It is primarily the latter who survived; although, as the persecution of the Renovationists in the 1930s showed, even complete obedience was no guarantee of survival.

---

[30]For obvious reasons, the names of the clerics and the circumstances in which these statements were made cannot be disclosed at the present time. The same informants believed that Pimen had spent around eight years in prisons and concentration camps and had suffered greatly. A secret inside report on Pimen of late 1967 or early 1968, apparently by A. Plekhanov, a senior official of the State Council for Religious Affairs, says that Pimen was imprisoned twice, from 1936 to 1938 inclusive and from 1944 to 1945 inclusive, while the years 1939-1940 he spent in Andizhan, Uzbekistan, obviously in exile. The document, "Spravka na mitr. . . . Pimena (Izvekova)," is in the Keston College Archives.

CHAPTER 4

The Schisms on the Right

The Emigré Church Schism

The apolitical stance adopted by Patriarch Tikhon at least since 1919, preceded by his refusal to give his blessing to any of the belligerent sides in the Civil War, was not to the liking of many right-wing elements in the Church, particularly among those who had emigrated with the White Armies.

The most extreme of the émigré church groups became known as the Karlovci Synod, after the town in Yugoslavia where it was formed. It evolved indirectly from the "Temporary Higher Church Administration of South Russia," organized among the local bishops in Stavropol (Caucasus) for the territories controlled by the Whites but within the Patriarchal jurisdiction. Tikhon did not question the sacramental validity of the administration, recognizing ordinations, consecrations and defrockings carried out by the administration on its territory in Russia after this territory reverted to the patriarch's direct control following the departure of the White Armies. The émigré Synodal apologists later used this as one of the arguments in favor of the Synod's validity.[1] But this is open to challenge on a number of grounds. First, all sacraments, according to the ecumenical councils, are valid as long as the bishops performing them have themselves been ordained and consecrated by valid bishops possessing the apostolic succession and have not fallen into doctrinal heresy. Secondly, while in Russia, the bishops making up the temporary

[1]Polsky, 113.

administration of the south were regular diocesan bishops either occupying their respective dioceses or having recently temporarily evacuated these under the pressures of the Civil War; Metropolitan Antony of Kiev, for example, left his diocese only toward the end of 1919. Finally, quite another matter is the recognition of a group of bishops as a canonical administrative structure, particularly an extraterritorial one. The canons require a bishop "to be married to his diocese"—in other words, the very concept of voluntary emigration of a bishop, leaving his diocese to its own devices, is uncanonical.[2]

Be it as it may, the beginnings of the future Karlovci Synod were laid by the ecumenical patriarchal locum tenens when, in December 1920, he permitted the émigré bishops in Constantinople to form a Temporary Higher Russian Church Administration Abroad, "under the supreme protection of the [Ecumenical] Patriarchate, whose duty it would be to supervise and administer the church life of Russian communities abroad both in non-Orthodox . . . and in Orthodox countries." The patriarchal decree made it clear that the new émigré church body would recognize the supremacy of the Patriarch of Constantinople, who retained all judicial prerogatives.[3]

This strange ecclesiastical body claimed to be a continuation of the church administration of the south and recognized Patri-

---

[2]A characteristic example of such canonical behavior is presented by the young Bishop Aleksii (Simansky)—the future patriarch—an aristocrat with a brilliant education and command of several western languages. When his father begged him to flee with him to nearby Finland, for "there is no room for the Simanskys in Bolshevik Russia," Aleksii utterly refused, saying: "A pastor does not flee from his flock. He must stay with it and accept it and accept all trials, however frightening they may be." See the memoirs of the Leningrad Professor Konstantin Kripton, "Zashchita kanonov pravoslaviya, 1922-1925," *VRKhD*, no. 128 (1979) 237. Paradoxically, the Metropolitan and later Patriarch Aleksii became the target of most aggressive attacks for his political compromises from the émigré Synod circles in general and from Polsky in particular. From their émigré safety, having abandoned their flocks, these pastors have accused Aleksii and his hierarchs of treason!

The relevant canons are: 1 Nicea, 15; Antioch, 21; and Apostolic Canon 14.

[3]Stratonov, *Smuta*, 16-20. Characteristically, Polsky does not mention the limitations imposed on the administration by Constantinople (Polsky, 113-4). It may be noted that in his 1923 encyclical, after his release from prison, Patriarch Tikhon states quite clearly that the Church Administration Abroad was created by the Patriarchate of Constantinople without Tikhon's knowledge (Stratonov, *Smuta*, 18; text in Levitin-Shavrov, 2:153).

arch Tikhon as its supreme head. But in reality, its sole source of legitimacy was the Patriarch of Constantinople. The Stavropol church administration of the south was the product of a sobor assembled in May 1919 in Novocherkassk, which consisted of all members of the Moscow Sobor available on the spot and of representatives of the local church, state and public organizations under the control of the Whites—a total of eighty persons (thirty-five bishops and forty-five priests and laymen)—followed, apparently, by a similar sobor (or a continuation of the former) in Stavropol. According to a Karlovcian source, the Novocherkassk Sobor was gathered and chaired by Metropolitan Antony. There are no claims, however, of his presence in Stavropol. Be it as it may, after the evacuation of Denikin's armies this body fell apart. Another Temporary Church Administration was somehow formed in 1920 in the Crimea for the territory controlled by General Wrangel's army. Archbishop Venyamin (Fedchenkov) became the head of this church administration. The statutes of the Stavropol body limited its jurisdiction only to the territory of the White Armies and only for the duration of the Civil War. The idea of forming an émigré church administration in Constantinople was Venyamin's, who suggested it to Antony. The latter initially replied: "Only an absolute fool can dream of a separate church administration in the capital of the Ecumenical Patriarch." However, under the pressure of Venyamin and other Russian émigrés, he reluctantly agreed to head a Russian delegation to the patriarchal locum tenens. None of the documents of the time claimed any continuity of this émigré church body from Stavropol; only much later did the Karlovci Synod begin to claim legitimacy on this basis.[4] Later, in 1921, it moved on to Yugoslavia along with the mass of Russian emigrants. Without requesting or receiving any release from the Ecumenical Patriarchate, Metro-

---

[4]The Karlovcian source is Fr. Vladimir Vostokov, a participant of both the Novocherkassk and the Stavropol sobors, both of which are claimed to have taken place in May 1919. See his memoirs, in the Vostokov Collection, Bakhmeteff Archives: "Na severnom Kavkaze i na Kubani s Donom," 5-6; and "Nezabyvaemye krymskie vechera letom 1920 g," 3. On the Stavropol Sobor see Glubokovsky, *op. cit.*

For a detailed negation of the Stavropol legitimacy see G. Lomako, *Tserkovno-kanonicheskoe polozhenie russkogo rasseyaniya* (New York: Russian Orthodox Metropolia of America, 1950) 3-16. For the Karlovcian claim of legitimacy see Polsky, 15 et passim.

politan Antony (Khrapovitsky), formerly of Kiev, the head of this administration, subsequently began to act as if there had been no such connection and no limitations on the prerogatives of his church body.[5] In July 1921 he drafted a fundamental document on the basis of which the first émigré laity-clergy conference would take place in November of the same year. The document declares unconditional loyalty and subordination to the Patriarch of Moscow, and that all decisions of the forthcoming assembly are to be submitted to Patriarch Tikhon for confirmation, and only in urgent cases will decisions take effect immediately on a temporary basis, subject to their validation or rejection by the patriarch. In addition to this fundamental platform, the administration issued an instruction (*nakaz*) for the assembly on the eve of its opening which unilaterally appropriated for itself the right "to take upon itself the question of spiritual renovation of Russia."

The representation at this assembly was very irregular—some members had been delegated by parishes and church communities, while others had been personally coopted by Metropolitan Antony and by other bishops. This latter category included thirty monarchists straight from their political conference in Bad Reichenhal, Bavaria, where they had set up a Higher Monarchist Council.[6] Arbitrarily, they were granted full voting rights by the presiding Antony, making up a high proportion of the total eighty-five delegates and giving a political-partisan tone to the whole "sobor." As an initial test of strength, they attacked the former Duma Chairman, Mikhail V. Rodzyanko, whom they considered a traitor to the monarchist cause for having been one of the initiators of the tsar's abdication. They demanded his departure from the sobor, and Rodzyanko complied, having received no support from the chairman. The point is, however, that the Moscow Sobor ruled on September 5/18, 1918 that all delegates to that sobor would retain their prerogatives until new sobor elections had taken place. Until such time, all the delegates

[5]*Deyaniya russkogo vsezagranichnogo tserkovnogo sobora* (Sremski Karlovci, 1922) 3-20. For instance, the Higher Church Administration—i.e., in fact, Antony —received the right to coopt any twenty-five persons to the sobor with full voting rights.

[6]E.V. Anichkov, "Na grani," in V.V. Zenkovsky, ed., *Pravoslavie i kul'tura* (Berlin, 1923) 131-2.

automatically become members, with voting rights, at any local ecclesiastical assemblies in the areas of their residence. Thus, the expulsion of Rodzyanko, a full delegate to the Moscow Sobor, alone rendered the legitimacy of the Karlovci gathering and its decisions highly questionable.[7]

Moreover, the monarchists forced on the assembly a resolution setting up as an aim of the newly established émigré Church the reestablishment of the Romanovs as autocratic tsars of Russia. Metropolitan Evlogy, recently appointed by Patriarch Tikhon as the head of the Russian parishes in Western Europe, protested that such a declaration by a body professing to be subordinate to the Moscow patriarch could result in tragic consequences for the Church in Russia. But he weakened his position by voting for the monarchist principle of the resolution, protesting only against the Romanov section. Failing in their attempt to change the wording of the resolution, Evlogy, five other bishops, fifteen priests and fourteen laymen abstained during the final voting. Thus, had it not been for the coopted monarchists, the resolution would not have passed.[8]

In addition to providing fuel for the barbaric acceleration of terror against the Church within Russia in 1922, including the execution of Metropolitan Venyamin of Petrograd, the Karlovci assembly precipitated major church schisms in the USSR,[9] one of them being the Renovationist one, as their adherents were able to claim that the patriarch was trying to restore the monarchy. On the other hand, the rightists within Russia now had the émigré Church to fall back upon.

[7]Ibid. The text of the relevant sobor declaration is in *TsV*, no. 10-11 (August 1922) 7.

[8]Half of the bishops and only one-third of the priests (six out of twelve bishops and seven out of twenty-one priests) voted for the resolution, but of the fifty-three laymen, thirty-eight voted for, one against, and fourteen abstained. This and details on the Rodzyanko conflict are in Irinarkh Stratonov, "Iskhodnyi moment russkoi tserkovnoi smuty poslednego vremeni," *Put'*, no. 12 (1928) 89-99. See also his *Smuta*, 23-32; Evlogy, *Put'*, 395-7; and *Deyaniya vsezagranichnogo sobora*, 46-53.

[9]Stratonov, *Smuta*, 34. An independent American Roman Catholic scholar, James Zatko, confirms: "Emigré Orthodox bishops and leaders did not make the situation of the patriarch any safer or easier." *Descent into Hell*, 106 and n. 19.

The USSR came into being in December 1922. Until then there was a Soviet confederation without a name, consisting of the Russian Soviet Federated Socialist

To add insult to injury, in response to the Soviet government's decree of February 26, 1922 on the confiscation of all church valuables (allegedly to alleviate the Volga famine), and Patriarch Tikhon's circular letter approving all confiscations but those of sacramental articles, the Karlovci administration issued its appeal of March 1 to the Genoa Conference to start a military crusade against the Bolsheviks rather than to organize food aid, for famine could help destroy the Bolshevik regime. The Soviet press immediately associated the patriarch with the Karlovci group, although the former issued a denial of any foreknowledge of the émigré church group's plans and actions, and issued his decree of May 5 ordering the dissolution of the Higher Church Administration in Karlovci, owing to its politicization. The decree subordinated all Russian parishes in Europe to Metropolitan Evlogy of Paris.[10]

The Soviet government paid no attention to the patriarch's decree. The Karlovcian group claimed that the decree was forced upon the patriarch by the Soviets, since he had had six months to condemn the Karlovci resolution and to dissolve the administration, yet he waited until May 5, when he was already virtually under house arrest. Consequently, they argued, the decree was invalid. However, in his 1923 encyclical, the patriarch explained that he had always opposed the Karlovci resolutions, but had at first been outvoted by the majority in his Synod of the time and could prevail over the opposition only after the second Karlovcian resolution, namely, after its appeal of April 1922 to the Genoa Conference for a crusade against the communist government of Russia and her confederal allies.[11] The probability that Patriarch Tikhon's decision to dissolve the Karlovci administration was his own is confirmed by his independent behavior in prison, namely,

Republic and other self-ruling parts of the former Russian empire federally associated with the RSFSR.

[10]Stratonov, *Smuta,* 46-9 and 60. The ukaz was numbered 348. See M. d'Herbigny, *Les evêques russes en exil* (Paris, 1931) 53.

[11]Prof. S. Troitsky argues that the Genoa address could not have been drafted or adopted at the Karlovci Sobor, because it had ended on December 2, 1921, while the allied declaration on the convocation of the Genoa Conference occurred in January 1922. He accuses the Synod of fraudulently backdating the address in order to give it a semblance of conciliar legtimacy. See his *O nepravde karlovatskogo raskola* (Paris, 1960) 99. The Karlovcian Genoa address is in *TsV,* no. 3 (April 1922) 2-4.

by his refusal to recognize the validity of the GPU-supported Renovationist Sobor of 1923. In the circumstances of the time, when the patriarch could have seriously expected execution as the "instigator" of the actions of such executed hierarchs as Metropolitan Venyamin, this was an extremely risky action. Moreover, even after Tikhon's death his immediate entourage assured a Vatican emissary in confidentiality that the late patriarch had in all sincerity condemned the Karlovcians and desired their dissolution.[12] Be it as it may, the Soviet press seconded the Karlovcians in claiming that the patriarch's condemnation of the Karlovci resolutions was insincere. Conveniently, they referred to Metropolitan Antony's opening speech, which allegedly assured the assembly that it had the blessings of Patriarch Tikhon (the speech was never published in full because Antony always delivered his speeches impromptu and no records were kept). It was these Karlovcian resolutions, along with the church valuables issue, that were used as pretexts to arrest the patriarch in May 1922 and to unleash another campaign of persecution against the Church.[13] But whether Antony indeed uttered these words or not, the fact remains that the Karlovcians always tried to give the impression of being the patriarch's close associates. All their decrees and resolutions at the early stage began with the caption "By the blessing of the patriarch . . ."; and on December 4, 1921, the Karlovci "sobor" resolved that Antony be named the "Viceregent of the All-Russian Patriarch."[14]

Canonically, once the patriarch had disowned the resolutions and ordered the Karlovci organization to dissolve itself and to transfer all authority over émigré churches to Evlogy, the organization should have ceased to exist. Indeed, Antony's first impulse was to fulfil the order. He even applied to be accepted as a regular monk on Mt. Athos, but the Greeks refused to admit

[12]See the Karlovcian position in Polsky, 21. For the opposing views, see Levitin-Shavrov, 2:258 et passim; d'Herbigny, *Les evêques*, 53, and quotations of his statements in the Renovationist *VSS*, no. 8-9 (1926) 13 and no. 10 (1926) 3. The patriarch repeats his condemnation of the Karlovci Synod again in his last testament. See Levitin-Shavrov, 3:7-16 and 123-7.

[13]Stratonov, *Smuta*, 47.

[14]*TsV*, no. 10-11 (August 1922) 12. They even published the text of the address to the Genoa Conference immediately next to Patriarch Tikhon's encyclical on church reforms, as if to show that the patriarch's and the émigré Church's affairs were one and the same thing.

him. Thereupon his lay monarchist entourage began to insist that he stay. Evlogy assured Antony that the patriarch's order should not be obeyed, for the GPU must have forced his hand, and he proposed that instead of Antony's retirement he should preside over a loose federation of autonomous metropolitan districts whose bishops would periodically meet for consultation under Antony's chairmanship. Later, he would explain his action by his deep personal respect and love for Antony, which prevented him from taking the reins of church administration from the aged metropolitan. Evlogy admitted that this had been a grave error on his part, the fruits of which would be felt almost immediately on his return from Karlovci to Paris. Back in Karlovci, Antony's lay monarchist advisers took full control of his office and, instead of enacting a federal structure, set up a new central body in Karlovci. In formal compliance with Tikhon's order, the September 1922 assembly of émigré bishops dissolved the administration, but replaced it with a Synod of Bishops of the Russian Church Abroad under Antony's chairmanship.[15] The sole difference was that the former had contained two laymen, while the latter had none. It was formally specified that meetings would not be valid without Evlogy's presence, because he alone held his appointment from the patriarch. But in practice, since the majority of bishops were on the periphery and would meet at best once a year for a Synod session, the day-to-day administration was in the hands of lay officials of the Higher Monarchist Council—Makharoblidze, and later Count Grabbe.

Karlovcian apologists would henceforth claim that this system was fully in accordance with the November 1920 resolution of the patriarch permitting the setting up of temporary autocephalies, in view of the uncertainty of the central church administration. This instruction would be reaffirmed by Metropolitan Agafangel on Tikhon's arrest. However, both instructions were addressed to dioceses within Russia and headed by regularly appointed or confirmed diocesan bishops, and neither applied to the émigré bishops, who had deserted their dioceses. Moreover, the latter had

---

[15]Evlogy, Put', 402-5 and 605-12; Elevfery, Moi otvet m. Antoniyu, 29-30. This act of insubordination makes Evlogy, in Elevfery's opinion, the actual architect of the Karlovci Synod and responsible for the subsequent church schism. More than two hundred protests were received against Antony's desire to leave for a monastery. TsV, no. 3-4 (February 1923) 8.

a clear order to dissolve their organization, not to retain it under a different name.[16] However, two years later, after repeated orders by the patriarch to dissolve the Synod and to cease its political activities, the Synod declared that the patriarch was not free and that his orders did not reflect his real intentions, and therefore:

> In future cases those orders from His Holiness relating to the Orthodox Church Abroad which would be insulting to her honor and bearing clear features of direct pressure upon the Holy Patriarch's conscience on the part of Christ's foes, should be ignored as originating not from the Patriarch's will but from a completely different will. At the same time full respect and devotion should be rendered to the person of the innocently suffering Holy Patriarch . . .

Even before that, the Synod had adopted functions of a completely independent and supreme church administration, invalidating the patriarch's orders of earlier years. For example, it interfered with the affairs of Metropolitan Evlogy's West European see, appointing vicar bishops there without his approval and against his will. These bishops were de facto responsible only to the Synod and not to Evlogy. All this, not to mention the practice of accepting only those orders of the patriarch which suited it, turned the Synod into a totally extracanonical, if not directly schismatic, body. These actions finally precipitated the émigré church split between the adherents of the Karlovci Synod and those who remained faithful to the patriarch and wanted to keep the Church out of politics. Stratonov argues that in principle there was no difference between the Karlovcians and the Renovationists in Russia: both subordinated the Church to their sociopolitical and ideological aims, destroying her unity and ecumenicity.[17]

In conformity with the above-mentioned policy vis-à-vis Patriarch Tikhon, the Karlovcians transgressed the patriarch's 1919

---

[16]See the Karlovcian view in Count D. Olsufiev, *Mysli soboryanina o nashei tserkovnoi smute* (Paris, 1928) 17-20. The opposing view is in Evlogy, *Put'*, 115-7.

[17]*Smuta*, 60-110. It may be of interest that, according to Stratonov, during the debates on the sincerity of the patriarch's orders in 1922 and 1923, both Evlogy and Antony published encyclicals confirming the validity of the patriarch's orders and stated that according to the canons they should be adhered to. Yet, in practice Antony followed the current of his church organization.

declaration of the Church's political neutrality to the Soviet government. This declaration stated that the separation of the Church from the state also freed the former from any obligations toward the latter and permitted members of the Church to side with any political movement or faction. Consistently with this stance, the patriarch refused to give his blessing to the White Armies. These acts, as well as his anti-Karlovci declarations of 1922, 1923 and 1925, and along with his emphatic declarations of civic loyalty to the Soviet regime and partial revocation of the anathema by proclaiming in 1923 that during the liturgy churches should say prayers for the government of the Soviet Union, were viewed by the Karlovcians as human errors committed under the impact of persecution.[18] They contrast Tikhon's weaknesses with the steadfastness of Metropolitan Peter, pointing to Peter's arrest in late 1925 and to the fact that he never returned from exile. On this ground the Karlovcians recognized Peter as the locum tenens and prayed for him as their head until his death in 1936, but never recognized his heir, Metropolitan Sergii. The irony of the situation is that out of the whole Tikhonite circle of the central ruling bishops, Peter appears to have been the most intolerant one toward the Karlovcians and the one who was most insistent on *positive* loyalty to the Soviet government. In the last few months of the patriarch's life, his Synod was greatly reduced in size by arrests and by the Soviet ban on provincial bishops' visits to Moscow, so that its membership was practically limited to Metropolitan Peter of Krutitsy and Archbishop Tikhon of the Urals. Since Peter was the more influential of the two, and since the patriarch had resisted the inclusion of the pro-Soviet passages in his last testament-appeal to the Orthodox people that Peter had wanted him to sign, Peter's hand and initiative behind it are more than obvious. The patriarch finally agreed to sign the appeal only after a scene at his bedside in the hospital, when Peter assured him that his refusal to sign would be interpreted by the authorities as a hostile demonstration, in which case he, Peter, would request the patriarch to release him from all his duties.[19]

This document emphatically stated that the Soviet regime was not an accident, for

[18]Polsky, 11-2.
[19]Levitin-Shavrov, 3:8-9. See also Polsky, 24.

nations' destinies are settled by the Lord, and the [Orthodox people] must accept all that has happened as an expression of God's will . . . in civic terms we must be sincere vis-à-vis the Soviet power and in our work in the USSR for the common cause . . . condemning all association with the enemies of the Soviet power and all overt agitation against it. . . .

Appealing to parish communities . . . to prevent any anti-government activities by disloyal elements, not to hope for the restoration of the monarchy . . . we call upon you to elect only those people to the executive organs of parishes who are honest, decent, dedicated to the Orthodox Church, not engaged in any politicking and who are sincere in their attitudes to the Soviet power . . . we cannot but denounce those who . . . abusing their positions in the Church, instead of serving the Divine, dedicate themselves to crude, human politicking . . . therefore . . . we give our blessing to establish a special commission attached to the patriarchate . . . to investigate and, if necessary, ban in the proper canonical order those archpastors and pastors who persist in their errors and refuse to repent before the Soviet power.

They have the full right to cherish any convictions they wish. But they have arbitrarily, and contrary to the canons of our Church, acted in our name and in the name of the Holy Church, claiming concern for the good of the Church. The so-called Karlovci Sobor has produced nothing good for the Church. Hereby we repeat our condemnation of it . . . we charge a special commission with the investigation of the activities of the pastors and archpastors who have run away from Russia, in particular: Metropolitans Antony, formerly of Kiev, and Platon, formerly of Odessa. . . .[20]

The Synod in Karlovci was obviously deeply perplexed by the tone and contents of the testament. Antony's official encyclical claimed that it was a forgery and therefore should be disregarded

[20]Levitin-Shavrov, 3:11-22.

in accordance with the émigré Synod's resolution of 1924, which directed that only those orders of the patriarch which appeared to be free from external pressure should be obeyed.[21] But three years later Count Olsufiev, an extreme right-winger who had already criticized Tikhon for his encyclical on the political neutrality and civic loyalty of the Russian Church of 1919, correctly assessed the testament as genuine on the grounds of its endorsement by Metropolitan Peter on June 28, 1925. And he saw a logical continuity from Tikhon's stance to the policies of Peter and eventually to Sergii's Declaration of Loyalty of 1927.[22]

As has already been shown, Metropolitan Peter considered the struggle against the Renovationists more important than that against the Soviet regime. He saw the possibility of ending the schism only in depriving the Soviet government of its reasons to support the Renovationists through adopting their attitude of complete civic loyalty, while retaining the doctrinal purity and the immunity of internal church life from active government interference, and without declaring ideological affinity between the Church and the Soviet power. Like most bishops of the time, Peter, apparently, still believed that there was some rational motivation behind the persecutions of the Patriarchal Church by the Soviet state and hoped that declarations like the above and a civically loyal behavior of the Church could rationally convince the regime to change its policy toward the Church. One must remember that these actions took place at the time of the still selective persecutions, prior to the large-scale terror of 1930s and the wholesale liquidation of the Church.

The Karlovcians at first refused to recognize the validity of Peter as the locum tenens, ostensibly on the grounds of the canonical illegitimacy of such appointments by outgoing patri-

[21]*TsV*, no. 9-10 (May 1925) 3-4. Antony says that the signature on the document is too legible, while Tikhon's handwriting in his last years of life was nervously uneven and illegible, owing to the pressures.

[22]*Mysli soboryanina*, 41-4 and 3. While Antony tried to convince himself and others that he and his Synod remained loyal to the patriarch, some of his associates from the Higher Monarchist Council made no such pretense. For instance, N. Talberg plainly stated that the Karlovci act of 1922 was direct insubordination to Tikhon and justified it by claiming that the 1919 formation of the Higher Church Administration for the White-occupied territories of Russia was likewise an act of insubordination to Tikhon's 1919 declaration of the political neutrality of the Church. *Tserkovnyi raskol* (Paris, 1927) 4-11.

archs, but more probably because they felt that Peter would continue Tikhon's anti-Karlovcian policies. There was even a proposal to declare Antony the new head of the Russian Church, which he would direct from abroad. They justified this by arguing that no patriarchal elections were now possible in the USSR, while Antony had received the largest number of votes at the 1917-1918 Moscow Sobor.[23] Only on November 12, 1925 did the Karlovcians recognize Peter as locum tenens, on the pretext that they had received confirmation from Russia of Peter's general acceptance by the Russian bishops, along with the text of Tikhon's secret will appointing Peter and a secret clause of the Moscow Sobor granting the patriarch the right to appoint locum tenentes under extraordinary conditions.[24] It is rather significant that Karlovci recognized Peter as their head only after he had been safely put behind bars. As long as he was free, his anti-Karlovci stance was inconvenient to them. There is a parallel here with the Grigorians: for both, Peter in prison was a convenient tool for legitimacy, and his martyrdom would serve as a flag around which to rally.

A further irony is that Metropolitan Sergii, later so uncompromisingly condemned by the Karlovcians, had begun his tenure as deputy locum tenens (deputizing for Peter after his arrest) by reversing his predecessors' anti-Karlovci policy. In a confidential letter of September 13, 1926 (which the Karlovcians published nevertheless, thus sending Sergii to jail in 1926), Sergii advised that, in the conditions prevailing in the USSR, relations between them and Moscow were impossible. Consequently, they should not look up to the Moscow Patriarchate for leadership. Instead, they ought either to form a joint central administration for church affairs abroad, or, if it proved impossible

[23]At first they resolved to pray for a locum tenens without elevating any name. Then there was the suggestion of elevating the name of Antony. In response, Prof. Kartashev of the Paris St. Sergius Theological Institute accused them of fomenting a new church schism. See, respectively, *TsV*, no. 15-16 (August 1925) 3-4; "Raskol russkoi tserkvi," *Vozrozhdenie*, no. 41 (1925); E. Makharoblidze, "Otkrytoe pis'mo g-ru Kartashevu," *TsV*, no. 15-16 (August 1925) 8-11.

[24]*TsV*, no. 21-22 (November 1925) 4-5. Some sixty bishops in Russia had signed the act, which stated that "the late patriarch, in the prevailing conditions, had no other means [but the appointment of locum tenentes] to preserve the succession of authority in the Russian Church." The act was dated April 12, 1925. Stratonov, *Smuta*, 126; Regelson, 97.

to form an organ that would be recognized by all the émigrés, then

> it is better to accept the will of God . . . and return to the proper canonical platform by subordination . . . to the local Orthodox churches, e.g., to the Serbian patriarch in Serbia . . .

> In non-Orthodox countries, independent local church bodies could be formed with international membership. Such separate local formations will provide better protection from mutual accusations and misunderstandings than attempts to keep everything under a single artificially organized center.

The latter system, he wrote, also suits the Russian Church better, since it was in a situation where any orders from Moscow might be suspected of deception or fraudulence.[25]

Although the metropolitan accepted the concept of an extraterritorial émigré ecclesiastical center with full powers, obviously on the grounds of *oikonomia*,[26] he indicated his preference for the territorial structure by stating that the canonical order of things favored the restoration of the principle of "one bishop in one city" and by suggesting the abolition of parallel émigré church structures in Orthodox countries. However, this letter gave the Karlovcians the opportunity to claim that they had legitimate supreme ecclesiastical authority over all émigrés. What they failed to "notice" was the proviso in the letter that such a body would be acceptable only if it were recognized by all émigrés, and a suggestion that otherwise the canonical order should be followed. Therefore, in view of the fact that not—by far—all the émigrés accepted the Karlovci authority, the Karlov-

[25]Rahr, 22-3.

[26]This term, which means "household" in Greek, is used in Orthodox theology in reference to an act called for by extraordinary need and performed for the good of the Church, even if it does not fully accord with the canons. By the same token, it has been stated that canons are applicable only for the good of the Church, and are not to be applied toward her destruction. See, for instance, Metropolitan Kirill's letter to Sergii of November 1929 in Regelson, 171.

cians should have absolved their central organization and adhered to the canons.[27]

Less than a year later it became evident how right Sergii was in his warning not to look up to Moscow for ecclesiastical leadership. This happened when his already mentioned Declaration of Loyalty was issued. In fact, it differed from the last patriarchal appeal only in its—obviously insincere—expression of thanks to the Soviet government for their care for the needs of the Orthodox Church. The schism on the right that it precipitated in Russia must have really been the result of the bitterness caused by the two documents combined, not by Sergii's declaration alone. In addition, it should be remembered that people always tend to be more forgiving to those who have died or become martyrs. Tikhon and Peter (the latter, most probably, was behind Tikhon's appeal), fitted into these categories. Sergii's position was very different: he had only four brief spells in prison,[28] he was not as beloved as Tikhon, nor did he possess the authority of a patriarch. Nevertheless, one of the declarations of the imprisoned bishops warning against too zealous an expression of loyalty to the Soviet state and spelling out the aspects and limitations of such loyalty appeared prior to Sergii's declaration, as a moderately negative reaction to Tikhon's appeal-testament of 1925. But we will speak more on the schism on the right in Russia later. For now, let us return to the divisions among the émigrés.

---

[27]Moreover, in the "Karlovcian" literature the letter is usually cited in an abbreviated form with the reference to the canonical order missing. See, for example, Polsky, 29-30; Mikhail M. Rodzyanko, *Pravda o zarubezhnoi tserkvi* (Munich, 1954) 7-8. In contrast, the émigré "Popular-Monarchist Movement" resolved that the Karlovci Synod fulfil this second suggestion of Sergii's and dissolve itself, in accordance with the late patriarch's earlier orders. This group blames the existence and actions of the Synod on a plot of the legitimist Higher Monarchist Council, which aims "at its partisan interests." "Tserkovnaya smuta," *Vozrozhdenie,* no. 649 (March 13, 1927). Even such a strict canonist as Stratonov takes the view that despite their uncanonicity the Karlovcian organization could be justified on the grounds of church *oikonomia* if it had been able to spiritually unify the Russian diaspora, but it failed in this at its very first "sobor" when politics took precedence over the Church in the Rodzyanko affair. "Iskhodnyi moment," 88-91.

[28]This author has been able to trace only two arrests, but Metropolitan Elevfery, who had visited Sergii in 1932, mentions four. *Nedelya v Patriarkhii,* 103.

Metropolitan Antony (Khrapovitsky)

A very important factor in assuring the longevity, importance and influence of the Karlovci schism was the personality of Metropolitan Antony himself, one of the most influential bishops and conservative theological reformists in the Russian Church before the revolution, whose influence and theological authority reached far beyond the frontiers of the Russian empire in the world of Orthodoxy. As rector of the Moscow Theological Academy, where he achieved much in emancipating Orthodox theology from the influence of the abstract and skeptical German scholarship, emphasizing instead the legacy of eastern patristics and the living existential theology of Orthodoxy, he created a whole school of disciples and admirers among the younger bishops and theologians. A passionate advocate of celibacy and monasticism, it was under his direct influence that a large number of theology graduates chose monastic life and thus later became bishops. One of them was Evlogy, the future émigré metropolitan of Western Europe.[29] But while in theological terms Antony fought against the post-Petrine legacy and was an active advocate of the restoration of the patriarchate and autonomy of the Church from government interference, in politics he was extremely conservative, even reactionary, and a rather narrow Russian nationalist.[30]

In 1905, while the majority of bishops, in their memoranda to the Synod on the necessary church reforms, favored a sobor with participation of the lower clergy and laity, Antony saw the sobor as a council of bishops, and at most agreed to tolerate laymen and the lower clergy as observers and consultants without voting rights. He was also in favor of emancipation of the Church from the state bureaucracy and wanted to see a reorgan-

---

[29]Evlogy, *Put'*, 37-46. He reproaches Antony, however, for having been too aggressive and unselective in tonsuring young people; consequently, there were many tragic cases among them.

[30]Ibid., 41; *K tserkovnomu soboru*, 72-148. The radical priest and sociomoralistic pamphleteer Grigory Petrov wrote that Antony, who had begun as everybody's hope in reforming the Church, had degenerated into "a defender of court-martials . . . executions, hater of foreigners and of the non-Orthodox and a collaborator of Pobedonostsev." *U pustogo kolodtsa* (Moscow, 1911) 227-63. Although much more restrained, similarly negative remarks regarding Antony are to be found in the memoirs of Shavelsky, *Vospominaniya*, 1:167 and 2:161-8.

ization of the Church into a decentralized federal-metropolitan system with a patriarch and a council of bishops at the top. In other words, he wanted episcopal hegemony, the very reverse of the aims of the Petersburg reformist priests and of the eventual Living Church schism.[31]

At the 1917-1918 All-Russian Church Sobor he had received the majority of votes as patriarchal candidate, and only the choice by lot resulted in Tikhon's enthronement. Once the Patriarchal Church inside Russia began to move toward compromises with the Soviet government, Antony and his church organization abroad, free from Soviet interference, would be the natural pole of attraction for those who had originally voted for him.

The degree of his theological authority abroad was demonstrated by the words addressed to him by Metropolitan Dorotheos, the locum tenens of the Ecumenical Patriarch in Constantinople, when he recognized the Higher Church Administration for the émigrés under Antony's leadership on December 29, 1920: "The Patriarchate permits any initiative under your leadership, because the Patriarchate knows that Your Grace will never commit anything that would contradict the canons."[32] It is most likely this attitude that precluded Constantinople from *publicly* censuring Antony's administration and later his Synod in Karlovci—at least until the acceptance of Metropolitan Evlogy's diocese under its jurisdiction in 1931—although it had full rights to do so, as the above document retained judicial powers for the patriarchate, i.e., it made the January 1927 Karlovci bans on Evlogy and his clergy null and void. In a private conversation with a Russian Orthodox bishop from America, the Ecumenical Patriarch (Vasilios) said: "The Ecumenical Patriarchate has never recognized the Karlovci Synod. We responded to Metropolitan Antony's letters because he was a Russian bishop, not because he chaired a Synod," and added that in view of the uncanonicity of Antony's administrative position, his interdicts and excommunications were invalid.[33] It

[31]*Otzyvy eparkhial'nykh arkhiereev*, 1:112-48 and 3:186-94. See also the eulogy on Antony as a great theologian by one of the most authoritative Orthodox theologians, Archimandrite Justin Popovich of the Belgrade faculty of theology: "Taina lichnosti M. Antoniya," *RAPV*, no. 8 (1941) 115-7.

[32]Rodzyanko, 5.

[33]"Vselenskii Patriarkh o tserkovnoi smute," *Vozrozhdenie*, no. 647 (March 11, 1927).

was apparently also out of personal respect for Antony that Constantinople refrained from passing any judgment on the arbitrary migration of the administration from Constantinople's ecclesiastical territory to that of the Serbian patriarch, although canonically the Patriarch of Serbia could not receive the émigré bishops as his guests, nor did the bishops have the right to leave the jurisdiction of the Patriarch of Constantinople without asking for and receiving formal leave from him. Having now arrived on the territory of another local Orthodox Church, canonically, Metropolitan Antony and his bishops became subordinates of the Patriarch of Serbia. Indeed, in his invitation to Antony to make Yugoslavia his home, Patriarch Dimitrije of Serbia specified that Antony's church administration would have authority only over those Russian priests in Serbia who had not joined the Serbian Patriarchate, over the military chaplains of the Russian refugee army, and over the matrimonial affairs of the Russian refugees in Yugoslavia.[34]

It must have been the imperial complex and the subconsciously contemptuous attitude to the "backward little Balkan churches" that allowed the old imperial claims to overshadow Antony's theological conscience. At the same time, the Serbian Church, in her warm hospitality, did not dare even to remind their Russian guests of their proper place. Canonically speaking, as soon as new bishops had been appointed by the Moscow Patriarchate to the Russian sees vacated by the émigré bishops, the latter became nothing more than vicars of the Serbian Patriarchate, unless they were appointed to other sees unoccupied by any other canonically appointed bishops.[35] This applied to Metropolitan Evlogy, appointed by Tikhon to head the Russian parishes in Western Europe, which had hitherto been a vicariate of the Metropolitan of St. Petersburg; similarly, Metropolitan Platon was appointed by Tikhon to administer temporarily the Russian Orthodox Arch-

<hr />

[34]Even this piece of information appears in *TsV* (no. 2 [April 1922] 8-9) under the caption: "By the blessing of Patriarch Tikhon . . ."

[35]*Kanonicheskoe polozhenie pravoslavnoi russkoi tserkvi zagranitsei* (Paris, 1927) 34-41. Canon 18 of the Council of Antioch and canon 37 of the Council *in Trullo* regulate the prerogatives of bishops who are forced out of their dioceses by hostile invasions. According to these, in the area of their new domicile they only retain the right to perform liturgical services and sacraments. Their episcopal authority relates only to their former diocesan territory, unless they are duly appointed to new dioceses.

diocese of America.[36] Hence, the agreement of émigré bishops to recognize the authority over them of the Karlovci administration and the Karlovci Synod rested entirely on the personal prestige and authority of Metropolitan Antony. This was vividly illustrated by Evlogy's uncanonical 1922 decision not to abide by Patriarch Tikhon's May 5 decree in Antony's favor, which was to have such tragic consequences in precipitating the continuing divisions within the émigré Church.

The inner conflict between Antony the outstanding theologian and bishop that he was, and Antony the monarchist politician, in the peculiar émigré conditions of nostalgia for the past and abhorrence of the present, led to the triumph of his political emotions over his theological judgment at the 1921 Karlovci "Sobor" and at the Bad Reichenhal Congress of Monarchists, which had preceded the former and which in fact had resolved to convoke this church assembly of clerics and laymen. There, Antony privately told Metropolitan Evlogy how nice it was to be "among one's kin," meaning the monarchists. Thus, the very initiative of this church conference, which was to regularize émigré church affairs, came from a political party conference— an ecclesiastical absurdity that Antony eagerly condoned because of his monarchist sentiments. The same was true of the resolutions on monarchy adopted by the Karlovci meeting, which declared itself a sobor, and on an anti-Soviet crusade, formulated later in accordance with the "sobor" decisions.[37] The *Double-headed Eagle (Dvuglavyi oriol)*, an organ of the Higher Monarchist Council edited by Rklitsky, the future Synodal Bishop Nikon of Florida, became a semiofficial voice of the Karlovci Synod, and from 1926 launched a wild campaign against the Paris St. Sergius Orthodox Theological Institute, the famous

[36]*Kanonicheskoe polozhenie*, 50-61. On Platon's appointment, in the Karlovci version, see Polsky, 156-7. Orthodoxy in America developed out of a Russian mission for the Alaskan natives; hence, strictly speaking, the Orthodox Church in America is not an organic part of the émigré schisms, although she is related to them inasmuch as she had been a part of the Russian Church. See Chapter 8 below.

[37]Evlogy, *Put'*, 604-5 and 396-7. See also N. Zernov's diary notes from the "sobor" in *VRKhD*, no. 114 (1974) 119-46; and Georgy Grabbe's "Karlovcian" response, *VRKhD*, no. 116 (1975) 146-52, with Zernov's comments, ibid., 152-3. It is ironical that the same bishop who in 1905 had been against voting rights for laymen at sobors was now coopting lay monarchists with voting rights for his Karlovci "sobor."

theologian Fr. Sergius Bulgakov and the YMCA Press, accusing them all of Judeo-Masonic connections. Indeed, the destructive and splitting activities emanating from the Karlovcian circles caused serious suspicions that the GPU "monarchist" Trust operation, launched to subvert the émigré monarchist organizations, may have also operated under the auspices of the Karlovcian Synod.[38]

Deprived of patriarchal (Moscow) recognition after 1922 and stained by an overtly partisan political course, the Karlovci Synod's claims to legitimacy began to be doubted by Evlogy, Platon and a number of their bishops, clerics, theologians and lay faithful. Although the personal authority of Antony and the failure of his critics to denounce his uncanonical acts in no uncertain terms, plus the highly charged anticommunist political atmosphere of the diaspora, made the struggle against Karlovci very difficult, Evlogy's West European church district lost only three or four parishes at the time to the Karlovcians. In fact, even in terms of numbers and prestige among the émigrés the claims of the Karlovcian bishops, presiding over literally a handful of parishes in the deep Balkan hinterland of Europe, were preposterous. The intellectual centers of the Russian diaspora were Paris, Berlin and Prague, in that order, while numerically the largest concentrations of Russians in Europe were in the Baltic states and in Poland, followed by France. None of these areas belonged to the Karlovcians ecclesiastically. For instance, at the diocesan clergy-laity conference of July 18, 1927, convoked by Evlogy to discuss the question of the loyalty pledge requested by

[38]On December 10, 1926, the Karlovci Synod began its attack on the St. Sergius Institute by refusing to approve its statute and appointing one of its bishops to draft another over the head of the autonomous diocesan bishop of France, Evlogy. Not only in the *Doubleheaded Eagle* but as late as the 1960s Talberg continued to maintain that Evlogy had fallen under the influence of Masons and that the Very Rev. Prof. Vasily Zenkovsky, the dean of St. Sergius Institute, was a Mason. See, respectively, *TsV*, no. 1-2 (January 1927) 2; Talberg, *Tserkovnyi raskol*, 3-9; and *K sorokaletiyu pagubnogo evlogianskogo raskola* (Jordanville, N.Y.: Holy Trinity Monastery, 1966) 27 et passim. One of Talberg's "sources" is D.N. Lyubimov, who had taken a Soviet passport in Paris after World War II, returned to the USSR and published there a book of "memoirs" full of slander. See also G.P. Fedotov, "Zarubezhnaya tserkovnaya smuta," *Put'*, no. 7 (April 1927) 119-20. On the Trust see V. Shulgin's *Tri stolitsy* (Berlin, 1927) passim; S.L. Woyciechowski, *Trest* (London, Ontario: Zarya Publishers, 1974) passim. On the Karlovcians and Metropolitan Platon see below in chapter 8.

Metropolitan Sergii (see below), eleven countries were represented, although Evlogy had parishes under his jurisdiction in
thirteen European states and in Australia. Prior to this controversy, it seems, only two or three parishes in Germany belonged
to Karlovci, besides a handful of their parishes in the Balkans.
Outside Europe, the Orthodox Church in China and only a handful of parishes in North America were likewise in the Karlovci
jurisdiction.

However, Sergii aggravated the issue in Karlovci's favor by
his above-cited 1926 letter, the first part of which could be interpreted as favoring Karlovci's position, and by his actions of the
subsequent years, which seemed to suggest that the émigrés
should follow his 1926 letter and break with Moscow. The
heaviest blow to Evlogy was Sergii's request that all émigré
clerics pledge loyalty to the Soviet state.

> Some refused to sign. One of such clerics logically formu-
> lated his refusal in the following terms: ". . . The minimal
> duty of the whole clergy is . . . to pray to God to deliver
> our beloved motherland . . . from the theomachistic Soviet
> power. . . . hence, it would be a hypocrisy on my part if
> I were to state that I recognized the legitimacy and bene-
> ficiality of the Soviet power for my motherland. The
> Church cannot be apolitical towards such a power."[39]

Metropolitan Evlogy

Like Antony, Evlogy (then still an archbishop) had not
deserted his flock voluntarily. Both were arrested by the Ukrainian
Petlyura government (Antony had been the Metropolitan of Kiev

[39]On the diocesan conference, see *Vozrozhdenie*, no. 777 (July 19, 1927). It
reports that only the parishes of Rome and Bari refused to take the pledge, even
in Evlogy's redaction. In fact, according to Evlogy's memoirs, there were more who
broke off, including the priest of the Geneva parish and two or three in France.
See also Rodzyanko, 14.

The original pledge, which Evlogy refused to accept, read: "I the under-
signed, do hereby give the present promise that being now within the jurisdiction
of the Moscow Patriarchate, I will not let myself do anything in public, and
particularly in my ecclesiastical activities, that might be taken as an expression of
my disloyalty to the Soviet government." Fletcher, *Study in Survival*, 40.

and Galicia, Evlogy the Archbishop of Volhynia) and transferred to a monastic Uniate detention in Lvov. After Lvov had been taken by the Poles, the latter apprehended both prelates and, accusing them of anti-Polish policies when in authority, transferred them to a Catholic monastic prison in Cracow. Under international pressure, the two prelates were finally released in the early spring of 1919. Expelled from Poland, Antony and Evlogy proceeded to southern Russia via the Black Sea. When Kiev was taken over by the Denikin forces, Antony briefly reoccupied his Kievan see, while Evlogy remained in the Don area because his Volhynian archdiocese, contested between the Bolsheviks, the Ukrainian nationalists and the Poles, was still inaccessible to him. With the evacuation of the Whites, Evlogy and many other bishops emigrated to Serbia on the invitation of its government. There Evlogy petitioned the Higher Church Administration for Russian Émigrés in Constantinople to appoint him administrator for Russian parishes in Western Europe. The appointment was duly granted, but some clerics in charge of Russian parishes in Western Europe, having been traditionally under the Metropolitan of Petersburg, legitimately doubted the validity of appointments made by an émigré church organization consisting of bishops without dioceses. It was in response to these doubts that Metropolitan Venyamin of Petrograd soon confirmed the validity of this appointment, and Patriarch Tikhon issued the appropriate circular appointing Evlogy "temporary administrator" of all Russian parishes in Western Europe—making him a vicar of the Petrograd metropolitan.[40]

Thus, of all the émigré bishops who would make up the Karlovci Synod, Evlogy and Platon of the Russian Church in

[40]Stratonov erroneously says that Evlogy's appointment by Tikhon of April 8, 1921 was based on a petition of the *inside-Russia* Higher Church Administration. The patriarchal order no. 424, appointing Evlogy, says: "owing to the decision of the Higher Church Administration *Abroad* [emphasis supplied], let all Russian Orthodox churches in Western Europe . . . be under the administration of Archbishop Evlogy . . ." However, the Karlovcian confirmation of Evlogy as an autonomous head of a metropolitan district (June 1, 1923) says that it is "based on the rights given Metropolitan Evlogy by the patriarch's ukaz no. 424 . . ." Hence, Evlogy was correct in claiming that his prerogatives originated from Moscow, and not from Karlovci. See, respectively, Stratonov, "Iskhodnyi moment," 82-3 and 88; *TsV*, no. 1 (March 1922) 2 and no. 17-18 (September 1923) 1; *Kanonicheskoe polozhenie*, 50-62.

America were the only members with canonically valid appointments originating from the mother Church. However, Evlogy's earlier application for appointment, addressed to the canonically questionable émigré body in Constantinople, had set a bad precedent of canonical inconsistency in his own behavior. Although he could argue that the émigré body in Constantinople had the approval of the Ecumenical Patriarch, he should have known that no patriarch or bishop had the right to accept clergy under his jurisdiction without the latter's release by its former canonical bishop, and the émigré bishops continued to regard themselves and be considered by others as subordinates of Patriarch Tikhon. This, along with his subsequent waverings between following the canonical order and his feelings of personal loyalty to and love for Metropolitan Antony—which caused him several times to stretch and at least once to break the canons[41]—further undermined Evlogy's authority. Whenever he would realize that the compromise was going too far and take action against the Karlovcians' arbitrariness, he would cite the canons as his authority and as the ultimate requirement for church discipline. In these circumstances, the Karlovcian accusation that Evlogy resorted to the canons only when it suited him appeared quite plausible. Such appears to be the case with the 1922 patriarchal decree to dissolve the Karlovci administration and to appoint Evlogy (elevated by then to the title of metropolitan) the sole administrator of all parishes in Europe. Evlogy's first response was a letter to Antony in which he wrote: "This decree . . . was undoubtedly issued under Bolshevik pressure. I do not recognize any obligatory validity in this document, even if it was indeed written by the patriarch. Its character is political, not ecclesiastical. Beyond Soviet borders it has no meaning or authority for anyone."[42]

But when the reformed Synod of Bishops, accepted by Evlogy (who even became its vice chairman), began to drift more and more to partisan monarchist political issues and to issue declarations that reflected its claims to speak not only on behalf of the émigrés but for the whole of Russia, Evlogy suddenly began to

---

[41]That is, when he did not abide by the patriarch's order and left the émigré church administration in Antony's hands.

[42]Rodzyanko, 6.

deny its validity on the grounds of Patriarch Tikhon's ukaz of May 5, 1922. The point is, however, that in these confused conditions everybody was straining or simply breaking the canons. Even Patriarch Tikhon and the All-Russian Sobor of 1917-1918 did so when the sobor asked Tikhon to secretly appoint a number of heirs for the patriarchal throne, in case the Bolsheviks prevented the election of a patriarch after his death or if he was arrested. The patriarch complied, although the canons expressly forbid the naming of any heirs or desirable candidates by outgoing patriarchs in their wills.[43] Yet, the unprecedented conditions under the Soviets and Tikhon's prestige were such that no one even thought of questioning the validity of these appointments. The real confusion began when every one of the above-named metropolitans, while in danger of arrest, made secret lists of their replacements, and the Soviet regime began to play leapfrog with them by arresting some and releasing others. But even then, despite the fact that these metropolitans had not been requested by any such church body to make such appointments, their validity was not questioned in the USSR, to the best of our knowledge.

It seems to have really been a situation where everybody understood that the canons could not be observed verbatim under the existing circumstances. The difference between those churchmen for whom the Church and her unity were of primary importance and those who placed political aims above those of the Church was that the former tried to invoke the canons whenever they felt it was necessary to do so in order to prevent total anarchy in the Church. The church "politicians" had no such restraining motives. This seems to be the key to the seemingly inconsistent behavior of Evlogy who, in the final analysis, always tried to put the Church above politics. But the trouble is that such a "flexible" attitude toward the canons, guided by one's ecclesiastic conscience rather than by any clearly definable criteria, can work only if the other participants are guided by similar considerations and restraints. The reality proved that it was not so, and the politicized Karlovci bishops and their lay advisers would

[43]Canon 23 of the Council of Antioch says: "A bishop is not . . . to appoint another in his stead even at the close of his life . . . such appointment will be null. . . . a bishop shall not be made without a synod and the decision of the bishops."

use Evlogy's waverings and changes of attitude against him, accusing him of inconsistency and of using canons only in his own interests.[44]

An official theological-canonical analysis of the conflict between Evlogy and the Karlovci Synod states that:

> The . . . Synod . . . wanted to have the full powers of the prerevolutionary Russian Holy Governing Synod in relation to the bishops abroad.

> This striving for centralization in the style of the . . . overprocurator era expressed itself already at the 1923 Sobor of bishops when Metropolitan Evlogy's project on separate independent metropolitan circuits was rejected . . . Metropolitan Evlogy aimed at coordinating the idea of organic ties with Moscow with the idea of a necessary and inevitable decentralization . . . "in conditions of diversified local state and social conditions . . ."

> The Synod . . . moreover, tried to adopt the full rights of an all-Russian church authority, not only in relation to the émigrés but even in relation to Russia, putting such questions on the agenda of every consecutive bishops' sobor, from 1923 to 1926:

> 1923: . . . "On the adoption by the Higher Church Administration abroad of functions of the all-Russian church authority temporarily, until Patriarch Tikhon or his heir is restored in his position" [passed when the Patriarch was under arrest].

> 1924: . . . "On the necessity and possibility . . . to grant the bishops' Synod . . . under Metropolitan Antony's chairmanship the rights and functions of an all-Russian church authority . . ."

> There was no bishops' sobor in 1925, but still on April 9 the Synod issued the following decree: "The . . . Synod

[44]See, for instance, the cited works by Polsky and Rodzyanko, passim.

considers it useful for the good of the Russian Orthodox Church . . . in case the Soviet government will prevent the canonical patriarchal locum tenens in Russia to govern the Church . . . to grant Metropolitan Antony the preroga- tives of the provisional . . . deputy patriarch, representing the whole Russian Church and governing, as far as possi- ble, the life of the whole Russian Church both abroad and inside Russia."

As already mentioned, the Synod hesitated to recognize the valid- ity of Metropolitan Peter's position as locum tenens in Russia. Then on November 12, under the pressure of sixty bishops inside Russia who had signed a statement recognizing Peter, the Synod agreed to recognize him temporarily, subject to the validation of the title by a sobor of Russian bishops *abroad*—i.e., thereby the "Synod appropriates for itself the function of recognition of a bishop as its head, which rightfully belongs only to the supreme administrative bodies of autocephalous churches." Metropolitan Evlogy, who, although a member of the Synod next in seniority only to Antony, was not even consulted prior to the issuance of such declarations, commented: "It is not Metropolitan Peter who is in need of recognition by a small group of émigré bishops, but we need his recognition." The Karlovci sobor of bishops, in June-July 1926, suddenly decided to deprive Metropolitan Evlogy of his autonomy, which it had no right to do, since he had been appointed directly by the Patriarch of Moscow, who alone could legally change his status. This was the final breaking point, after which both Metropolitan Evlogy and Metropolitan Platon of North America walked out and discontinued their ties with the Synod.[45]

The émigré Synod immediately interpreted this as an act of insubordination—a rebellion by Evlogy and Platon against the authority of their Church. But, canonically, this accusation was invalid, for the authority of these two metropolitans originated from the Moscow Patriarchate—hence, technically speaking, they had never been subordinates of the Synod, only its voluntary associates. In fact, they were the only ones among its members who held canonically valid positions, not infringing on the terri-

---

[45]*Kanonicheskoe polozhenie*, 14-22.

tories of other autocephalous Orthodox churches and granted by the Moscow Patriarchate.[46]

In the meantime, as already noted, Metropolitan Sergii resumed his duties as locum tenens after his release from prison in 1927, and Metropolitan Evlogy reaffirmed his subordination to him, while the Karlovci Synod, from then on, refused to recognize Sergii, condemning out of hand Sergii's Declaration of Loyalty and, in particular, his request of a pledge of loyalty to the Soviets from the émigré clergy.

Evlogy responded to this request in a sermon at his Paris cathedral (September 4, 1927) and in a letter to Sergii (September 12). In the former he stated: "we cannot . . . be loyal to the Soviet government . . . being political in nature, [the request] is not obligatory for us from the canonical point of view. As to the second request . . . not to turn the Church into a political arena . . . it is purely ecclesiastical . . . [to fulfil it] is our sacred duty to our suffering mother Church." In his official response to Sergii, Evlogy pointed out that:

> we Russian émigrés are not citizens of the Soviet Union . . . and our membership in the Russian Orthodox Church cannot be grounds for requesting of us émigrés "loyalty," i.e., legal obedience to the Soviet power.

> In full recognition of my duty to the mother Church and in the name of my limitless love for her, I pledge to stand firmly by . . . the position of noninterference of the Church in political life, and to prevent the use of the pulpit for political purposes.

In his reply, Metropolitan Sergii accepted the above formulation, stating that "the term 'loyalty,' of course, cannot mean any subordination to Soviet laws." He also added that he did not care about the wording of the pledge, as long as all of the clergy signed a promise regarding the noninterference of the Church in politics.[47] This correspondence was followed by a

[46]Ibid., 45 and 61-3, et passim, where relevant canons are cited. The opposing view is in *Russkaya pravoslavnaya tserkov' v severnoi Amerike* (Jordanville, N.Y.: Holy Trinity Monastery, 1954) 6-9.

[47]This, for the time being, made superfluous Evlogy's other option in his reply

diocesan conference, convoked by Evlogy, which approved his actions and his formulation of the pledge. The latter was then signed by all of Evlogy's clergy except for two or three in France and the already mentioned cleric in Geneva.

From that moment on, however, the Karlovcians began an active seizure of Evlogy's diocesan territory—a blatant breach of the canons, particularly since, being canonically invalid, the Karlovci Synod had no jurisdictional territory of its own to begin with.[48] Nevertheless, the Synod even arrogated for itself the prerogative of banning bishops in the jurisdiction of the Moscow Patriarchate. In 1927, the Karlovcians placed an interdict on Evlogy for his insubordination to them—to which Evlogy responded that, as he had never been their subordinate, the ban was invalid.[49]

Soon, however, Evlogy's position did become rather vulnerable. Ever since his interpretation of the pledge of loyalty as one of political neutrality, his relations with Moscow began to be strained. Sergii kept reproaching him for engaging in anti-Soviet politics, while Evlogy repeatedly responded that his statements on church persecution in Russia were acts of pastoral duty and were of a religious, not political, nature. The matter dragged on, until Evlogy participated in joint Anglican-Orthodox public

to Sergii—namely, to allow his diocese to temporarily exist as a separate church organization outside of the Moscow Patriarchate should Sergii find Evlogy's version of the pledge insufficient. Evlogy's letter to Sergii and the summaries of his pledge formula are in *Vozrozhdenie*, no. 836 (1927) 1 and 3; no. 869 (1927) 1; no. 1123 (1928). The official declaration of Evlogy's diocesan administration of August 26, 1928 is in the Bakhmeteff Archives, Vysheslavtsev's Collection, box 7, folder 9. The full texts of Evlogy's sermon and the Sergii-Evlogy correspondence is in *Tserkovnyi vestnik* (the official organ of Evlogy's diocese), no. 3 (September 22, 1927) 1-11; and no. 4 (October 31, 1927) 1.

Sergii later confirmed to Metropolitan Elevfery of Lithuania (during the latter's visit to Moscow) that he had meant by a pledge of loyalty nothing more than that contained in Evlogy's interpretation. He added: "We are suspected of illegal relations with the émigrés, we're distrusted; but we must go on building up our church life." *Nedelya v Patriarkhii*, 56-8.

[48]Evlogy, *Put'*, 418-23 and 610-48; and *Kanonicheskoe polozhenie*, 65-79. In 1926 the Karlovci Synod unilaterally carved out most of Evlogy's parishes in Germany and set them up as a diocese under their control via the Karlovcian Bishop of Germany Tikhon (originally consecrated officially as Evlogy's vicar for Germany). The canons expressly forbid the setting up of any new dioceses on the territory belonging to another bishop without that bishop's permission (canon 3 of the Council of Carthage).

[49]Evlogy, *Put'*, 615-8; and the above-cited diocesan declaration.

prayers in Britain on behalf of the persecuted Christians in
Russia, at the time of the particularly harsh attack on the Church
begun by Stalin in 1929. These prayers contradicted Sergii's
(obviously enforced) statement at a press conference in Moscow
just before, at which he had assured western journalists
that his Church was not being persecuted. Metropolitan Evlogy
spent a week in England in such public prayers and gave many
sermons to the British public on the sufferings of believers in
Russia. Shortly afterward, a letter was received from Sergii requesting an explanation of Evlogy's actions and of his attitude
to the question of Church and politics. Evlogy replied that it was
his pastoral duty to plead for the silent sufferers and martyrs in
Russia. Metropolitan Sergii responded by ordering Evlogy to
retire and to hand over his duties to Archbishop Vladimir, the
next bishop in seniority in the Western European archdiocese
(strictly speaking, a vicariate, since no decree of the Moscow
Patriarchate ever officially elevated it to the status of an independent archdiocese). Archbishop Vladimir refused to accept, whereupon Sergii requested that Evlogy pledge never again to participate in public actions such as the one described above. In the
meantime, he gathered an archdiocesan conference of delegates
of clergy and laity. The conference begged him not to retire and
to derive the legitimacy of his position from Patriarch Tikhon
and not from the current orders of Metropolitan Sergii. Evlogy
then addressed a letter to Sergii, requesting permission to organize a temporarily independent diocese by the authority of Metropolitan Agafangel's above-cited 1922 decree on temporary autocephalies, which would thus be extended to territories outside
Russia.[50] Instead, Sergii interdicted Metropolitan Evlogy and all
bishops and clergy remaining loyal to him, and ordered all
parishes in Western Europe remaining loyal to Moscow to subordinate themselves to Metropolitan Elevfery of Lithuania, who
had remained in the jurisdiction of Moscow.

The fact that Evlogy, who had earlier insisted on abiding by
the orders of the Moscow Patriarchate (except once in 1922, as
already mentioned), now failed to fulfil Sergii's order himself
gave the Karlovcians grounds to attack him for canonical inconsistency. The canonical side of the issue will be discussed in

[50]Evlogy, *Put'*, 622-3.

chapter 8.[51] Be it as it may, Constantinople ruled that Sergii's interdiction of Evlogy was unjustified and accepted the latter into its jurisdiction. Thereafter, the Archdiocese of Paris and Western Europe remained a Russian exarchate of the ecumenical see until 1965, when Patriarch Athenagoras, under Moscow's pressure, unilaterally severed jurisdictional ties with it, advising it to join the Moscow Patriarchate. Instead, the archdiocese proclaimed itself an independent Church of France, with which, surprisingly, Constantinople remained in communion. In 1973, soon after Patriarch Athenagoras' death, the new patriarch, Dimitrios, re-accepted the archdiocese, only, however, as a Russian vicariate of the Greek Metropolitan of France.[52]

The Schism on the Right in Russia

Although Regelson, showing a bias similar to that of the Karlovcians and like-minded schismatics in Russia, writes that Sergii's July 1927 declaration "painfully shocked the Orthodox by its transition from the position of apoliticism to that of internal spiritual solidarity with the government,"[53] the fact that it was preceded by the May memorandum of the bishops imprisoned in Solovki indicates that Tikhon's will had already created an atmosphere of alarm that the patriarchate was slipping from a position of neutrality to one of active collaboration with the Soviet state. The memorandum, addressed to the Soviet government, dealt with the whole problem of Church-state relations in the Soviet Union and their relation to the teachings and canons of the Church. It is so directly relevant to the whole subsequent conflict within the Church that its summary is in order. It will

[51]But see the attacks in Rodzyanko and Polsky, passim. The canons are numbers 9, 17 and 28 of the Fourth Ecumenical Council. See *Kanonicheskoe polozhenie*, 26-31.

[52]Evlogy, *Put'*, 625-9; and Prof. A. Knyazev, "Otkrytoe pis'mo redaktoru," *VRKhD*, no. 114 (1974) 114-8, where he says, inter alia, that in 1949 Metropolitan Vladimir, the head of the Paris archdiocese after the death of Evlogy, offered Metropolitan Anastasy, the chairman of the post-Karlovci Synod, the subordination of himself and his archdiocese to the émigré Synod on the condition that the latter enter the jurisdiction of the Patriarch of Constantinople. Anastasy refused, thus perpetuating the émigré schism and his own uncanonical status.

[53]Regelson, 117-8.

also help to remove the onus of blame for the persecutions from the Church, as laid upon her by Professor Curtiss, and to return it to where it belongs: to Marxism-Leninism and its first state.

The document begins by stating that it is the government, not the Church, that violates its own law on the separation of Church and state by refusing to allow the Orthodox Church to run her regular central, diocesan and parish organs of administration. Consecrated bishops are prevented from residing in the dioceses to which they were appointed by the patriarch or his locum tenens. The Church is not permitted to hold religious instruction classes for children, although her duty is to bring the gospel message to all. The locum tenens and about half of all the existing bishops are under arrest. Monasteries are being forcibly closed, even though all of them have become monastic working communes, feeding themselves by the fruits of their own labor. The Orthodox Church suffers more than any other, because the state, in contradiction of its own law and declarations that it is opposed to all religion, artificially supports the schismatic Renovationists, recognizing them as a sort of state Church by the virtue of having confiscated all city cathedrals from the Patriarchal Church and giving them to the schismatics. As a result, the cathedrals stand empty, since the faithful ignore the Renovationists. Delegates to the Renovationist "sobors" are granted free railway tickets by the state and are lodged in Moscow at government expense. Most of the bishops and clerics in prison are there in punishment for their refusal to recognize the Renovationists. The duty of the Church is to spread Christian teachings while remaining politically neutral and loyal to the state in the civic sector, but the government's dealings with the Renovationists indicate that it wants the clergy to be the servants of the state and to act as police informers. Hence, although the government accuses the Orthodox Church of meddling in politics, in real fact it is the latter that tries hard to keep out of politics, while it is the Renovationists who have become politicized. An example is their "defrocking," in 1923, of the patriarch and of the émigré clergy, and Archbishop Solovei's letter containing fraudulent charges fabricated by the GPU against the late patriarch and Metropolitan Peter.

The whole history of the Church shows that she is capable of

leading a politically separate but loyal existence in as diverse po-
litical systems as the Moslem Turkish empire and the democratic
USA, rendering to God what is God's and to Caesar what is
Caesar's. She could do likewise in the Soviet state, despite the
deep contradictions between the teachings of the Church and the
Marxist ideology of the Party that heads the Soviet state:

> The Church recognizes spiritual principles of existence;
> communism rejects them. The Church believes in the living
> God, the Creator of the world, the leader of its life and
> destinies; communism denies his existence, believes in the
> spontaneity of the world's existence and in the absence of
> rational, ultimate causes of its history. The Church assumes
> that the purpose of human life is in the heavenly father-
> land, even if she lives in conditions of the highest develop-
> ment of material culture and general well-being; com-
> munism refuses to recognize any other purpose of man-
> kind's existence but terrestrial welfare. The ideological
> differences between the Church and the state descend from
> the apex of philosophical observations to the practical . . .
> sphere of ethics, justice and law: communism considers
> them to be a conditional result of class struggle and
> assesses the phenomena of the moral sphere exclusively
> in terms of utility. The Church preaches love and mercy;
> communism, *camaraderie* and merciless struggle. The
> Church instills in believers humility, which elevates the
> person; communism debases man by pride. The Church
> preserves chastity of the body and sacredness of repro-
> duction; communism sees nothing else in marital relations
> but satisfaction of the instincts. The Church sees in reli-
> gion a lifebearing force which . . . serves as the source for
> all greatness in man's creativity, as the basis of man's
> earthly happiness, sanity and welfare; communism sees
> religion as opium, drugging the people and relaxing their
> energies, as the source of their suffering and poverty. The
> Church wants to see religion flourish; communism wants
> its death. Such a deep contradiction in the very basis of
> their *Weltanschauungen* precludes any intrinsic approxi-
> mation or reconciliation between the Church and state,

as there cannot be any between affirmation and negation
. . . because the very soul of the Church, the condition
of her existence and the sense of her being, is that which
is categorically denied by communism.

Therefore, no compromises or even concessions by the Church
would ever be able to reconcile these diametrically opposed
doctrines, as was demonstrated by the futility of all the pitiful
attempts of the Renovationists to change the words of services
and prayers so that they would reflect republican rather than
monarchic relations between God and man, and to purge the
church calendar of all saints of a "bourgeois" class background,
etc. All this resulted only in the estrangement of the believers
and the failure of the schismatics to take the place of the traditional Church in the hearts of the nation.

The imprisoned bishops, however, see a possibility of coexistence of the two bodies, but only under the conditions of strict
observance of the separation of Church and state. Under such
conditions, the Church will not interfere in the socioeconomic
activities and reform of the state and in the fulfilment by the
citizens of their civic duties, while the state will cease to interfere
in the spiritual activities of the Church and to hinder the religious
life of its citizens. The memorandum admits that the Church did
interfere in the civic-political life of the state and opposed the
new regime, but this was in the chaos of the Civil War, when

the revolution expressed itself only destructively . . .
Groups of suspicious individuals were active everywhere,
claiming to be the new government's agents, but in actual
fact turning out to be impostors with criminal records.
They beat and murdered innocent bishops and priests,
attacked private houses and hospitals, killed residents and
patients, robbed houses and churches and then disappeared without a trace. It would have been very strange
if in such tension of political and self-interested passions,
in such hatred tearing people apart, in the midst of this
struggle of all against all, the Church were to have alone
remained an indifferent observer.

The Church, say the authors of the memorandum, appealed to peace and order and condemned those who were the agents and activators of chaos, disorder and suffering. "But with time, as some form of civil authority became apparent, Patriarch Tikhon, in his appeal to the faithful, declared his loyalty to the Soviet government and resolutely stated that he would not attempt to exert a political influence on the life of the country." A further confirmation of this was the patriarch's condemnation of the political activities of the Karlovci Synod and his order that it be dissolved. This was the maximum the Church could do, for the Church cannot try and condemn people, even clerics, for political declarations and views—she can only dissolve church organizations for attempting such activities. The obedience of the Church inside Russia to the declaration of loyalty by the patriarch has been demonstrated by the fact that since that time (1923), *not a single cleric* has been sentenced for anti-Soviet activities by a Soviet court. All those in prison are there by *administrative action.*

The memorandum concludes that if the Soviet government accepts these conditions of coexistence, then the Church "will rejoice at the justice of those on whom such policies depend. If . . . not, she is ready to go on suffering, and will respond calmly, remembering that her power is not in the wholeness of her external administration, but in the unity of faith and love of her children; but most of all she lays her hopes upon the unconquerable power of her divine Founder."[54]

Although this memorandum preceded Sergii's Declaration of Loyalty, it contained all the seeds of the future conflict between Sergii and the schism on the right that would develop from that declaration. The memorandum, while proclaiming civic loyalty to and coexistence with the regime, stressed the importance of spiritual steadfastness and no compromises in subjects of faith and mission even at the cost, if need be, of the formal disintegration of the Church as an organization. Sergii, however, decided to sacrifice the essence of the Church's opposition to the atheist state, i.e., the internal freedom of the Church, in order to

[54]Regelson, 417-28. The initiator of this memorandum was Archbishop Illarion (Troitsky). See S.A. Volkov, "Arkhiepiskop Illarion," *VRKhD*, no. 134 (1981) 227.

save the external organizational forms. But the almost complete annihilation of the Church in the 1930s showed that all Sergii succeeded in gaining at the cost of such great sacrifices was a "general staff" without any "army": a Holy Synod recognized by the state, at the top, whose members nevertheless kept disappearing in the dungeons of the NKVD, so that by 1939 it consisted of only two metropolitans—Sergii (Stragorodsky) and Aleksii (Simansky)—and two archbishops—Sergii (Voskresensky) and Nikolai (Yarushevich). All the others had either been killed by various means, imprisoned, or lived in retirement, either as laymen or as legal or illegal priests (depending on whether they were registered with the authorities).[55]

In justification of Sergii's act, it must be admitted that much more than merely an external form of the Church was at stake. After the metropolitan's arrest in December 1926, all three of the bishops whom he had appointed to replace him if he were to be arrested followed him behind bars. They were in turn followed by ever increasing numbers of detained Patriarchal bishops, with only a small and constantly diminishing minority remaining at large. In the message to the bishops of December 31, 1927, rationalizing his declaration, Sergii and his Synod explain: "The disintegration of church affairs had reached the ultimate limit . . . the center knew little about the peripheral dioceses, while the dioceses often had to base their ideas about the center on rumors. There were dioceses . . . which did not know whom to follow in order to preserve Orthodoxy."[56]

The situation was not unlike that of 1923, when Patriarch Tikhon was forced to seek release from prison even at the cost of his own declaration of loyalty. After he had been released and

[55]Regelson, 187. The Soviet government, in addition, ever since the mid-1920s widely practiced a policy of preventing the bishops from actually governing their dioceses by not allowing them to leave Moscow for Russian and other dioceses, while forcing the Ukrainian bishops to reside idly in Kharkov. Thus, in the late 1920s more than sixty nominal diocesan bishops were forced to live in Moscow. Ibid., 121-2.

[56]Bogolepov, *Tserkov'*, 30; Regelson, 127-8. The crux of the argument between Sergii and the opponents of his policies can be compared to the fifteenth-sixteenth-century debate between St. Nil Sorsky and St. Joseph of Volokolamsk and their disciples, the nonpossessors and possessors, respectively. Whereas the former favored the material poverty of monasticism and its spiritual, otherworldly aspect, the latter emphasized the wealth, glory and worldly influence of the Church upon the state and its policies.

informed of the fact that the laity and much of the clergy were
not supporting the Renovationists and were returning to the
Patriarchal fold, he said that had he known that the actual position of the Renovationists was so weak he would have rather
remained in jail than signed his declaration.[57] The inner spiritual
cohesion—the fact that the masses were on the side of the Patriarchal Church—was much more important for a spiritually oriented man like Tikhon than the state of the formal organization
of his Church. In contrast, Metropolitan Sergii—the author of a
dissertation "On the Orthodox Teachings on Salvation," in which
he had preached the precedence of a personal, subjective road
of salvation over the institutional, and criticized Western Christianity for formalism and institutionalism—now after ten years of
confrontation with the Soviet regime became an "organization
man," a more "western" formal churchman in his actions. He
now refused to visualize the survival of the Church without a
modicum of structured, formal organization. We do not hear of
any later statements by Sergii that could compare with the above
by Patriarch Tikhon. Therefore, whereas Tikhon continued to
fight the regime over the issue of the independence of the Church
even after the 1923 declaration, Sergii gave in more and more to
the regime after his 1927 declaration—all for the sake of preserving and reviving the *organization* of the Church.

   However, even if we adopt an entirely pragmatic-utilitarian
platform regarding Sergii's concessions, it still becomes obvious
that the trouble was that Sergii always gave the Soviet government an advance credit in the belief that it would pay dividends,
but the regime constantly broke faith. The declaration of 1927
resulted only in the legalization of the Synod, not of the whole
Church under Sergii's jurisdiction, while 1929 brought a new
Soviet Law (Code) on Religious Associations, which not only
reiterated the state's recognition of groups of twenty laymen or
more making up a parish and leasing a church building from the
state, but also explicitly stated that "religious unions and executive organs elected by them do not have the rights of a legal
person." They continued to be deprived of the right to set any
church membership dues or collections, and all church communities and parishes were strictly required to register with the local

[57]Levitin-Shavrov, 2:215.

soviet. Unless a group of twenty laymen was founded and registered with the local government bodies within a year, the parish
community was to be deemed illegal and to be closed. At the
same time, there was no legal proviso obliging the local government either to permit a reopening or recognize an already existing church. This provided broad opportunities for the local
governments not only to prevent the opening of new churches
but also to close the already existing ones.

At least in theory, however, there were some concessions and
gestures in Sergii's favor in this legislation. It was the first Soviet
legislation to recognize episcopal control over the clergy and to
make obstruction of religious services punishable by up to six
months in prison. The law required the registration of each religious community and priest in order for the parish to be able to
legally function. But whereas it permitted the local Soviet government organs to reject certain members of church committees, it
did not give the government such rights regarding the clergy.
Ostensibly, the purpose of the act of registration of the clergy
was to keep the government informed, but in practice, it was
soon to be used as a measure of approval of a priest by the
government, which would often abuse this arbitrarily assumed
privilege in order to blackmail the bishops, the priests and the
believers. Altogether, the following decade showed that the
regime did not mean to observe its own legislation on religions.
In addition, 1929 saw the passing of a constitutional amendment
banning all religious propaganda and confining all religious activities within church walls, but reconfirming the unlimited rights
of atheist propaganda.[58] This limitation of religious rights remains
in force to the present day (as reflected in the Constitutions of
1936 and 1977).

Judging by the fact that, after the death of Metropolitan-
Patriarch Sergii and the election of Patriarch Aleksii, at the time
when churches and seminaries were opening and government
pressure against the Church was eased, many of those who had
broken with Sergii in the late 1920s—including one of their most
widely recognized leaders, Bishop Afanasy (Sakharov)—returned
to the Patriarchal Church, it could be surmised that had the
Soviet government not defaulted on Sergii's credit of 1927-1930,

[58]Bogolepov, *Tserkov'*, 12-3; Spinka, 70-6; Shafarevich, 10-60.

the schism on the right would have folded up, or at least would not have taken such magnitude as it did.[59]

The schism took many forms, from the most extreme groups, which had begun to break away from the Patriarchal Church as early as 1925 in protest against Patriarch Tikhon's appeal, and which would become known as the True Orthodox Church (*Istinno-Pravoslavnaya Tserkov'*) or the IPTs, to moderate ones, like those of Metropolitans Agafangel and Kirill, with their many followers, known as the "Noncommemorators." The latter condemned Sergii's declaration and his policies and refused to commemorate either him or the Soviet government in their prayers, but they recognized the canonical validity of the Patriarchal clergy and the sacramental validity of their services. Consequently, they did not prevent their followers from attending the official churches and from partaking of their sacraments. Both metropolitans had been candidates to the locum tenens position, according to Patriarch Tikhon's will, and in fact were senior to Sergii.[60]

Of the two, Metropolitan Agafangel assured Sergii that, although he himself would not enter into administrative collaboration with him, he recognized Sergii as the administrator of the Russian Church while Peter was in prison and actively advised all appealing to his own authority to recognize Sergii's Church spiritually, to attend its churches and not to create a new schism. Shortly before his death, he responded to a telegram asking whether it was true that he had made peace with Sergii by reply-

[59]Evlogy, *Put'*, 194-5 and 568-74.

[60]Returning from prison in 1926, Agafangel declared that since Peter was in prison he, Agafangel, would assume the functions of the locum tenens. Sergii responded that once Peter had assumed the functions (when, at the time of Tikhon's death, both Kirill and Agafangel had been in prison) and as a legitimately ruling locum tenens had appointed Sergii as his deputy in case of arrest, Sergii was now the de facto locum tenens and had no right to give up his functions to Agafangel as long as Peter was living and did not abdicate. Agafangel complied. According to an anonymous Tikhonite bishop from the Ukraine, Sergii resisted Agafangel not because of his greed for power but because, first of all, Agafangel was a naive person who sincerely believed that his honesty and sincerity had won the sympathy and trust of Tuchkov. (The bishop had said to Agafangel: "There are sixty-two idle bishops now in Moscow. Tuchkov will allow you to appoint only those to active service who agree to work for the GPU, while exiling others.") Secondly, having spent three years in prison and exile, Agafangel was out of touch with the Church-state reality of the time. See Chrysostomus, 2:125-30.

ing: "Yes, this is true." Six months later he died.[61]

Kirill's attitude was much less conciliatory, and he lived on until 1944 (though mostly in exile under surveillance and in prison) to practice and preach it. He disagreed with Sergii at least as much on the interpretation of the canons in relation to Sergii's legitimacy as de facto locum tenens as on Sergii's capitulation to the Soviets. The point was that Metropolitan Sergii's policy to reinstate hierarchical order and discipline in the Church at any cost led him to issue a number of administrative sanctions, including suspensions of those bishops and clergy who had refused to abide by his policies and who proclaimed their independence from his Synod on the grounds of the 1920 patriarchal decree on local self-proclaimed diocesan autocephalies in case of breakup of the central authority or loss of contact with it. Sergii argued that this decree did not apply, for there was a canonical center—he and his Synod—and contacts with it were possible.

Kirill disagreed. He held that Sergii's overscrupulous use of canons to condemn and suspend his opponents was unfair, because, first of all, the situation the Church found herself in under the Soviet regime was unprecedented in history, and therefore one should be guided by the spirit of the Church and use the canons cautiously; and secondly, in terms of the needs of and usefulness for the Church under the prevailing conditions, Sergii's own claim to legitimacy as chief administrator of the Patriarchal Church was uncanonical both in letter and in spirit. The uncanonical appointment by the patriarch of heirs-apparent to his position in case of the impossibility of holding a proper electoral church council was generally accepted in these special conditions as necessary for preserving the unity of the Church,[62] and the rights of the three candidates to the position of locum tenens thus became reflections of the patriarch's rights. But no provision whatsoever had been made by the 1917-1918 Sobor or the patriarch to allow similar appointments of further candidates to the locum tenens position by the locum tenentes themselves. Hence, Sergii's legitimacy as deputy locum tenens appointed by Metropolitan Peter is valid only as long as Peter is alive. The moment Peter dies or abdicates, all of Sergii's prerogatives disappear, and it is he,

[61]See the Sergii-Agafangel correspondence in Regelson, 109-13 and 152-60.
[62]See note 27 above.

Kirill, who must and will assume the title of locum tenens.

Kirill also suggested in one of his letters to Sergii that Sergii's administration would have been accepted by the feuding churchmen had it been strictly conciliar, had he negotiated his decisions and policies with the bishops at large, corresponded with them as brothers, accepted some of their advice and showed himself ready to retract those of his actions that caused the most disagreement. In such circumstances the bishops would even have recognized, in the name of expediency, a Synod formed by Sergii, again provided it were formed in consultation with them and filled with bishops acceptable to them and commanding their faith and respect. Instead, Sergii kept ordering them about as if he had formal and canonically undisputable authority. In the case of Kirill, Sergii responded by declaring him to be under an ecclesiastical trial (which never took place) and removing him from the position of diocesan bishop (metropolitan) of Kazan. Kirill considered these acts canonically invalid and continued to consolidate the Noncommemorators under his guidance, if not administration (the latter was impossible in view of his exile under surveillance), until his final imprisonment in 1934.[63] This milder treatment of Kirill, in comparison with the suspension and banning of Metropolitan Iosif (Joseph), Bishop Aleksii Bui and others, reflected, on the one hand, the fact that Kirill commanded such general respect and authority among the clergy (he had received the majority of the bishops' votes in their clandestine polling in an attempt to carry out the election of a patriarch by correspondence in 1926) that Sergii simply did not dare to deal with him as summarily as with others, and, on the other hand, his less rigid attitude to Sergii and his recognition of Sergii's sacramental and ecclesiastical, though not administrative, validity.

The case of Metropolitan Iosif (Petrovykh) deserves separate treatment. To complicate matters, he was another deputy locum tenens, only second to Sergii according to Peter's instruction of December 6, 1925. And, after Sergii's arrest in the autumn of 1926, Iosif did briefly replace him in that position, and shortly

[63]Regelson, 166-72, 181-4, 466-7, 468-77, 493-5, and 559-60. Inter alia, Kirill reproaches Sergii for forbidding full Christian burial to those who died while in schism, whether Renovationist or "on the right."

before that he had been appointed Metropolitan of Leningrad by Sergii. In his turn, Iosif, expecting arrest sooner or later, issued a secret instruction appointing three archbishops—Kornily (Sobolev), Faddei (Uspensky) and Serafim (Samoilovich)—as his deputies in case of his arrest. Regelson, one of the most authoritative investigators of the subject, comments:

> This document shows the extreme reached by the application of the false idea of deputizing . . . Metropolitan Iosif's instruction leaves the impression that it concerned an army, with the necessity of retaining one-man rule at any cost, not the Church. . . .
>
> Metropolitan Iosif does not seem to realize that by establishing the new system of succession of the supreme ecclesiastic administration (following, by the way, in the steps of Metropolitan Peter) he supersedes the act of the holy patriarch, which was performed in strict fulfilment of the Sobor's decision.[64]

Obviously, the same accusation could be directed against Sergii and his acts, the precedent for which was set by Iosif and his deputy, Serafim, who assumed power after Iosif's arrest. Seeing the impossibility of a solid administrative base in Moscow owing to the "imprisonment-leapfrog" played by the Soviets, a Siberian archbishop, Dimitry of Tomsk, proclaimed the temporary autocephaly of his diocese, whereupon Serafim suspended him from all clerical functions.[65] It is an irony, therefore, that the very same bishops later accused Sergii of uncanonical behavior when he exercised similar clerical interdicts against them for their refusal to accept him as their administrator. Yet that is precisely what happened.

Although appointed to Leningrad, Iosif was forced by the Soviets to live under surveillance in the small but ancient city of Rostov-the-Great. On September 13, 1927, on the grounds that the metropolitan had no means of administering his diocese

[64]Ibid., 115. In all, he names four hierarchs who are to replace Metropolitan Peter, one by one, in special circumstances, and six who shall replace the deputy locum tenens in a certain order of seniority.
[65]Ibid., 116.

in the absence of permission from the civil authorities to proceed there, Metropolitan Sergii and his Synod relieved him of his title and appointed him Metropolitan of Odessa in the Ukraine. The metropolitan refused to accept the order, considering it illegal, for strictly speaking a bishop cannot be removed from his diocese against his will and that of his flock by any other means except an ecclesiastical trial for serious offenses. The practice of the prerevolutionary Church, however, was to move bishops around from one diocese to another, usually under the direction of the imperial government, or rather the emperor and his overprocurator of the Synod. Thereafter, Iosif became the leader of the most uncompromising opponents of Sergii, rejecting not only his administrative but also his sacramental functions, on the erroneous assumption that the alleged abuse of power by Sergii as well as his uncanonical adoption of the authority of a de facto locum tenens affected his sacramental status as a bishop and hence invalidated the rites performed by him.

The weakness of Iosif's position lies in the fact that (1) he had recognized the validity of his own appointment to Leningrad in 1926 by Sergii; (2) it was Iosif himself who, in his instruction discussed above, extended the powers of a deputy locum tenens to those of a de facto patriarch; and (3) Iosif had not protested against Sergii's Declaration of Loyalty when it had at first appeared, but only after his removal by Sergii from the see of Leningrad.[66] On the latter point, however, there is an explanation in a letter from his steadfast supporter, Bishop Dimitry of Gdovsk, who wrote that when the declaration first appeared, "we took it as but another confirmation of the Church's noninterference in civic affairs, characteristic even of the late patriarch. But we had to change our attitude to it when we realized that the declaration was beginning to seriously affect purely church affairs, distorting the Church not only canonically but also dogmatically." There follows an enumeration of such dogmatic distortions, including the illegitimate formation of a Synod, a request to commemorate Sergii in liturgies along with Metropolitan Peter and up to forty uncanonical removals and reappointments of bishops under the pressure of the civil authorities alone. One of the main reasons for the Noncommemorators' objection to

[66]Ibid., 134-6, 451 and 456-7.

the Synod was its composition: some of its members were suspected of being GPU agents, and others of Renovationist sympathies.[67] On these grounds Bishop Dimitry suspected that Sergii's freedom was circumscribed by this Synod, and he saw a similar limitation of the bishops' freedom in the newly created diocesan councils. Finally, he accused Sergii of exerting pressure on the believers and the clergy to identify the interests of the Church with those of the atheist state, which was impossible.[68]

The schism was spreading and involving huge masses of clergy and believers. This latter fact was in marked contrast to the case of the Renovationists, and should have been of particular concern to the Soviet authorities. A 1965 Leningrad Theological Academy dissertation admits that "in many dioceses, the majority of Orthodox parishes returned Sergii's declaration to its author in protest . . . in some dioceses (in the Urals) up to 90 percent of parishes" did so.[69] One of the consequences of the declaration was the offering of prayers for the Soviet government in the

[67]The members of the Synod who caused the greatest objections were Metropolitan Serafim (Aleksandrov), "whom everyone suspected of ties with the GPU"; Archbishops Sylvester (Bratanovsky) and Aleksii (Simansky), the future patriarch, because of their former ties with the Renovationists; and Archbishop Filipp (Gumilevsky), who had been a member of an Old Believer sect for a while. Ibid., 117.

Regelson erroneously continues to label Archbishop Aleksii "a former Renovationist" despite the documentation of Aleksii's case by Levitin. When, after the arrest of Metropolitan Venyamin, Bishop Aleksii became the administrator of the Petrograd diocese (1922), he was threatened by the GPU that unless he removed the bans from three priests (including Vvedensky and Krasnitsky) who had begun the Renovationist schism in Petrograd, Venyamin would be shot. Aleksii consulted the diocesan council, which decided that any action would be justified in order to save the metropolitan. Aleksii, on the strength of this decision, issued a decree reinstating these Renovationists into full communion with the Church and into their priestly orders. When Metropolitan Venyamin was shot nevertheless, Aleksii "broke into tears like a child." Later, left on their own, Bishops Aleksii and Nikolai (Yarushevich, future Metropolitan of Krutitsy, second in rank to Patriarch Aleksii) declared a temporary autocephaly of the Petrograd diocese, based on the relevant patriarchal encyclical of 1920. They emphatically declared the civic loyalty of the diocese to the Soviet government, condemned the Karlovcians, avoided the name or offices of the arrested Patriarch Tikhon, but clearly dissociated themselves from the Renovationists. Most of the Petrograd believers flocked into the fold of this "autocephaly." In 1923 (when Aleksii was in enforced exile in Central Asia) this "autocephalous" diocese returned fully into the Patriarchal fold. Levitin-Shavrov, 1:103-14 and 218-24; and 2:223-8.

[68]Regelson, 136-51.

[69]Ibid., 434.

liturgy. The faithful reacted violently against that. When Bishop Sergii of Serpukhov tried to include such prayers, he was dragged out of the church by the believers, manhandled and thrown into the snow.[70] According to Metropolitan Iosif, twenty-six of the ruling Orthodox bishops joined the schism on the right, while of the hundred or so bishops imprisoned on the island of Solovki, forty agreed to adhere to Metropolitan Sergii, while some sixty broke with him.[71] Fletcher thinks that Metropolitan Sergii remained in Nizhny Novgorod until 1934 instead of moving to Moscow in 1927, with the permission of the Soviet authorities, owing to the opposition of the Moscow clergy and faithful. Numerous public demonstrations of protest against Sergii's policies took place in many Moscow churches in the late 1920s.

Orthodox Russia was divided into three groups, distinguished by their attitudes to Sergii. Some believed that Sergii's capitulation was a disaster for the Church; others that it was an act of personal cowardice; and still others that it was a wise decision, which alone would allow the continuing function of the Church in the Soviet state.[72] Regelson enumerates six groups of bishops representing various types and degrees of opposition to Sergii and heading or leading such factions—from the Yaroslavl diocese headed by Agafangel, which eventually made an uneasy peace with Sergii, and the Kazan diocese headed by Kirill (who affirmed the sacramental validity of Sergii's Church but would not con-celebrate with Sergii on the grounds that it would be blasphemous to accept the sacrament from the same chalice while having no spiritual peace and accord with him), to the most extreme groups of the Danilov Monastery in Moscow headed by Archbishop Fedor (Pozdeevsky), which had been in open opposition even to Patriarch Tikhon since his own declaration of loyalty in 1923, and Iosif (Petrovykh), who even denied the sacramental valid-ity of Sergii and his clergy. This was a heresy, since administrative

[70]Chrysostomus, 2:205-11.

[71]Regelson, 452; and Chrysostomus, 2:205-11. Since Sergii claimed in 1930 that he had 163 bishops loyal to him, presumably including the forty in Solovki prison camps (Regelson, 477), the schism on the right included over 35 percent of the Patriarchal bishops in its ranks (if we exclude the ten to fifteen bishops who supported the Grigorian schism from the total).

[72]Fletcher, *Study in Survival*, 37.

acts and policies have no relation to the sacramental and charismatic functions of a cleric, according to Christian dogma.[73]

In this turmoil, the reaction of the bishops imprisoned in Solovki was important particularly in terms of the formulation of their ideas. Their letter, in fact, proved surprisingly moderate, with no evidence of bitterness or intolerance—which might be expected from people who, at least in their own opinion, were suffering imprisonment without any guilt. They agreed with the general course of civic loyalty, but criticized Sergii only for the tone of its expression, which

> could be interpreted in the sense of a complete intertwining of the Church and the state . . .

> . . . the deep gratitude expressed to the Soviet government for its attention to the spiritual needs of the Orthodox Church . . . cannot be sincere when expressed by the head of the Russian Orthodox Church and therefore does not correspond to the dignity of the Church . . .

> . . . the declaration unquestionably accepts the official version placing guilt upon the Church for the clashes between the Church and the state . . .

> The threat to ban and suspend the émigré clergy contradicts the decision of the Sobor of August 16, 1918, which explained the uncanonical nature of such punishments . . . applied for political crimes.[74]

Three months later, in December 1927, practically the entire Leningrad diocese was in revolt against Sergii in response to Iosif's appeal to them, in which he declared his refusal to retire from the Leningrad see. Their views were expressed in their appeal to Sergii, formulated and signed by the Rev. Professor V. Veryuzhsky. The appeal repeated most of the complaints already heard (including the one against the Synod and the legality of its function as a ruling body, when it should only have been an

---

[73]Regelson, 471, 559-608 et passim.
[74]Ibid., 436.

advisory body since it had not been elected but appointed by Sergii), and in addition requested: (1) that three bishops, including Aleksii Simansky (the future patriarch) be removed from the Synod; (2) that Metropolitan Iosif be reinstated to the Leningrad see; (3) that the name of Metropolitan Sergii not be commemorated at services next to that of Peter; and (4) that the orders to cease public prayers for imprisoned bishops and to pray for the Soviet government be repealed. Sergii responded with a flat refusal, claiming that the Synod had the same functions as under Patriarch Tikhon, when it was likewise appointed and not elected; that his political course was in the interest of the Church as he understood it; and that the frequent transfers of bishops were a temporary measure that would cease once the relations between the Church and the state were normalized.[75]

None of this could pacify the conscience of the believers, and the schism continued to grow. Metropolitan Iosif was its recognized leader, and whole dioceses joined him, including most of the diocese of Voronezh with Bishop Aleksii Bui who, by 1929, would become the de facto leader of the anti-Sergiites in this huge south Russian area engulfing the provinces of Voronezh, Tambov and Kursk. The rebelling bishops declared temporary autocephalies of their dioceses. As already stated, the Iosif-Aleksii movement became the most uncompromising one among the anti-Sergiites, and according to some Soviet atheist scholars, the Aleksii Bui movement in the Voronezh area gave birth in 1929 to the IPTs (the True Orthodox Church), which survives to the present day as one of the more extreme forms of the "catacomb" Church.[76]

At first the Soviet regime tried to "help" Sergii by carrying

---

[75]Ibid., 136-7. Perhaps the best illustration of the eventual reconciliation of Sergii's Orthodox opponents with the official Church is the fact that this very Veryuzhsky later rejoined the patriarchate—probably becoming a theology professor, for he published theological articles in ZhMP, e.g., in no. 7 (1979) 58.

[76]Regelson, passim, in particular 134-6, 166-8, 447, 454-5, 477 and 595. Also: Fletcher, Church Underground, 58-76; and A.I. Klibanov, "Sovremennoe sektantstvo v Tambovskoi oblasti," Voprosy istorii religii i ateizma 8 (1960) 60-99. Klibanov distinguishes between the IPKh as having originated in 1925 in the Danilov Monastery opposition to Patriarch Tikhon, and the IPTs as originating with the Bishop Aleksii Bui 1929 schism. Other Soviet atheist religiologists claim that both are but two terms for one and the same thing and that its adherents use both terms indiscriminately.

out wholesale arrests of bishops and priests disloyal to him.
During OGPU interrogations, the investigators first asked what
the given cleric's attitude was to "our" Metropolitan Sergii and
"the Soviet Church," and then often engaged in theological
discussion(!) trying to convince the defendants that Sergii's
administrative acts and his declaration were fully in accord with
the canons.[77] Obviously, the purpose of these provocative actions
was to cause further dissension within the Orthodox Church, by
further antagonizing the anti-Sergiites through giving currency
to the rumor that Sergii and/or his Synod were GPU agents.
The general consensus of even the strong opponents of Sergii's
policies, both at the time and even today within the USSR, has
been that Sergii was not personally and directly involved in any
collaboration of this kind with the OGPU. But it is ironic that
while in 1926 bishops had been arrested for supporting Sergii,
two years later they were being arrested for opposing him.[78]

An unidentified bishop, who remained in opposition to the
Moscow Patriarchate right into the 1960s, thus assessed the Soviet
secret police actions of the 1930s:

> After Sergii's opponents had been arrested, those who had
> hoped to save themselves by supporting him followed in
> their steps. Churches and monasteries were being shut
> one by one, and ten years after the declaration, which had
> promised the Church a "peaceful and happy existence,"
> only *several churches* in big cities remained open in the
> huge expanses of the USSR. They even became known as
> "show churches." With them survived also Metropolitan
> Sergii with his illegally organized Synod. . . .

> Thus it would have continued, had it not been for the war.
> In the areas occupied by the Germans there began a spon-
> taneous church reconstruction . . . by the believers them-
> selves . . . Stalin . . . understood that the continuation of
> his former policies toward the Church could be too dan-
> gerous for him . . . and he ordered Metropolitan Sergii to
> reopen the churches, the shutting of which Sergii had only

[77]Regelson, 465, 599.
[78]Ibid., 406-13 and above.

recently justified in his press statements by the allegedly voluntary decisions of the parishioners themselves.

The example of Khrushchev's renewed attacks on the Church convince the writer that Stalin's new policies were mere tactics, not a change of heart, and that therefore it was right to abstain from communion with Patriarch Aleksii and his Church. Then the writer tries to justify this position canonically by arguing that the canons forbade secular governments to exert pressure upon the decisions of sobors and that such decisions, made under pressure, were canonically invalid.[79] (Practically the whole post-Petrine and most of the earlier Russian and Byzantine Church and their decisions should be ruled invalid by these standards.)[80]

Evaluating the OGPU-NKVD total purge against the Church after 1934, their practical annihilation of Sergii's opponents as well as of churches and clerics loyal to him, of Renovationists and Grigorians, the conclusion is clear: the Soviet government wanted to liquidate all religion. But there seems to be another side to it as well. It appears that, having realized the extent of the popularity among the religious masses of the anti-Sergii, i.e., of the more uncompromisingly anticommunist line, they soon realized that leaving Sergii's clergy alone would only further compromise him and his Church in the eyes of the believers and produce a repeat of the story of the Renovationists, deprived of their flock. Therefore, Sergii's Church had to go, in order to regain some believers' confidence. And when the moment of reckoning came during the war, when a Church became necessary for the survival of the Soviet state, there was available the "general"

[79]Ibid., 187-93.

[80]In fact, Archbishop Illarion, who had been a leading Patriarchal policymaker after Patriarch Tikhon's release from prison (as a result of which he was soon to be arrested, never to be fully released until his death in 1929), argued along the same lines in a letter from his exile of July 21, 1928: "There were probably many canonically much more questional acts of the Synod from 1721 to 1917; yet there were no schisms." On the shifts and reappointments of bishops by Sergii he also points out that this was the usual practice before the revolution, and no one protested; while Sergii was now being forced to do it by external circumstance. This statement is particularly valid, because Illarion was highly critical of some aspects of Sergii's Declaration of Loyalty and of his subsequent acts and policies in his letter of December 10, 1927. See both letters in Regelson, 460-1 and 130-3, respectively, and appendix 2. Apparently, his position was that Sergii's transgressions of the canons were not of such a magnitude as to warrant a schism.

and his reduced staff, who could be entrusted with the resurrected "army." This is not to say that Stalin and the NKVD were so consciously prophetic in the mid-1930s as to foresee the war and the necessity of allowing the Church to revive. Just as Hitler's insane *Untermensch* policy helped Stalin to win the war, so the accidental survival of the badly mutilated but politically loyal faction of the Church allowed Stalin to tolerate the revival of *this* particular church organization, which in turn helped him to win the war by providing his side with a national-spiritual aspect. It is not unlikely that had Sergii's Church not been persecuted in the 1930s, she would have been unable to spiritually mobilize and patriotically consolidate tens of millions of Orthodox believers.

As to the anti-Sergiite factions, the incomplete biographies of those of their bishops whom Regelson was able to trace show that most of them eventually made peace with either Sergii or his successor, Patriarch Aleksii. The most prominent and probably most significant case was that of Bishop Afanasy, who, between his consecration in 1921 and death in 1962, had been at large for some thirteen years while spending twenty-eight years in prison and exile.[81] In 1927 he was sentenced to three years' hard labor for supporting Sergii. In the 1930s he broke with Sergii and adopted a platform similar to that of Kirill of Kazan. In 1945, after the election of Patriarch Aleksii, Bishop Afanasy, who was recognized by most of the "catacomb" clergy and laity as their leader, forwarded a circular letter to all these secret churches and sketes, instructing them to return to the fold of the official Church. He argued that the election of Patriarch Aleksii had been valid, and Aleksii could not be held directly responsible for Sergii's usurpation of patriarchal authority. A very respectable *samizdat* source tells us: "According to rumors of questionable credibility, in the provincial depths there still remain small scattered groups who refuse any contact with the patriarchate. Even if this is true, their influence is negligible."[82]

[81]Ibid., 568-74; and "Krestnyi put' preosvyashchennogo Afanasiya," *VRSKhD,* no. 107 (1973) 170-211.

[82]V. Ya. Vasilevskaya (an aunt of the Moscow priest Alexander Men'—a scholar, a convert to Orthodoxy from formal Judaism in the 1930s and a member of a catacomb church in Zagorsk until Bishop Afanasy's above-cited instruction), *Katakomby XX veka,* ed. A.S. Dubina (who died in a concentration camp in

Indeed, there still are such groups. They may be less negligible than the cited author thinks (this subject will be discussed under a separate heading). But even the already cited letter of 1962 by an unnamed catacomb bishop admits that these groups have been left practically without clergy and churches and that therefore the true believers ought to seek out those sincere priests in the official Church who "try to squeeze through the needle's eye" of Soviet control and to truly serve God, and join their parishes.[83]

Hence, in the eyes of theological authorities (e.g., Metropolitans Kirill and Agafangel, Bishop Afanasy, and all others, it seems, except Iosif), Metropolitan Sergii's maneuvers, compromises and lies did not affect the sacramental validity of the Church and the charisma of clerical consecrations. A further evidence of this feeling is the fact that the bishops in schism did not consecrate any new bishops in the postwar period (although they did in Solovki in the 1930s), apparently in order not to perpetuate the schism. This goes to show that they recognized the sacramental validity of Patriarch Aleksii's Church,[84] to say the least.

1977, according to one source), ms. in Keston College Archives, pp. 2-8. The main catacomb monastic priest on whom Vasilevskaya reminisces and who had brought her to the Church was a father-confessor to Bishop Afanasy. The above-cited unidentified catacomb bishop's letter of 1962 likewise says: "Times have changed: our churches do not exist in the USSR anymore" (192).

[83]Ibid., 193.

[84]This author was told by a very respectable Russian (Soviet) monk who had spent many years in prisons and secret monasteries—though always recognizing the canonical administration of the official Patriarchal Church—that the reason why the IPTs and IPKh schisms of today are so short of priests and have no bishops is that the bishops who had joined the schism on the right, eager to avoid its perpetuation, did not consecrate any new bishops for the schism. But apparently this was true only of the post-1945 situation—i.e., after the election of Patriarch Aleksii and his recognition by Bishop Afanasy—for Regelson cites a memoir reporting secret episcopal consecrations by Iosifite bishops in the Solovki concentration camps at least in the late 1920s (599).

CHAPTER 5

The Holocaust of the 1930s

"On taking power, the Bolsheviks immediately declared war on the Church. This was, probably, the only honest act in their whole political activity, for, because of the contradictions that separate them, there can be no agreement between these two camps (what intercourse can there be between Christ and the Satan?)."[1] As early as 1922, the Bolsheviks declared that the Communist Party was equally and militantly hostile to all religions. But, "We have nothing against the current schism. We shall make use of it to tear the masses completely away from all clergy, from any church, from every religion."[2]

The subsequent years, however, as we have already shown, proved the inability of the Communist Party to tear the masses away from religion. The masses, in fact, demonstrated a remarkable capacity to judge and choose for themselves the Church they trusted. And twice the bulk of religious believers demonstrated that their choice was of that Church which would attract the greatest enmity of the regime. In the early to mid-1920s, it was the choice of the Patriarchal Church rather than the Renovationists; in the late 1920s it expressed itself in violent reactions against prayers for the Soviet government (although originally called for by Patriarch Tikhon) or for Metropolitan Sergii after his Declaration of Loyalty. It took the 1930s, with their wholesale persecution and destruction of all churches, to force the

[1]A 1962 letter by an unidentified bishop of the "catacomb" Church, in Regelson, 119.

[2]See above in chapter 2, n. 44.

believers to accept any functioning church remaining in a given district, be it Sergiite, Iosifite, Renovationist or any other. This situation made possible the Sergiite 1943 concordat with the Soviet government and the acceptance by the believers and the surviving clergy of a Church totally loyal and submissive to the state.

Apparently, in return for his 1927 Declaration of Loyalty, Metropolitan Sergii hoped also to gain the right to expand the sociocultural and private educational activities of the Church. According to the émigré press of July 1928, a special program was drafted over the signature of a Bishop Evgeny, obviously on Sergii's instructions, detailing religious instruction for children, special sermons for them in churches, pastoral-theological seminars for parents, church-organized sports, excursions and public lectures.[3] But the new laws on "religious associations" of April 8, 1929, and the Instructions of the People's Commissariat of Internal Affairs of October 1, 1929, dealt a heavy blow to these hopes, demonstrating Sergii's tactical error in extending the Soviet regime a credit of trust instead of bargaining a quid pro quo prior to the signing of his declaration. As stated in the previous chapter, these laws explicitly forbade any religious activities outside the church walls, classifying these as propaganda, which henceforth was to remain the exclusive domain of the atheists. The legislation explicitly forbade church groups or the clergy to instruct any special children, youth, women or other study circles or conduct special religious services for such groups. The same applied to literary, handiwork, bible-study or general religious education groups. Nor was the Church allowed to organize any hikes, playgrounds, libraries, reading rooms, sanatoria or medical services. Henceforth, the clergy was allowed to function only within the area of their residence and of the residences of the members of the parish by which the given cleric was employed. Thus, any missionary journeys to areas deprived of churches and clergy became illegal. The only religious services outside the church building permitted to the clergy without the necessity of applying each time for specific permission from the local soviet were visits to the sick and the dying. Although this legislation again explicitly denied the status of a legal person to the Church,

[3]N.S. Timasheff, *Religion in Soviet Russia* (London, 1943) 62.

it nevertheless stipulated that "all religious associations actually functioning in the territory of the RFSFR on the day of adoption of this legislation are required to apply for and receive registration from the state within one year." The local governments had the right either to register the congregations or to refuse such registration. In the latter case, a parish would cease to exist and its church building would be confiscated. Moreover, the local soviets once again received the right to reject individual members of church councils elected to their offices by parish meetings—i.e., to control the membership of the "twenties" as well as of the parish executive organs, infiltrating them with their agents. Furthermore, "Religious associations . . . may not: (a) organize any sort of central booking offices for the collection of voluntary offerings of believers; (b) establish any compulsory collections . . .; (c) conclude any sort of agreement contract." All forms of charity work, even vis-à-vis needy clergy and their families, were likewise forbidden.[4]

Obviously, if these laws had been strictly adhered to, the Church could not have survived, economically at least. For instance, the same legislation stipulated that since church bodies had no legal status, contracts for repairs of a church and the like could only be concluded by individual members of the parish organs, not by the whole body, and would be treated as regular private commercial deals, not as part-and-parcel of the functioning of the church. Thus, they would be subject to the exorbitant taxation to which all private enterprise was being subjected at the time, in the drive to strangle all such activities. Because, in order to survive, parish organs would henceforth have to try to evade the law, church organizations became permanently vulnerable to attack on the grounds of illegal activities. The total subjection of the Church to the state was thus achieved by means of this legislative blackmail.

In the drive against private enterprise of the first five-year plan, which began in 1929, the Church was treated as a private

[4]See the April legislation in *Zakonodatel'stvo*, 10-24. This and the October instructions are in N. Orleansky, *Zakon o religioznykh ob'edineniyakh RSFSR* (Moscow, 1930) 6-25, 170-1, et passim. Various 1929 decrees also deprived the clergy of all state insurance and pension benefits, while allowing parishes no delays or reductions in paying the full premiums into the insurance funds applying to civilians working for the Church.

enterprise. Absolutely unrealistic rates of income tax were levied against individual priests, bishops and parishes, as "profit-making" private businesses. Failing to pay these taxes, priests, bishops and lay members of parish councils would be arrested and their churches closed. The destruction of all well-to-do peasants under the label of *kulaks* in the course of collectivization also deprived the Church in the rural areas of her last base of material support, as only individually earning and well-to-do peasants could make donations. This first wave of blanket closure of rural churches was slowed down in 1930 as a result of protests and prayer-appeals by major western church leaders, including the pope, as well as by Stalin's tactical decision to slow down the collectivization drive, expressed in his March 1930 *Pravda* article, "Dizziness from Success."[5] An ingenious maneuver by Metropolitan Sergii must have also contributed not inconsiderably: first he gave a press conference to foreign journalists assuring them that there was no religious persecution in the USSR, but four days later, on February 19, 1930, he directed a secret memorandum to the Soviet government complaining bitterly about the harassment and the impossible situation of the Church and requesting the right to revive theological schools and church publications and to set up a normally functioning church organization on all levels. Then, to reassure the government of his complete civic obedience, in hope of some cooperation on the part of the government, Sergii attacked Metropolitan Evlogy and deposed him as his exarch for his participation in the campaign of prayers for the persecuted Russian Church. Of all his requests, Sergii was granted only the right to publish an official monthly, the *Journal of the Moscow Patriarchate*. It began its irregular appearance in 1931, but folded up four years later for another eight years.[6]

[5]See the message of Pius XI (February 2, 1930) in Regelson, 475; also Evlogy, *Put'*, 619-21.

[6]Ibid., 622-3. The contents of the memo are mentioned in Regelson, 475-7; Bogolepov, *Tserkov'*, 32; Struve, 48-52.

Metropolitan Evlogy writes that soon after this mendacious statement by Sergii he received a letter from a priest in Russia—whom he had intimately known for many years and whose testimony he did not doubt—claiming that the statement was composed by the Bolsheviks and only given to Sergii for editorial corrections and signing. The effect of it was such that at the next liturgy he celebrated the priest could not elevate Sergii's name, for the congregation would have attacked him and thrown him out of the church. When he came to Sergii to explain his

The *Journal,* with a meager circulation of three thousand copies, illustrates the general atmosphere of terror and secrecy of the time. It published most of its diocesan and parish reports with blank spaces in place of the names of the priests, bishops, dioceses and parishes concerned. Was Metropolitan Sergii thereby hoping to divert the attention of the Soviet officialdom from the personalities of his clerics and thus protect them from the OGPU? Or was it the central censorship's work, with its paranoid mania for secrecy? There are also many reports on the decline of canonical and administrative discipline among the clergy—e.g., acceptance of clerics returning from the Renovationist schism without a proper examination of their moral record, without the necessary penance and even without informing the diocesan bishop of their acceptance by a local parish or senior priest. Metropolitan Sergii issued orders annulling such acts unless done through the proper channels, and insisting on canonical order and discipline. Cases have been cited of priests who, while in the Renovationist schism, had divorced and remarried and therefore could not be accepted as priests in the regular Orthodox Church. All this may shed more light on the question why Sergii chose to sacrifice so much for the sake of restoration of the central organization of the Church.

Other interesting materials in the *Journal* include a decision of Sergii's Synod to permit funerals in absentia in extraordinary circumstances, when there is no physical possibility of giving the deceased a proper Christian burial and yet it is known that the deceased had been, and died, a Christian.[7] In almost every issue of the periodical there is a fine scholarly theological article of considerable length by Sergii himself. One issue opens with Sergii's message of October 15, 1931 to Photios II, the Patriarch of Constantinople, concerning the latter's acceptance of Evlogy with his West European Russian parishes under his jurisdiction. Sergii disputes the validity of the claims of the ecumenical see

reasons for not mentioning his name in public prayers and to ask why he made the statement, the latter explained that he had been kept under arrest for a week before signing the statement and was made to understand that if he refused to give the press conference, *all* the remaining Tikhonite bishops would be arrested and the whole church organization would perish. Instead, he chose to be branded a liar by the clerics and the believers. *Put'*, 621.

[7] *ZhMP*, no. 4 (April 1931) 2.

to jurisdiction over Orthodox churches in the non-Orthodox diaspora, whereby the churches that had belonged to the Moscow Patriarchate had been unilaterally accepted by Photios. Sergii pointed out that canon 28 of the Fourth Ecumenical Council gives the ecumenical see jurisdiction only over the Barbarian lands of the Black Sea region, while the Barbarians of Western Europe belonged to the Patriarch (Pope) of Rome. But, of course, the real reasons for Evlogy's appeal to Photios and his acceptance by the latter were political. This is also clear from the context of Sergii's letter and from its friendly and fraternal tone, with a request at the end to help "return Metropolitan Evlogy . . . onto the road of obedience to his canonical ecclesiastical authorities."[8]

Even as the metropolitan was preoccupied with restoring some order and discipline in the Church against all odds, a new attack was being launched against the churches, particularly in the cities, in 1932. This was followed by some respite in 1934, although in the same year began the first arrests of the Renovationist clergy. The mass liquidation of all religions began in 1936, leading to their almost total annihilation by 1939.[9] Some of the reasons for the regime's decision to change from selective sup-

[8]"Address to the Patriarch of Constantinople," no. 7623 (October 15, 1931), *ZhMP*, no. 7-8 (1932) 2-6. *ZhMP*, no. 22 (1934) also contains a curious reminder of the activities of the monk and ex-bishop Vladimir (Putyata), a former military officer and friend of Nicholas II, who as a bishop was involved in a number of moral scandals and escaped defrocking before the revolution only by the direct intervention of the tsar. Patriarch Tikhon finally defrocked him and reduced him to the status of an ordinary monk. Vladimir then founded his own "People's" Church, declaring complete dedication to Soviet socialism. From Sergii's order no. 58 (p. 2) it transpires that Vladimir had later repented and returned to the Orthodox Church as a monk, but then joined the Grigorian schism and began to officiate as a cleric. Sergii's order finally strips Vladimir of his monastic status and excommunicates him.

[9]Levitin writes that the 1929-1932 drive against the Church hit only rural areas and was not felt in Leningrad, for instance, although three most outstanding and popular priests were arrested there in 1930: Nikolai Chukov (later Metropolitan Grigory of Leningrad), Nikolai Chepurin and Mikhail Cheltsov. The latter, who was shot in 1931, was a great scholar and historian of the early Christian Church. Chepurin, also a scholar, was appointed rector of the Moscow Theological Academy fifteen years later on his release from the camps, but he survived in freedom for only six months. In Leningrad the mass closure of churches began in 1932, simultaneously with the liquidation of the monasteries. That year also saw the large-scale liquidation of the Iosifite-Buievite schism through mass arrests of its bishops and clergy. Both Metropolitan Iosif and Bishop Aleksii (Bui), and thirteen other bishops supporting them, were arrested in 1929. Regelson, 464-5, 486-505; Levitin, *Likhie gody*, 210-64.

pression to total destruction have already been discussed. There was also the very important fact that the existence of a Church, particularly a Church with some internal independence (even after Sergii's declaration, for Sergii subsequently stressed in several letters that the loyalty request had only a civic-political character, while spiritually, theologically, morally and liturgically the Church would remain free),[10] was incompatible with the unidimensional, totalitarian monolith that Stalin was building up at the time. Finally, there was the wrath of the Soviet leaders at their own helplessness, aggravated by the failure of the Marxist interpretation of religion as a class phenomenon determined by material conditions.

Instead of dying out, religion, deprived of property and legal rights, was growing—not only during the semicapitalistic NEP of the 1920s, but even in the 1930s, prior to its physical destruction in 1936-1938, right in the midst of the process of the construction of "classless socialism."[11] We have already mentioned the remarkable religious revival of the 1920s, when the believers clung around their popular pastors in an unprecedented mood of closeness, unity, love and harmony between the clergy and the laity. In accordance with the instructions of the 1917-1918 Sobor, but probably more because of the prevailing sense of the seriousness of the moment, the quality and quantity of sermons reached unprecedented heights, not only in the capital cities but on the periphery as well.[12] Bishops were carefully protected by unpaid volunteer guards organized by the parishioners.

> When our bishops traveled in luxurious carriages, people
> . . . did not greet them . . . And now they humbly walk
> . . . but how much honor and veneration do they now
> receive from the people! . . . They have been deprived of

[10]Regelson, 443-4, 153, 445-6, 456-8.

[11]M.M. Sheinman, "Obnovlencheskoe techenie v russkoi pravoslavnoi tserkvi posle Oktyabrya," *Voprosy nauchnogo ateizma* 2 (1966) 63.

[12]According to the already mentioned *Ostraya luka* ms., in the rural and semi-rural areas of the Volga region there had been a considerable estrangement of the laity from the Church during World War I, as the masses had blamed the priests for the war. But everything changed with the persecutions. By 1921 believers began to gather around their priests in ever-growing numbers. Sermonizing played an important part in this revival of the priest's role as the leader of the masses, who felt more and more estranged from the new regime (272 et passim).

worldly goods, and have themselves become not of this world.[13]

Christian youth groups and youth choirs, as well as youth conferences organized by popular bishops and priests, were widespread. Levitin says that if he were asked what was his vision of "an ideal church community, I would always recall Petrograd of the 1920s." Sermons were delivered not only on Sundays, as before the revolution, but on weekdays as well. In many churches, one or two days a week would be set aside for serious theological lectures, discussions and debates between the clerics and the laity after brief services, for which benches and chairs would be set up in the churches. Practically every church had at least one such popular priest-preacher or priest-teacher around whom believers flocked, until these priests disappeared in the prisons by the late 1920s or early 1930s. The practice of the GPU was to liquidate precisely such priests, until each church was left with mediocre clergy, who would then mostly be left to serve undisturbed until the mid-1930s, when the blanket destruction began. The temporary detentions and deportations of the 1920s still left enough popular priests around, as there were no registration permits: a priest or bishop would turn up (often after a spell in prison), conclude a contract with a parish council and begin his work.[14] It was against this freedom that the government's insistence on registrations was aimed, opposed consistently by the patriarch and all his deputies, until Sergii gave in. Similarly, the 1929 legislation was a tacit recognition that the regime had no other resources in its arsenal but brute force, terror and suppression.

Simultaneously, Soviet published data on religion and atheism here becomes totally unreliable. For example, one source states that convinced atheists amounted to no more than 10 percent of the population in 1929, but another source, for 1930, claims 65 percent, and still another 98.5 percent of the population as atheists. These estimates were simple propagandists' fancies. Official statistics showed something else. The Moscow Registry Office, for instance, supplied the figures given in table 5-1.

[13]Levitin-Shavrov, 2:165 and 167-204, et passim; Regelson, 92-5.
[14]*Likhie gody*, 73-9.

TABLE 5-1
<small>PERCENTAGES OF TOTAL MOSCOW POPULATION PARTICIPATING IN RELIGIOUS RITES</small>

	1925	1926	1927	1928
Baptisms of babies	56%	59%	60%	58%
Unknown (baptized or not)*	2	1	7	4
Religious burials	58	59	67	66
Unknown	1	0	3	1
Religious marriages**	21	22	16	12

*In the given circumstances, and in view of the increase in this category, "unknown" should most likely be deciphered as christened but concealed.

**Christenings could be blamed on religious "grandmothers," burials on the "backward views" and wishes of old people. Weddings were the sole responsibility of the young, and hence persecutions and fear of repercussions affected them the most.

At least one Soviet source states that "in the 1930s the Patriarchal Church began to grow," and an internal, secret memorandum of the League of Militant Godless (LMG) confirms that there were signs of a new religious resurgence toward the end of 1929-1930.[15] If this is so, then there seems to be a direct correlation between the unpopular measures of the Soviet regime, which resulted in a climate of general dissatisfaction with the regime, and the religious resurgence. We have already discussed the religious resurgence, which began around 1923, elsewhere. Now there was the forced collectivization, dekulakization and mass deportations of millions of peasants to distant areas of the country or directly to the concentration camps. The quoted documents try to present this process purely as a suppression of the exploiting *kulak,* and the activization of the Church as a sign that the "religious organizations are counterrevolutionary agencies of the *kulak* and the *nepman.*" But then they contradict themselves by admitting that the Church has been successfully "recruiting industrial workers and the poorest and landless peasants into the church councils and other elected church offices."[16] If there was such a direct link between collectivization and the religious resurgence, as the documents imply, then it showed that not only

[15]Sheinman, "Obnovlencheskoe techenie," 63; and the "Resolution on the Aims of Antireligious Work in the Western Oblast'," appendix 3, protocol 14 (December 16, 1929), in the Smolensk Archives, XT 47/460. See also V.F. Elfimov, *O prichinakh i usloviyakh sushchestvovaniya religioznykh perezhitkov v SSSR* (Vologda, 1971) 376.

[16]Ibid. Other Smolensk documents of 1929-1930 confirm this problem.

the richer elements but the nation as a whole was upset and unhappy over the state policies, that it was rejecting its promises and values.

School surveys revealed in the years 1927 to 1930 that 11 percent to 92 percent of school children were religious, with no inverse correlation between urbanization and religious affiliations. It was a Moscow secondary school that revealed the highest proportion of religious pupils—92 percent. Army recruits showed a 70 percent adherence to religion.[17] Even in 1937-1940, the official leaders of Soviet atheism estimated religious believers to constitute some 80 to 90 million—i.e., 45 to 50 percent of the total population of the time.[18] Hence, the frequent claims that the closure of churches reflected a proportional decline in the numbers of religious believers can have no currency whatsoever, as can be seen from the fact that in 1920 there were still over forty thousand functioning Orthodox churches on postrevolutionary Soviet territory, and that in 1930 Metropolitan Sergii claimed thirty thousand churches—which would still bring the figure to perhaps forty thousand, taking the Renovationists and the Iosifites into consideration.

Sergii's figures were probably based on the 1929 estimates, because by the end of 1930, Yaroslavsky, the leader of the League of Militant Godless of the USSR, boasted that in some areas the number of open churches had decreased by 50 percent over the year. This would leave, at the most, 20 to 25 thousand churches still functioning in 1931. It was at this time that the LMG boasted: "In the course of 1930 we must turn our Red capital into a godless Moscow, our villages into godless collective farms . . . a collective farm with a church and a priest is worthy of a comic strip . . . The new village does not need a church."[19]

In order to bring this promise closer to reality, in addition to all the above legislation, there were a number of administrative

[17]This and the above table are from Curtiss, *Russian Church,* 219-24.

[18]Yaroslavsky's figure, for 1937, was 80 million; Prof. N.M. Nikolsky's, for 1940, was 90 million (presumably including the newly acquired territories in the West). See Fletcher, *Study in Survival,* 74-5; and B.N. Konovalov, *K massovomu ateizmu* (Moscow, 1974) 62.

[19]I. Lagovsky, *Kollektivizatsiya i religiya* (Paris: YMCA Press, 1932) 1-3, citing from the factory workers' LMG journal *Bezbozhnik u stanka,* nos. 4 and 2 (1930).

decrees also aimed at squeezing the priests out of existence. A number of decrees by the Ministry of Finance of 1928 to 1931 raised the taxes on priests and other uncollectivized rural elements to such an extent that the Communist Party organ *Bolshevik* stated that these measures increased the rural tax income of the state by 31.6 percent. In 1929, priests were practically deprived of the possibility of earning extra income to support their families by taking civilian jobs. A decree of that year allowed local officials to dismiss all persons who have been harmful to Soviet society and the working class. This affected not only the clergy, but lay practicing believers as well, for they were likewise treated as holding views hostile to the working class and the socialist state. Furthermore, on January 3, 1930, *Pravda* declared that all disenfranchised people (priests as well as members of the pre-revolutionary "exploiting classes") were to be evicted from all state and nationalized housing, as well as from housing belonging to cooperatives or to industrial enterprises. This, of course, included houses that had formerly been the property of the Church or of individual parishes, as all of them were nationalized.[20] Thus, the priests, overburdened by absolutely unrealistic taxation rates, were now forced to rent housing privately, where the rent was regulated by the free market rules of supply and demand in conditions of an acute housing crisis! And in these conditions, according to reports in the *Journal of the Moscow Patriarchate,* priests were still joining the Patriarchal Church, including some who had earlier given up their clerical vocation.[21]

Nevertheless, with all these measures and terror combined, the 1930s saw the realization of the closest approximation to the above promise of creating, at least in external appearances, a godless country. If Moscow, where by 1933 there remained 100 open churches out of nearly 600 in the early 1920s, and Kargopol, an ancient city in northern Russia where none out of a former 27 remained, can be used as measuring sticks, then there could not have remained more than 15 to 25 percent of the prerevolutionary number of open churches in the country by that year. Even this was a luxury compared with 1941, when according to an official Soviet statement there remained only 4,225 open

[20]Curtiss, *Russian Church*, 230-73.
[21]E.g., *ZhMP*, no. 7-8 (1932) 11-16.

Orthodox churches in the whole USSR. This included well over 3,000 on the territories annexed in 1939 and 1940 (the Baltic republics, western Ukraine and western Belorussia, Moldavia and portions of eastern Finland). The statement, which also claimed that there was a total of 8,338 functioning houses of prayer of all religions, could be interpreted as evidence that the Orthodox Church had been subjected to greater persecution than others, for the Orthodox population constituted well over 75 percent of the total, while the number of Orthodox churches in the above total was only slightly over 50 percent.[22] Thus, according to this statement, less than a thousand churches remained on pre-1939 Soviet territory by 1939, or under 2.5 percent of the 1920 figure. Other sources claim that even this was an exaggeration, as illustrated, for instance, by the following cases: the Tambov diocese had only two functioning churches of the original 110; the city of Moscow, "no more than fifteen"; Leningrad, five of the original three hundred or so, etc. Here, only Moscow, a showcase for foreigners, falls within the category of 2.5 percent. The Tambov case is more typical, as a provincial area out of reach of foreign correspondents, for whom a facade of freedom of religious practice had to be kept. Obviously, the reduction of the number of open churches to a figure of less than two thousand could not have had any approval of a mass of 80 million believers![23]

As to the fate of the clergy, some western sources estimated that no fewer than 42,000 Orthodox clerics were killed between

[22]Shafarevich, 14, 21; see also n. 20.

[23]Levitin gives the figure of ninety-six functioning Orthodox churches in Leningrad in the late 1920s, but many of these were, in fact, monasteries with several functioning churches. What he gives then is the total number of parishes, some with several functioning churches and chapels, rather than individual houses of prayer (*Likhie gody*, 61-8). Shafarevich cites a figure of 425 churches in Petrograd in 1917, but that figure must have included non-Orthodox houses of prayer—of which there were very many in Petrograd with its large minority population (65). For information on churches open in 1941, see Mark Popovsky, *Zhizn' i zhitie Voino-Yasenetskogo, arkhiepiskopa i khirurga* (Paris: YMCA Press, 1979) 350-1 and 384. Popovsky erroneously gives the prerevolutionary number of functioning Orthodox churches in Moscow as 480, and speaks of several hundred churches remaining still open across the 1939 Soviet territory (prior to western annexations). A petition of Soviet Christians to the 25th Congress of the CPSU claims, however, that only several scores of Orthodox churches remained open in 1939. See "Obrashchenie . . . gruppy khristian russkoi pravoslavnoi tserkvi," *VRKhD*, no. 118 (1976) 279.

1918 and the late 1930s.[24] While no solid statistics exist to either confirm or refute this figure, circumstantial evidence tends to corroborate this estimate. In his 1930 statement, Metropolitan Sergii said that the number of clergy in *his* jurisdiction exceeded that of the functioning churches. In addition, as we know, by the early 1930s some ten thousand priests still belonged to the Renovationist schism, and at least as many must have been in the various schisms on the right. This would bring the figure of active clergy in 1930 close to sixty thousand (i.e., approximately equal to the prerevolutionary figure—another sign of a highly active church life). In 1941, the number of officially active priests, including the Renovationists and those in the newly acquired western territories, amounted to 5,665,[25] of whom probably fewer than three thousand were original Soviet citizens—i.e., some 5 percent of the 1930 estimate. The situation was so desperate that a city of half a million residents like Odessa had only one church still open but no permanent priest. The functioning church represented Stalin's concession to the great oculist, the practicing believer Academician Filatov, who had treated Stalin's eyes and, in return, had asked to have at least one church preserved in the city. The church stayed open and, each Sunday at first, and later just at Easter, a priest would show up from the crowd of believers and celebrate the liturgy, only to disappear in the NKVD dungeons the following day. After all the priests who dared martyrdom had disappeared, there remained a few deacons who could perform the whole rite except for the eucharist, until they likewise disappeared. These were replaced by psalmists, who would also be liquidated. In the last few months before the German attack there remained only laymen, who prayed the best they could in the church.[26]

[24]Kurt Hutten, *Iron Curtain Christians* (Minneapolis: Augsburg Publishing House, 1967) 11.

[25]See n. 22 above, and Wassilij Alexeev, "The Russian Orthodox Church, 1927-1945: Repression and Revival," *RCL* 7:1 (Spring 1979) 29-30. Alexeev erroneously omits Moldavia and Bukovina, with their three million-plus Orthodox population, and the Finnish Karelia in his list of 1939-1940 annexations, and hence he arrives at an inflated figure of 2,700 open churches on the original Soviet territory.

[26]Story told this author by a priest of the Russian Orthodox Church who was born in Odessa in the mid-1920s in a religious family and used to frequent the church in question up to the Romanian occupation in 1941.

Obviously, in these conditions there could have been only very few ordinations in the 1930s, and hence a fairly high natural mortality rate among the original aging clergy could be expected during the decade—perhaps up to 30 percent of the 1930s cadres, assuming that the majority of the priests were not young even in 1930, since no regular theological schools on any extensive scale existed after 1921. This would still leave some 37,000 priests unaccounted for by 1941, even if the ordination rate for the 1930s had been zero, which was not the case. For instance, all the remaining monastic communities across the country were being disbanded and the monks and nuns either shot, incarcerated, exiled or (in the minority of cases) expelled and dispersed. But in several monasteries the bishops had time to ordain all the monks to the priesthood so that they could continue the priestly mission in whatever circumstances they might find themselves.[27] (The current patriarch, Pimen, seems to be an example of such an ordination: seventeen years of age in 1927, he was tonsured at a skete of the Holy Trinity-St. Sergius Monastery, which seems to have been closed in 1930, when he was ordained priest at one of the Moscow churches. Then, there follows a conspicuous fourteen-year hiatus in his official biography, which is normally interpreted as prison and exile.)[28] Now, even if we were to assume that a good proportion of ex-priests went into hiding, joined the secret "catacomb" churches—these could have added up to perhaps 20 percent of the "registered" clergy by the end of the decade[29]—or lived as private individuals,

[27]In a conversation with an American correspondent, Wallace Carrol, Metropolitan Sergii said that, in the absence of seminaries, if a high school graduate wanted to enter the clerical profession he applied to the patriarchate or other bishops, was in return provided with a list of books to read and a program of study (the books would often be provided by the Church) and then had to pass a pastoral examination (Fletcher, *Study in Survival*, 86-91). On ordinations of monks, see, inter alia, ibid., 92-4. Levitin calls the year 1932 in particular the St. Bartholomew night of Russian monasticism (*Likhie gody*, 222-3).

[28]See *ZhMP*, no. 6 (1971) 23; see also chapter 3 above. The controversial document on which it is based says that Pimen was drafted into the armed forces from 1932 to 1934, again served as an army officer from 1941 to 1943, and was imprisoned in 1936-1938. It remains unclear what his status was from 1934 to 1936, and again from 1939 to 1941.

[29]The prominent Soviet atheist "religiologist" A.I. Klibanov claims that the "True Orthodox" became particularly active toward the end of the 1930s (*Iz mira religioznogo sektantstva* [Moscow, 1974]); another source claims that they tried to influence the elections of 1939 (Fletcher, *Study in Survival*, 92-4). Popovsky

we would still end up with some 30 to 35 thousand priests who were either shot or incarcerated in the 1930s. Extrapolating the Leningrad figure of the disappearance by 1941 of 131 out of the 100 Patriarchal and 50 Renovationist priests that had still served the churches there in 1930 (and there is no reason to assume a higher rate of terror against the Church in Leningrad than elsewhere in the country), we arrive at a rate of 80 to 85 percent incarcerations and executions of priests in the USSR in that decade—over 45,000 persons.[30] At least another five to ten thousand should be added for the period 1918 to 1929, and a few thousand, particularly among the "catacomb" priesthood, for the 1940s through 1964. As the survival rate in Stalin's prisons was no more than 10 to 20 percent—and even those who survived had their lifespans substantially curtailed by the hunger and overwork in the labor camps—the total toll could easily have reached some fifty thousand over the first forty-five years of the Soviet state—i.e., up to the end of the Khrushchev era, with its renewed persecutions.[31]

With all these persecutions, the gains of the atheists were very questionable at best. In 1930, two trumped-up trials of

maintains that more than ten underground priests were active in the Moscow area by 1941 (355-60). At that time there were only fifteen churches functioning in the city of Moscow, and perhaps none in the Moscow province; hence, the proportion of the underground priests to the registered ones could have easily been 1:5. Former participants in unofficial church life claimed that in the 1930s there was also the widespread phenomenon of wandering priests, who called on believers and performed secret church services in private homes. Fletcher, *Study in Survival*, 86-91; see also Regelson, 506.

[30]Levitin estimates that a total of at least 670 Orthodox and Renovationist bishops (280 and 390 respectively) perished between the late 1920s and early 1950s in camps, prisons and exile, or were executed. He does not take the natural death rate into consideration, however, which could have accounted for up to 50 percent of the deaths over a twenty-five-year period, as most bishops are consecrated at forty to fifty years of age. Hence, 300 would be a figure closer to the truth. *Likhie gody*, 321-2. For illustrations of the almost total liquidation of the clergy of all the three major jurisdictions in the Ukraine, see Heyer, 108-29.

[31]In 1943 almost all the catacomb priests of the Moscow area were arrested and imprisoned. See Vasilevskaya, *Katakomby XX veka*, and Popovsky, 357. During the early 1960s many arrests of priests and even bishops did take place, and some were reported in the Soviet press at the time. In 1960, forty-six priests of the Orenburg diocese alone were under arrest. In the same year, a priest was sentenced to a labor camp term for Christian work with young people (Shafarevich, 64). Every political prisoner of the Khrushchev and post-Khrushchev eras has met a number of priests serving long prison terms for missionary work.

fictitious anti-Soviet organizations alleged to be associated with counterrevolutionary activities of the clergy took place: one in the Ukraine, of the so-called Society for the Liberation of the Ukraine, alleged to be associated with the Ukrainian Autocephalist Church; and the other in Leningrad, of a fictitious liberation organization. It was alleged that among the founding members of the latter organization were former students of the Leningrad Theological Academy, which was closed in 1925, the others being priests and former tsarist officials. Both organizations allegedly aimed at overthrowing the Soviet regime by terrorism and had ties with the émigrés.[32] Insinuations against the Church and the clergy as active enemies of the Soviet state continued throughout the 1930s, with only some discord among atheist authors toward the very end of the decade, when the threat of a major war suggested the future need to make peace with the nation and its religion at least to some extent.[33] During the same decade, the LMG membership grew from half a million to its top figure of over five million in 1932, but instead of reaching the planned figure of 22 million members in 1937, it dropped back to two million in 1938, despite the fact that between 1928 and 1940 over 140 million copies of specialized antireligious literature were put out by the LMG. At the same time, there were numerous reports on the generally fictitious membership figures in the LMG. The proportion of members who paid their dues was at first reported to be 45 percent, but then fell to 13 percent.

[32]G. Obichkin, *Kto skryvaetsya za religiei* (Moscow, 1930) 7-11. He accuses the Fedorovtsy sect also of perpetrating terrorism against the Soviets. The fraudulency and fictitiousness of the Society for the Liberation of the Ukraine has been exposed by the late Soviet-Ukrainian writer and son of one of the participants in the trial, Ghely Snegirev, in "Mama moya, mama!" *Kontinent,* nos. 11, 12, 13, 14, 15 (1977 and 1978) 11-54, 163-212, 173-203, 152-92, 90-122, respectively.

[33]The line that the Church is a class enemy was continued, for instance, by F. Putintsev, *Vybory v sovety i razoblachenie popovshchiny* (Moscow, 1937) 20 etc., and *XX-letie otdeleniya tserkvi ot gosudarstva* (Moscow, 1938) 20-3. One of the leading official Soviet philosophers of the time, P. Fedoseev, stated that religion would not die of its own—i.e., it had to be actively fought against. See his article in *Ob antireligioznoi propagande* (Moscow, 1937) 58-9. The more moderate line is represented by F. Oleshchuk, *Bor'ba tserkvi protiv naroda* (Moscow, 1939), and *Sputnik antireligioznika* (Moscow, 1939), which cites Lenin against the physical persecution of the Church. Another collection, *Komsomol i antireligioznaya propaganda* (Moscow, 1937), argues that religion is the domain of the most backward elements and is caused by deficiencies in Soviet social relations, rather than by any particular hostility toward the Soviet system.

And it was reported that the Komsomol, which should have stood behind the LMG, generally shunned participation in the latter's activities, while many Komsomol members were found to be religious believers.[34]

The Church in the 1930s: Catacomb and Sergiite

According to an official Soviet estimate, by the late 1930s, 75 to 80 percent of all Orthodox were Sergiite, 15 to 20 percent Renovationist and under 5 percent "Grigoriite."[35] This estimate, however, is highly suspect, for it does not mention the Iosifites-Buiites and the less radical Noncommemorators—the followers of Metropolitan Kirill and his supporters[36]—whose numbers must have been well in excess of 5 percent.

All Noncommemorators, known as "catacomb" Christians, possessed no registration, were "underground" and therefore led a much more spiritually intensive life than the official part of the Church, severely controlled and curbed by the state. In their secrecy they engaged also in the spiritual upbringing and education of children, which the official Church could not do. A fine example of their work is Fr. Alexander Men, one of the most outstanding, intellectually brilliant and prolific priests of the contemporary Moscow Patriarchal Church, who had been baptized and spiritually educated by catacomb priests in the vicinity of Moscow in the 1940s.[37]

As the example of Fr. Men suggests, "catacomb" did not necessarily mean a fanatical and total break with the official

[34]Oleshchuk says that only 10 percent of all nominal members of the LMG are active. See his article in *Revolyutsiya i kul'tura*, no. 3-4 (1928). See also Spinka, 73-87;. Curtiss, *Russian Church*, 237-80; D. Ledin, "S chego nachinat'," in *Komsomol i antireligioznaya propaganda*, 64 et passim; N. Amosov, *Antireligioznaya rabota na poroge vtoroi pyatiletki* (Moscow, 1932) 45.

[35]Curtiss, *Russian Church*, 284-8.

[36]I.e., those who refused to commemorate Metropolitan Sergii as the acting head of the Church.

[37]See n. 27 above and chapter 4, pp. 150ff. On Men, see *Katakomby XX veka*, by Vasilevskaya—Men's aunt, an outstanding scholar in the field of child psychology. Men is a Jewish convert to Orthodoxy, who publishes theological (on the history of religions) books in the West under the pseudonym of E. Svetlov (with the Belgian Roman Catholic press Life With God, publishing in Russian).

Church. Indeed, it was an all-inclusive term for all unofficial and hence uncontrolled church activity. It included the extreme movement of total rejection of even the episcopal charisma of Metropolitan Sergii, which, like most schismatic and protestant movements, soon produced out of its midst a number of sects—e.g., the *Fedorovtsy,* after Fr. Fedor of the Bishop Aleksii (Bui) schism; the *Imyaslavtsy* (Name-glorifiers), who appeared in the northern Caucasus, had clear promonarchist inclinations (as did most of the rightist schismatics) and an eschatological tendency; and the *Molchalniki* (Silencers), who have survived well into the 1960s, but about whom very little is known because they refuse to speak. (We shall treat these movements in more detail in chapter 11.) The majority of those not in communion with Sergii, however, looked at their schism as a temporary situation, as illustrated by their already discussed return to the Patriarchal Church in 1945-1946 on an appeal from Bishop Afanasy.[38]

But, it seems, by far the largest part of the catacombs consisted of elements who had never formally broken with Metropolitan Sergii (some of them rejecting his political course, but not his charisma, and others not going even that far), but who had gone underground simply because of the impossibility of performing religious rites openly. Probably, most of them recognized Sergii as the legal temporary head of the Russian Church and reestablished regular canonical and liturgical contact with him after 1943, when this became technically possible and practical from the point of view of participating in the life of the revived Church. There can be no other explanation for the sudden mushrooming of thousands of lay believers' associations ("twenties") petitioning the government to reopen churches and the reappearance of thousands of priests acceptable to the new communities (hence in many cases personally known to them) in places where there had been no open churches for periods of five to fifteen years. Obviously, most of them had been active in the religious underground prior to 1943-1944. In the opinion of at least one reliable Russian church historian, even the few

---

[38]See chapter 4, and Fletcher, *Study in Survival,* 38. The other term for the Molchalniki appears to be *Skrytniki* (Concealers), about whom one Soviet author writes that they have several dozen secret sketes in the Siberian taiga. See Zybkovets, *Natsionalizatsiya monastyrskikh imushchestv v sovetskoi Rossii (1917-1921gg.)* (Moscow, 1975) 111-2.

hundred parishes of the Sergiite jurisdiction still open in 1939 and his skeleton church administration were tolerated by Stalin's regime at least partly owing to the existence of the underground Church. The Soviet regime obviously did not want to see the whole Church disappear from under its purview and regular oversight—an open, controllable Church was less dangerous than an underground one.[39]

In place of monasteries closed by the government, many clandestine monastic communities appeared in the 1930s, some in the depths of Siberian forests, others in the cities—e.g., in Smolensk.[40] Underground seminaries also existed. One such, in Moscow, was finally disbanded in 1938, although its leader, Bishop Varfolomei (Remov), had been executed two years earlier.[41] A certain Bishop Peter, clandestinely ordained by Patriarch Tikhon, on returning from a long spell in prison in 1936 was provided by the believers with a secret dugout, where he lived and prayed with a few disciples. The NKVD began a hunt for him in 1937, interrogated hundreds of people, and yet could not discover him—although he was in contact with hundreds of believers across the country. In 1943, when the church situation had improved, he left for the Tien-Shan Mountains, where he established an unofficial monastery with some three hundred secretly tonsured monks. The community recognized Sergii and Aleksii as the heads of the Russian Church and prayed for them. It existed until 1951, when it was spotted from a helicopter; all the monks received prison sentences, while the bishop died or was killed in prison.[42]

[39]Alexeev, "The Russian Orthodox Church," 29-30. Indeed, the same became the crux of the open argument of some Soviet propagandists of atheism for the discontinuation of direct church persecutions in the aftermath of Khrushchev's frontal attack against the Church.

[40]According to a Soviet source, the Smolensk monks "were fighting against the deputies of the Block of communists and the Nonpartisans to the Supreme Soviet," i.e., they were apparently attempting to put forward their own candidates for "elected" government positions. *Sbornik materialov po antireligioznoi propagande* (Leningrad, 1938) 105. "Dispersed monks and nuns often organized . . . kolkhozes and sovkhozes," which in fact were continuations of their monastic communities. "In 1937 one such sovkhoz was one of the best in the Caucasus." Prof. Krypton, a former catacomb Christian, describes a secret convent in a Leningrad apartment: "The services and even the singing were whispered. The organization had several branches in the city." Fletcher, *Study in Survival*, 86-91.

[41]Ibid.

[42]The source has to remain unnamed, for obvious reasons; but the existence

The few remaining "registered" priests, in order to satisfy somehow at least a fraction of the religious needs of the population, and to protect them from persecutions for attending a church, began to practice mass baptisms, funeral services in absentia on the basis of a message from a believer, confessions by correspondence or general confessions. Even baptisms and marriage ceremonies were performed by some priests in the absence of the babies or couples.[43]

The 1936 Constitution, the approved discussion of the Constitution that had preceded its adoption and the subsequent electoral campaign were taken seriously at first by many sectors of the population, including the clergy, particularly since it at last granted the clergy and their families equal rights with all other citizens, including voting rights. Hostile reports soon appeared in the atheist press that article 141 of the Constitution, to the effect that candidates to the Supreme Soviet should be put forward by "social organizations," was interpreted by many priests as applying to the Church as one of such social organizations. The atheist authors sternly warned that the term "social organization" cannot be applied to the Church because of

> the reactionary, anticultural character of her activities . . .
> Although the priests have received civic rights, they continue to support and disseminate views and concepts hostile and contrary to science. . . . religious organizations are permitted . . . only as private associations for the performance of the religious cult. Religious organizations as such have no right to participate in the social and political life of the country. Priests should not be elected either to the Council of the Union, to the Council of Nationalities or to the workers' councils. They cannot express either the general interests of the toiling masses . . . or the special interests of the individual nationalities . . . [for] religious associations are very handy for the activities of anti-Soviet elements, because they are legal, *are headed by people*

and current growth of secretly tonsured monasticism has been confirmed to us by Tatyana Goricheva, a thirty-five-year-old religious philosopher recently expelled from Leningrad, whom we interviewed in Frankfurt am Main, September 29, 1980.

[43]Fletcher, *Study in Surival,* 86-8.

hostile to socialism, have funds, active groups of believers and a central apparatus.[44]

These attacks were a response to the reports that in some areas priests instructed local populations that now they could request the reopening of the churches, as the new Constitution ceased to treat the Church and her servants as hostile elements. In some rural and urban churches, straw votes were organized by secret ballot of the parishioners, resulting in the forwarding of priests and deacons as candidates for the future elections to the Supreme Soviet. Ironically, one article accused the churchmen who initiated these straw votes of infringing on the secrecy of the ballot![45]

Metropolitan (Patriarch) Sergii

Mark Popovsky, in his fascinating biography of the professor of medicine and Archbishop Luka (Voino-Yasenetsky), "explains" Metropolitan Sergii's subordination to the Soviet regime in 1927 by dismissing him as "a career-making bureaucrat of the prerevolutionary Synod."[46] Nothing could be further from the truth.

Sergii, in fact, was one of the most significant and influential theologians among the Orthodox bishops of this century. His magisterial dissertation, "The Orthodox Teachings on Salvation," was recognized as a major contribution to Orthodox theology and to the understanding of the essential differences between it and the theology of the West. He maintained that the difference was not so much in the papal dogmatic innovations as in Roman

[44]F. Oleshchuk, *O zadachakh antireligioznoi propagandy* (Moscow, 1937) 12-7; Yu. Kogan and F. Megruzhan, *O svobode sovesti* (Moscow, 1938) 64-5. According to Putintsev (*Vybory v sovety,* 20-2) some bishops even rewarded priests for conducting public discussions of the Constitution in parishes. "The Metropolitan of Vitebsk sent nearly forty priests to the rural districts of Belorussia" for this purpose. Levitin likewise confirms that priests cherished some hopes in connection with the new Constitution, which did remove the clergy from the status of "untouchables," which had deprived their children of higher and even secondary education, social insurance benefits, etc. *Likhie gody,* 299-300.

[45]Oleshchuk, *O zadachakh,* 15-7, etc.

[46]*Zhizn' i zhitie,* 353.

legalism and formalism, which, in the final analysis, substitutes codification of sins and deeds and contractual relations for love. In two major articles on the Old Catholics he presented clear and definitive theological issues that distinguish them from Orthodoxy and that make a mechanical unification with them impossible.[47]

His stature as a theologian among Russian bishops was probably even higher than that of Antony Khrapovitsky, but Sergii was never as conservative in his political views or even in his attitudes to the intelligentsia and social movements as was Antony. When the secular intelligentsia decided in 1901 to have a dialogue with the Church, it was the young Bishop Sergii, rector of the St. Petersburg Theological Academy, who became the chairman of these joint Religio-Philosophical Meetings. And the intelligentsia, still mostly distant from the Church at the time, had nothing but praise for Sergii's understanding, tolerance and love for them all: "He was not a chairman . . . but a Christian. . . . Vanity and pride vanished, replaced by a living font of spiritual interests . . . Bishop Sergii poured good weather upon our meetings from the depth of his soul."[48]

In 1904 he gave his blessing to Gapon's St. Petersburg workers' movement. As Bishop of Finland, he vocally welcomed the 1905 legislation granting toleration to Old Believers and sectarians.[49] In his correspondence with the Paris-based Orthodox theologian Vladimir Lossky in the 1930s, Sergii enthusiastically endorsed Orthodox missions in the West, the adoption of the western calendar and local languages for these churches, and even the establishment of a Western Rite Orthodoxy for converts raised in western traditions. He suggested the use of the pre-Roman Gallican liturgy or even the Latin mass, enriched, however, to accord with Orthodox liturgical theology.[50]

But the most telling document on Sergii's theological broadmindedness and undogmatism is his memorandum on church reforms for the Preconciliar Commission. His suggestions are among the most far-going of all the bishops' memoranda. The

[47]*Patriarkh Sergii*, 99-102.
[48]Ibid., 102-3, citing from *Zapiski religiozno-filosofskikh sobranii*, 245.
[49]Spinka, 54.
[50]*Patriarkh Sergii*, 72-6.

future sobor, he writes, should begin by abolishing the Synod, its tyranny over the Church and all intimate links with the government. Voting rights in the sobor, he says, should have been the prerogative of bishops, had they enjoyed the fulness of love and trust of the faithful. However, the lay believers and the clergy have no such faith in the Russian bishops, and the post-Petrine, bureaucratic, centralized structure of the Church has brought about a terrible alienation, on the one hand between the laity and the clergy, and on the other between the married clergy and the monastic bishops. Therefore, both lay and lower clergy members of the sobor must have equal voting rights with the bishops in the general chamber on all questions, except fundamental ones of faith, canons and dogma. A council of bishops should form a second chamber at the sobor, to which all resolutions approved by the sobor majority should go for verification and approval on theological grounds. Those bills that the bishops did not approve would go back to the chamber of the whole. In case of disagreement between the two, the bill would be relegated to the following sobor. He strongly advocates the *sobornost'* principle to be embodied in a decentralized federal-metropolitan circuits system, with a representative central council at the top presided over by a patriarch, who would be elected by one of the last sessions of the sobor,[51] i.e., by the time its members had become acquainted with each other and knew whom they were electing. He also suggests far-reaching reforms in theological education, including the abolition of the clerical estate (*soslovie*).[52]

The fact that he was so often moved around from one position to another suggests that he did not entirely fit into the prerevolutionary episcopal-synodal establishment. He had been a missionary in Japan, a Russian embassy priest in Athens, a professor and rector of St. Petersburg Theological Academy and the Bishop of Finland—a position on the fringes of the Russian diocesan structure, although close to Petersburg with its reformist clergy.

Spinka suggests that there was one blemish on the progressive-reformist image of Bishop Sergii: circumstantial evidence that he was partly instrumental in the episcopal consecration of Varnava, a Rasputin protégé. He is also on record as a defender

---

[51]Note that the 1917-1918 Sobor practically enacted Sergii's program.
[52]*Otzyvy eparkhial'nykh arkiereev,* 3:259-90.

of Sabler, the highly unpopular overprocurator of the Synod who was criticized for cooperating with Rasputin.[53] Were these early signs of Sergii's conclusion that in order to achieve his aims for the Church he had to win support from the powers of this world? If so, then such is also the case with his other self-discrediting act, which occurred under the Provisional Government, when he had at first pledged not to participate in the Synod arbitrarily dissolved and reassembled by V. Lvov, its new revolutionary overprocurator, but then sat on the Synod when invited by the same Lvov.[54]

Although he was one of the first Orthodox bishops to have been arrested by the Bolsheviks, as early as November 1917, he was soon released. In 1922 he joined the Living Church. During the 1923 Sobor he was in a Soviet jail, which protected him from signing any of its documents as well as from suspicion of collaboration with the Soviet state. In January 1924 he returned to the patriarch by means of a humiliating public penitence.

If the main reason for the relative success and survival of the anticanonical émigré Karlovci Synod should probably be sought in the personal charisma and magnetism of its head, Metropolitan Antony (Khrapovitsky), it similarly could be said that it was owing to the great personal charisma and status of Sergii that the highly unpopular 1927 Declaration of Loyalty was eventually, although reluctantly, accepted by the majority of the Church.[55] Some additional illustrations of its unpopularity are that in a January 1928 letter Sergii begged Metropolitan Agafangel not to break with him, to have a little more patience, "until it becomes clear where we are leading the ship of the Church: to a relatively bearable existence in the given conditions, or to a catastrophe."[56]

[53]Spinka, 55-9.

[54]The Grigorians made use of this to attack Sergii in one of their letters. Regelson, 407.

[55]Levitin-Shavrov, 2:112. On Sergii's prestige, see Metropolitan Peter's letter to him of February 26, 1930, in Regelson, 480-1. The Karlovcian *Tserkovnoe obozrenie* (their semi-official organ, again edited by Makharoblidze, replacing the defunct official *Tserkovnye vedomosti*) reported that even such a radical critic of Sergii's declaration as Archbishop Serafim of Uglich, who had replaced Sergii as deputy locum tenens while the latter was in prison in 1926, made peace with him (no. 2 [February 1932] 10). According to Regelson (584-5), his recognition of Sergii was conditional. In 1932 Serafim was arrested and eventually perished in the camps.

[56]Regelson, 153.

In another message, he promised that his uncanonical removals and appointments of bishops and other policies were a temporary expediency that would soon be abandoned once the church situation had been normalized.[57] There is none of that tone that he was to adopt in his interviews with foreign correspondents, beginning with the one in 1930 when he so grievously insulted all the imprisoned bishops, priests and laymen by claiming that there was no persecution of religion and that all punishments of clerics were caused by their transgressions of the political law. This he would repeat once more in his war-time publication *The Truth about Religion in Russia.*[58]

We have already cited one explanation of the reason why Sergii agreed to utter such a lie in 1930. The question could be asked, however, why did he not refuse to continue to utter such lies, at least when he saw that none of them were helping the position or safety of the Church and her clerics, when nothing remained but a shadow of the Church? The most hostile explanation is that by Fr. Polsky, who compares his subsequent behavior to that of a man condemned to death but permitted to live on without the annulment of the sentence: "he lives each day on the mercy of his conqueror and does everything that is ordered."[59] Sergii's right-hand man and exarch to the occupied Baltic republics would, under the German occupation, make the following explanation of this behavior:

The feasibility of putting the brakes on the destruction of the Church undertaken by the Bolsheviks was always the

---

[57]See his response to the Rev. Prof. V. Veryuzhsky in Regelson, 137-8.

[58]This caused more resentment among the clergy and bishops, as a betrayal of the martyrs, than his 1927 declaration. See the reactions in Regelson (477-81), particularly Peter's letter of February 26, 1930, requesting Sergii to return to the policies he was pursuing prior to his arrest in 1926.

[59]Polsky, 100. But even he quotes a late 1920s conversation with a Sergiite bishop, who told him that rejecting Sergiism and choosing prison would change nothing, except that the people would remain without any Orthodox pastors, for "only the Sergiite temples remained under the sign of Orthodoxy" (ibid., 65)— the others, of course, being the Renovationists, the Grigorians and the Ukrainian "Self-consecrators." It is interesting that Polsky does not correct this assertion by arguing that a vast number of churches did not accept Sergii's declaration and yet remained Orthodox. Apparently, he himself felt that they would not survive for very long and that, being in the underground, they could not perform even any passive missionary work (in the sense of merely being visible).

main concern of the patriarchate . . . we [were like] chickens in a shed, from which the cook snatches out her victim in turn . . . For the sake of the Church we reconciled ourselves to our humiliating position, believing in her certain victory and trying somehow to preserve her for better times, for the downfall of Bolshevism.[60]

Strangely enough, this tallies with the Moscow Metropolitan Sergii's own confession: "I act in accordance with the need of each day"; in another place, he compared the life of the Church in the USSR with the times of the apostles.[61]

The state, however, continued to use the Church for its needs on the foreign relations front from time to time, to show that all was well and that the only reason why churches were being closed was the disappearance of believers. Indeed, even Sergii made a statement to this effect, which was also mendacious, as the above statistics show.[62] To demonstrate how free the Church was, Metropolitan Sergii was instructed or permitted to perform a splendid ceremony in the patriarchal cathedral on April 27, 1934 to bestow on himself the title of "His Beatitude the Metropolitan of Moscow"—i.e., the de facto Patriarch of Russia (although Metropolitan Peter was still living in detention). Twenty bishops, forty-four priests and fifteen deacons participated in the ceremony.[63] Ironically, only four of these bishops remained in their positions by 1941.

On June 22, 1934, Sergii and his Synod at last fulfilled the long-lasting request of the Soviet government: namely, they banned the Karlovcian clergy from all clerical functions and declared them schismatics. Details of this act will be discussed later, in chapter 8. One point, however, which adds to the profile of Sergii as an Orthodox theologian and a dedicated churchman, may be brought up here. It relates to Sergii's correspondence with the Serbian Patriarch Varnava, his former pupil from the days when Varnava had been a student at St. Petersburg Theological Academy and Sergii was its rector (Sergii had also tonsured him

[60]Statement by Metropolitan Sergii (Voskresensky), cited in Fletcher, *Study in Survival*, 101-2.
[61]*Patriarkh Sergii*, 253; Popovsky, 355 et passim.
[62]Polsky, 88.
[63]Popovsky, 353-4.

a monk). In one of his letters to Varnava, Sergii terms the Russian postrevolutionary emigration "a spiritual emigration" rather than a political one—i.e., he sees the revolution as a spiritual cataclysm and communism as a secular religion. Similarly, in the same context, he sees as the primary God-given purpose of the Russian emigration the "opening to Western Christendom of the treasures of the Orthodox faith," and he reproaches the emigration with engaging instead in senseless schismatic activities "with mutual bans and baiting . . . in the press and from the church pulpit."[64]

Another event in Sergii's assertion of his position as the leader of the Church occurred on December 27, 1936. On the news of the incarcerated Metropolitan Peter's death, Sergii's Synod transferred "all the rights and duties of the patriarchal locum tenens . . . to his deputy, Metropolitan Sergii." In 1931, however, Sergii had argued that the deputy locum tenens, having been appointed to this post personally by the locum tenens, "retains his prerogatives only as long as the locum tenens retains his post. The moment the locum tenens leaves his post (by death, retirement, etc.), the prerogatives of the deputy cease." Therefore, argues Regelson, it was Metropolitan Kirill, the late Patriarch Tikhon's other choice for locum tenens, who should have assumed the title on Peter's death.[65] This was also the view of many bishops in the Russian Church, who refused to recognize Sergii's new title, and, consequently, his subsequent election as patriarch. This is particularly true, for instance, of the already mentioned Bishop Afanasy (Sakharov), who recognized Patriarch Aleksii as properly elected, in contrast to Sergii.

But were these purists right? To begin with, on purely theological-canonical grounds, Sergii argued in the same 1931 article that, whereas the appointment of locum tenentes by outgoing patriarchs was uncanonical and had been accepted by the Russian bishops only as an extraordinary measure necessitated

[64]Sergii's message to the Serbian Patriarch, no. 311, March 23, 1933, in *ZhMP*, no. 14-15 (1933) 1-8; and his resolution on the Karlovci group, no. 50, of June 22, 1934, *ZhMP*, no. 22 (1934) 1-2.

[65]Regelson, 185-6; see the text of Sergii's elevation in "Sovremennoe polozhenie rossiiskoi tserkvi," *Put'*, no. 53 (1937) 66-7. On the prerogatives of locum tenentes and their deputies see "O polnomochiyakh patriarshego mestoblyustitelya i ego zamestitelya," *ZhMP*, no. 1 (1931) 3-5.

by the historically unprecedented situation of the time, the election of locum tenentes by synods of bishops for an interim period was a normal practice of the historical Church. Hence, one could argue that what happened in 1936 was precisely such an election of Sergii as the temporary locum tenens by a synod of bishops, until the time when it became possible to elect a patriarch. There is also a pragmatic side to the issue: what would have happened to the barely surviving Synod, at the time of Stalin's greatest terror of 1936-1938, if an imprisoned metropolitan (Kirill) were to be elected the leader of the Church? Would it not have been interpreted by Stalin as further evidence of deliberate hostility of the Church toward his regime? Moreover, how would an octogenarian, imprisoned bishop administer the Church and appoint his deputies? Was it not Metropolitan Kirill himself who stated in one of his earlier letters to Sergii that only those canons should be observed which were beneficial to the Church at the given moment, not those that harmed her? This was not the time for canonical niceties. The situation was desperate. Archbishop Sergii (Voskresensky), the future Moscow Patriarchate's exarch for the Baltic republics, met a monk returning from Arctic imprisonment in 1935 with the words, "the last days have arrived," and he strongly advised the Kievan monk to choose a civilian vocation if he wanted to survive. Describing the situation on the eve of the German invasion, this monk, Leonty, a future bishop in the Ukrainian Autonomous Church under the German occupation and later Bishop of Chile, says that in most major cities only one Orthodox church was still functioning, while smaller towns were left without any as a rule. In each of these open urban churches the NKVD had left two priests, and only ones who had agreed to collaborate with it. They were to report on the contents of confessions, on believing Soviet civil servants and on underground clerics and believers. There were to be two rather than one, so that the priests would watch each other. Leonty cites the confessions of two priests of the only surviving Kiev church. One, apparently, did not do the job properly, because he was so badly beaten up by the NKVD that he died from the consequences. Before dying, he confessed his sins to fellow patients in the hospital. As to the other priest, his wife and son deserted him and took along his rough notes for the

NKVD. She denounced him to the Germans in 1941; he was arrested, confessed and was executed. It was for these reasons that, toward the late 1930s, the believers' loyalties toward the clergy were undermined, as observed by Soviet atheist authors and explained by Bishop Leonty.[66]

By that time Sergii must have likewise developed second thoughts regarding his 1927 declaration and its fruits, for he said to a Russian priest visiting him in May 1941: "Formerly they used to strangle us, but at least they fulfilled their promises. Now they continue to strangle us, but they no longer fulfil the promises they give while strangling us."[67]

[66]Leonty, 127 and 134-6. On the "indifference" of the laity toward their clergy, see Fedoseev, 58-9.

[67]Rev. V. Vinogradov's testimony, cited in Chrysostomus, 2:311. The strangling went so far that the frightened Metropolitan Aleksii of Leningrad (the future patriarch) issued a diocesan instruction in 1936 forbidding his clergy to administer communion to children. Levitin, "Slushaya radio," *Posev* (September 23, 1966) 3; also AS 735.

CHAPTER 6

The Church during the Second World War: Soviet Territory

The Soviet destruction of the Church was at least halted by the annexation of Orthodox or partly Orthodox territories in the West beginning in September 1939—as it was necessary to assimilate or at least politically neutralize these millions of new citizens. The Soviet government realized it could not hope to achieve this by attacking their churches point blank. Indeed, it was through unity in a single Orthodox Church that the western Ukrainians and western Belorussians could be most organically reunified with their eastern compatriots. The same is true of the large Orthodox minorities in the Baltic republics—some of them were ethnic Russians, and others Orthodox Estonians, Latvians or Karelians who, however, by virtue of their religion had a strong cultural affinity with the Russians. To a lesser extent this was also true of the Moldavians.[1] That the regime was at least not ignoring these considerations was demonstrated by the fact that of the only four still functioning members of Metropolitan Sergii's Synod, two were dispatched to the occupied territories: Metropolitan Nikolai (Yarushevich), as exarch for the western Ukraine and western Belorussia; and Metropolitan Sergii (Voskresensky), as Moscow's ecclesiastical overseer for the Baltic territories and, on the death of Metropolitan Elevfery of Lithuania, as exarch for the Baltic republics. The "specific

[1]Because the Romanians, with whom they had formed a single state between 1919 and 1940, were also Orthodox.

193

gravity" of the Orthodox Church in the occupied territory in relation to the Russian Orthodox Church as a whole—or rather to what remained of it by 1939-1940—has already been mentioned: of the four thousand-odd Orthodox churches functioning in 1941, probably well over 70 percent were in the newly occupied territory. But, in order not to antagonize these Orthodox masses, some religious tolerance had to be demonstrated on the part of the regime, not only in the occupied territories, but in the whole of the USSR as well. Thus, a lull in the persecutions had to take place. Also, for the first time since his assumption of administration over the Church, Metropolitan Sergii (Stragorodsky), as William Fletcher remarks, was in a position to bargain with the state,[2] although there is no evidence that he really tried or that the government was willing to respond to such attempts at that time.

It was the war, the German attack, that brought him out of this state of despair. The head of the traditional, historical, national Church knew how to react to the enemy attack. He knew this better than the political dictator Stalin, who went into hiding for at least a week and dared address the nation over the radio for the first time only ten days later. In a trembling voice, Stalin delivered an appeal to the nation that sounded rather like that of a priest: "Brothers and sisters! My dear friends! . . ."[3]—this was not from the Marxist-Leninist verbal arsenal. Metropolitan Sergii, in contrast, delivered his appeal to the nation on the very first day of the war: Sunday, June 22, 1941, the feastday of All the Saints of Russia. In the form of a pastoral letter he disseminated the appeal-sermon to all the existing parishes across the country, thereby, strictly speaking, breaking the law, which bans all activities of the Church outside church walls and any interference in the affairs of the state and nation.

This letter does not even once mention the Soviet Union or its government. There is even an indirect reproach to the unnamed powers of the USSR in the passage: "we, the residents of Russia, have been cherishing the hope that the blaze of war, which has engulfed nearly the whole globe, would spare us . . ."

---

[2]*Study in Survival,* 98. In fact, church attendance was facilitated in 1939 when the regime reestablished the regular seven-day week in place of the continuous work week, where one worked for five days and then had the sixth day off.

[3]Popovsky, *Zhizn' i zhitie,* 359.

Clearly, it was Stalin who, by means of his 1939 pact with Hitler, cherished most the hope of avoiding direct involvement of the Soviet Union in the war (after having antagonized the nation by the forced collectivization, the artificial famine of 1933, the terror of 1934-1938, and after having weakened his armed forces by liquidating over 60 percent of the officer corps in 1937-1938). Then Sergii goes on: "Our Orthodox Church has always shared in the destinies of the nation . . . Together with it she has borne both trials and successes. Neither shall she abandon her people today. She is giving this impending national struggle the heavenly blessings."

The message reminds the nation of her past heroes and assures her that their strength and victories were inspired by their sense of duty to their nation and to their faith. The message then tells the clergy not to remain just silent observers, let alone indulge in calculations "regarding some possible profit on the other side of the border." Such calculations, in Sergii's words, would be an act of "direct treason to the motherland and to one's pastoral duty." These are obvious hints that after all the horrors and persecutions many will be tempted to try the other side.[4]

Four days later he held a special Te Deum service at the patriarchal cathedral, after which he delivered a sermon with an even more direct implication that far from everything was satisfactory at home: "Let the storm come. We know that it will bring not only misfortune, but alleviation also; it will cleanse the air and blow away noxious vapors. . . . We already see certain signs of this disinfection."[5] This began his and his Church's active engagement in the patriotic effort. In October, when the Germans had penetrated to within sixty miles of Moscow, Sergii wrote another address to the nation, condemning all those churchmen who, like Judas, had become active collaborators with the enemy on the German-occupied territory. It seems that, whatever his genuine loyalties, Sergii was trying by this address to neutralize the effect of the defection to the Germans of Metropolitan Sergii (Voskresensky). The latter was considered to have been only

[4]See the collection of church documents, *Russkaya pravoslavnaya tserkov' i velikaya otechestvennaya voina* (Moscow, 1943) 3-5.

[5]*Pravda o religii v Rossii* (Moscow, 1942) 83-94; translation taken from Struve, 60-1.

second to his senior namesake in importance in the hierarchy and certainly was the one most trusted by the NKVD of all the hierarchs, having been the liaison between the Synod and the Soviet authorities.[6]

Apparently, the Soviets were not entirely convinced, for in the face of the German advance, on the very day of the above address, Sergii (Stragorodsky), despite high fever, was forced to board a train and evacuate to Ulyanovsk. Probably, the Soviets wanted thereby to prevent him from following in the footsteps of his namesake deputy. It was already from his Ulyanovsk semi-exile that on November 11 he wrote his third address to the Russian faithful, in which he was suggesting, as it were, a new war propaganda-policy line: "Progressive humanity has declared a holy war against Hitler in the name of Christian civilization, for freedom of conscience and religion."[7] The thought behind it probably was that if Stalin adopted this line, it would oblige him to change his own policy toward the Church.

Stalin, however, was very slow and cautious in changing his policy toward the Church, and the major alterations he would eventually make in 1943 were probably caused more by the necessity to match the mass opening of churches and the religious revival under the German occupation than by Sergii's overtures. So far all that changed was that, soon after the German attack, vocal and printed antireligious propaganda disappeared from the Soviet media, and no attempts were made to prevent Sergii from issuing his patriotic addresses or to hinder their distribution and public reading in all functioning churches across the country. According to the 1929 legislation (in force, with minor amendments, to the time of the writing of this book), these acts of the metropolitan were illegal. While Sergii was not allowed to return to Moscow until the late summer of 1943, long after the Germans had retreated, Metropolitan Nikolai was permitted to return to Moscow as early as November 1941. He immediately set down to the business of active cooperation with the Soviets in external propaganda matters, and soon became the patriarchate's foreign

---

[6]Wassilij Alexeev, "Russian Orthodox Bishops in the Soviet Union, 1944-1953," Research Program on the USSR, Mimeographed Series, 61 (New York, 1954) 88-92.

[7]Popovsky, 361.

policy spokesman—in fact the main Soviet foreign policy spokesman and propagandist, in clerical garb. His first position in this field, as early as November 2, 1942, was membership on the Extraordinary State Commission of Inquiry into German Crimes on the Occupied Territory. It was as a member of this commission, for instance, that he later cosigned an obviously fraudulent document claiming that the murder of eight to ten thousand Polish officers in the forest of Katyn had been the work of the Germans, whereas all evidence points to this as an act of the NKVD *prior* to June 1941.[8]

The only other Soviet concession to the Church in 1942 was the publication of a large volume under the title *The Truth about Religion in Russia,* which simultaneously appeared in several languages. Ironically though, it was the printing house of the by then practically defunct League of Militant Godless that was handed over for church use.[9] The volume was never widely available for sale in the USSR; it was meant as a propaganda piece for abroad. But its thorough perusal leaves a sad impression: photographs of worn, tired, sad, elderly faces of the lay church activists; the meager quantity of active churches photographed. The statements assuring the reader of complete religious freedom in the USSR sound hollow and unconvincing in the face of these photographs and of the total absence of church statistics. There is much emphasis on the continuity of patriotism in the historical role of the Russian Orthodox Church from Alexander Nevsky to the current war. Significantly, there is much praise of Patriarch Tikhon as a leader of the Church, affirming that he enjoyed great authority not by display of power and severity but through the force of love. Tikhon's conflict with the regime and his persecutions by the latter are passed over in silence, which only serves to further emphasize the unfree state of the Church.

It may be of interest that at least two photographs of Metropolitan Sergii (Stragorodsky) with groups of bishops include Sergii (Voskresensky), with the latter's name spelled out under

---

[8]See *The Crime of Katyn* (London: Polish Cultural Foundation, 1965) passim. On Nikolai's testimony, see Fletcher, *Nikolai,* 43-4. On his appointment to the commission see Alexeev, "Russian Bishops," 108.

[9]A part of the edition (*Pravda o religii v Rossii*), apparently inadvertently, contained a statement in small print on the last page in Russian: "Put out by the Antireligious Press of the USSR." Fletcher, *Study in Survival,* 111-2.

the photographs, at the time when he was actively collaborating with the occupying forces in the German-occupied Baltic region. Only on September 22, 1942, did the senior Sergii issue a message addressed to all faithful, "particularly those in Lithuania, Latvia and Estonia," which criticized the Baltic bishops, with the younger Sergii at their head, for collaborating with the enemy. Even Russian émigrés and other Slavs in America, said the message, who disagree with the Bolsheviks on matters of faith and ideology, supported the Soviet war effort against the Nazis. The message stresses that the Russians have no option but to fight against the Nazis, because their racism aims at the biological destruction of Russia. As for himself, Sergii does not need any arguments to be convinced of the necessity of resisting fascism: love for his country and his people takes care of that. On the same day, a resolution (no. 27), signed by twelve bishops in addition to Sergii, condemned the Baltic bishops, but rather mildly for the conditions: "Should the information [on their collaboration] prove to be true, let the bishops take the necessary measures to correct their line of behavior . . . and present an accurate report to the patriarchate, so that the future ecclesiastical court will have before it not only the misdeed, but also its correction." The resolution then banned any further elevation of the exarch Sergii's name at that Moscow church where he used to officiate as its bishop. The mild and conditional tone of the whole resolution demonstrates an involuntary submission to Soviet pressures and the senior Sergii's unwillingness to condemn his personal friend, who, even under the German occupation, continued to defend the Moscow Patriarchate and remained under its jurisdiction. In contrast, the Moscow Patriarchate's condemnation of the Ukrainian Archbishop Polykarp on March 27, 1943 was much more definitive. But this was because Polykarp was guilty of a serious canonical breach by reestablishing the uncanonical Ukrainian Autocephalous Church on the German-controlled territory.[10]

To return to *The Truth about Religion in Russia*, it must be mentioned that despite its propagandistic purpose, a Christian message was not entirely absent—for instance, in its condemnation of war as a matter of principle. It does this by criticizing the German World War I Field Marshal Ludendorff, who "came

[10]*Russkaya tserkov' i voina*, 32-6.

to the conclusion, that . . . Christianity . . . with its teachings on love toward one's enemy inevitably weakens animal cruelty . . . Wherefore the general appealed to the Germans to give up Christ and revere the ancient German idols instead." Was not this also a hint at the Bolsheviks, who attacked Christianity so often precisely for the "love thy enemy" doctrine?[11] The emphasis is placed on the bond between the Russian nation and its Church throughout history, on sacrifices to fellow man in the name of God as the source of strength of the nation—as if to hint, turn back to God, for only by His help can you hope to win this war, not by material power alone.[12]

There is no available evidence of church reopenings on the Soviet side of the front until 1943. The first visible concession to the Church on the home front was the permission to hold the traditional candlelit processions around the churches (at least in Moscow) the night of Easter eve in 1942 despite the danger of German air raids, and the lifting of the curfew for that night.

However, the Church went on with her appeals to patriotism. Particularly active in this field was Aleksii of Leningrad, permitted by the authorities to stay in the besieged city, apparently to help lift the morale of the people. His sermons are full of patriotic zeal, often alluding to historical parallels. Thus, in his Easter sermon (April 9, 1942) he points to the day's coincidence with the 700th anniversary of Alexander Nevsky's battle on the ice of Lake Peipus against the Teutonic-German knights, which saved Novgorod—the Leningrad area—from German invasion.[13] He seems to have pioneered the practical effort of church collections to aid the defense of the country by sermon-appeals as early as summer 1941, urging the people to donate all that they could to save the country. In a singular response, an anonymous pilgrim left 150 prerevolutionary ten-ruble gold pieces under the icon of St. Nicholas at Aleksii's cathedral.[14] In his sermons, Aleksii constantly stresses that Dimitry Donskoi and Alexander Nevsky

[11]See, for example, *My porvali s religiei* (Moscow, 1963); and M. Novikov, *Pravoslavie i sovremennost'* (Moscow, 1965) 91-4.

[12]*Pravda o religii*, 42-56, 84, etc.

[13]Patriarch Aleksii, *Slova, rechi, poslaniya, obrashcheniya, doklady, stat'i*, 1 (Moscow, 1948) 18.

[14]Ibid., 40-6; and Serafim, Metropolitan of Krutitsy, "Ikh podvig bessmerten," *Golos rodiny*, no. 25 (March 1975).

won their historic victories not just because of patriotism, but thanks "to the great faith of the Russian people in God's help to the just cause, . . . similarly today, we believe, therefore the whole Heavenly Force is with us."[15]

In the meanwhile, Metropolitan Sergii decided to make an important stride toward the de facto legalization of the Church on the basis of the Church's *illegal* charity collections for defense: on January 5, 1943, he sent a telegram to Stalin asking that the Church be permitted to open a bank account in her own name to deposit the collections for defense being made in all the churches across the country. Stalin granted this permission in writing, while thanking the Church on behalf of the Red Army for all her efforts. Having gained the right to have a central bank account, the Church had become de facto a legal person. By January 15, 1943, in the besieged and starving city of Leningrad alone 3,182,143 rubles had been donated by the faithful for the Church's Fund for the Defense of the Country, plus another half-million rubles expressly for the building and arming of a tank column named after Dimitry Donskoi. The total church donations to the above fund reached 150 million rubles by October 1944.[16]

It seems that it was after the exchange of telegrams between Sergii and Stalin in January 1943 that the fortunes of the Church in the USSR began to change for the better. In the distant Siberian city of Krasnoyarsk, the brilliant surgeon, professor of medicine and bishop, Luka (Voino-Yasenetsky), still technically a prisoner for his religious views but practicing as the chief surgeon of a military hospital, was received by the provincial first party secretary, who told him that Church-state relations would soon change for the better and that he, Luka, would soon be able to function as a bishop again. Indeed, on March 5, 1943, Bishop Luka sent a happy message to his son: a church had at last been reopened in a suburb of the city (the first one since the late 1930s), and after a sixteen-year forced separation from the church through imprisonments and exile, he was again celebrating the liturgy.[17]

[15]Aleksii's sermon of August 10, 1941, in *Slova,* 1:46.

[16]See Metropolitan Aleksii's letter to Stalin, written while he was the locum tenens, in *ZhMP,* no. 10 (October 1944) 3.

[17]Popovsky, 339-41.

But the main changes occurred after September 4, 1943, when Stalin invited the only three Orthodox metropolitans functioning at the time on Soviet territory—Sergii (Stragorodsky), who was brought from Ulyanovsk only on the eve of this meeting and thereafter remained in Moscow, Nikolai (Yarushevich) and Aleksii (Simansky) of Leningrad—to discuss and arrange the conditions for a controlled but more solid existence of the Moscow Patriarchate. No detailed report of any kind was ever published on the proceedings of the meeting. The most authoritative information on it, however, is probably that of Levitin, who heard the story from the late Metropolitan Nikolai, a participant, whom Levitin had known personally for many years.

On September 3, Sergii arrived in Moscow by train from Ulyanovsk and was whisked off in a government car—to his surprise, not to his old modest wooden house but to the luxurious former residence of the German ambassador, which would henceforth become the residence of the patriarch and the seat of his offices. The next day, he and the other two metropolitans were informed that they would be taken to the Kremlin later in the day. When, at 9 p.m., they were picked up by a Kremlin limousine, they had only a faint idea of where they were being taken. They were brought straight into Stalin's study, where the Foreign Minister Molotov was also present.

It was Molotov who began the conversation. He said that the Soviet government and Stalin personally would like to know the needs of the Church.

While the other two metropolitans remained silent, Metropolitan Sergii suddenly spoke up . . . The metropolitan spoke calmly . . . in a businesslike manner . . .

The metropolitan pointed out the need for the mass reopening of churches . . . for the convocation of a church council and the election of a patriarch . . . for the general opening of seminaries, because there was a complete lack of clergy.

Here Stalin suddenly broke the [ensuing] silence: "And

why don't you have cadres? Where have they disappeared?" he said . . . looking at the bishops point blank . . .

. . . everybody knew that "the cadres" had perished in the camps. But Metropolitan Sergii . . . replied: "There are all sorts of reasons why we have no cadres. One of the reasons is that we train a person for the priesthood, and he becomes the Marshal of the Soviet Union."

Stalin smiled with satisfaction: "Yes, of course. I am a seminarian . . ." Stalin began to reminisce about his years at the seminary . . . the chat lasted on until 3 a.m. . . . It was during this chat that the future Statute of the Russian Orthodox Church and the conditions in which she would operate were [orally] drafted.

Levitin realistically concludes that, although these conditions have subsequently been justifiably criticized, in the context of 1943 they were a very major improvement on what had prevailed up to then.

The old Metropolitan Sergii was absolutely exhausted. Stalin took him under the arm like a proper acolyte, led him carefully down the stairs and said the following on parting: "Your Grace, this is all I can do for you at the present time."[18]

[18]See the second volume of Levitin's memoirs (1941-1956), *Ruk tvoikh zhar* (Tel Aviv, 1979) 105-7.

Another version—much more hostile toward the metropolitans but less likely to be authentic, as it originates from A.V. Vedernikov, a former editor of *ZhMP* who had not participated in the meeting—is retold by Popovsky, whose hostility toward Sergii has already been demonstrated. This version claims that the metropolitans were silent most of the time and that it was Stalin who told them that their primary need was to replenish the clergy by opening seminaries and academies, whereas the metropolitans had only asked for permission to open short-term training courses for clergy. Also according to this version, Sergii had asked only for a monastic house attached to the patriarchate in which to tonsure future episcopal candidates, while Stalin replied that they should reopen real monasteries, a press, a library—"create a Vatican of sorts." Allegedly, the bishops, terrorized by decades of persecution, missed their chance: "Had the bishops been Jews, they would have bargained a better deal and today we would have had legalized religious education for children."

The Vedernikov-Popovsky story, however, contains a detail missing in Levitin's

Within four days a sobor of nineteen bishops gathered and, on the suggestion of Metropolitan Aleksii, unanimously elected Sergii the patriarch. But where did the nineteen bishops come from?

By the spring of 1942, in addition to the three metropolitans there were, apparently, eight other active diocesan bishops. At least two more were consecrated between the above date and the sobor, and six others must have been either released from prison or exile, or permitted to return to active church life from enforced retirement. Indeed, probably all the participating bishops except the three metropolitans had been either in exile or enforced retirement prior to 1942.[19] But there must have been at least several scores more still alive in imprisonment and exile. The four days that lapsed between the meeting and the sobor were obviously insufficient to obtain the release and transportation from prisons to the sobor for some of them; while others apparently continued to refuse to accept Sergii's post-1927 policy of cooperation with the regime as the condition of release. The catacomb Church was still a dynamic reality at that time.[20]

Patriarch Sergii and his Church, 1943-1944

The brief period between Sergii's "election" as the second postrevolutionary patriarch of the Russian Orthodox Church and

—perhaps because Nikolai had simply forgotten to mention it—and which may well have been true. According to it, in the middle of the conversation Georgy Karpov—the former head of the very department of the NKVD that had arrested and shot churchmen—appeared, and Stalin told the metropolitans that he would be appointed to head a liaison department between the Church and the state. "But," Sergii is alleged to have retorted, "is this not the same Karpov who had persecuted us?" "Precisely," replied Stalin, sadistically happy with the effect. "The Party used to order Karpov to persecute you, and he fulfilled the will of the Party. Now we shall order him to be your protector-guardian. I know Karpov, he is an obliging subordinate." Although this sounds very much like Stalin, the story may have been overdramatized, as it contradicts the amicable mood of the chat described by Levitin, particularly Stalin's last words to Sergii. See Popovsky, 373-5 and 505n.

[19]*Pravda o religii,* 141-2; and *Patriarkh Sergii,* 240-3. Information on Luka is from Popovsky, as above. None of these bishops' names appeared anywhere between 1939 and 1942.

[20]For instance, Bishop Afanasy (Sakharov) had refused to recognize the legitimacy of Sergii's administration but accepted Aleksii's election in 1945. Most

his death on May 15, 1944 was marked by the further consolida-
tion of the Church into a single unit by reestablishing regular
dioceses and appointing bishops to them. Some of these bishops
may have come out of exile and prisons, after having finally
agreed to accept Sergii and his pledge of total loyalty.[21] Others
were received back into the Church from the Renovationist schism
via repentance.[22] Some were newly ordained from the ranks of
widowed priests and surviving monastics with the necessary
education.[23] All in all, by the time the sobor gathered to elect the
new patriarch in January 1945, the number of diocesan bishops
recognizing the Sergii patriarchal administration had risen to
forty-one.

Sergii did not live to see the fulfilment of his main dream:
the reestablishment of regular theological education in Russia.
The first pastoral school and theological institute opened one
month after his death at the former Novodevichy Convent in
Moscow, later to be moved to the restored Holy Trinity-St.
Sergius Monastery, some forty-five miles northeast of the city.

Considerable efforts were made to achieve for the patriarchate
full and active recognition by the other local Orthodox churches.
Success in this field was reflected in the participation of the eastern patriarchs and/or their representatives in the 1945 Sobor.
More important perhaps was the recognition of the self-declared
autocephaly of the Georgian Orthodox Church by the Moscow
Patriarchate on November 10, 1943. The Georgian Church had
lost her ancient autocephaly upon the death of the last Georgian
patriarch, after the incorporation of Georgia into the Russian

"catacomb" clerics recognized Afanasy as their spiritual leader and therefore rejoined the Patriarchal Church with him in 1945. See Vasilevskaya, *Katakomby*,
2-8; also Regelson, 194-5.

[21]An anonymous catacomb bishop wrote in 1962 that Sergii's "concordat" with
Stalin caused much confusion and torment among fellow bishops in prison and
exile. Some returned to Sergii. One did so with the following comment: "All that
Metropolitan Sergii is doing is a very dirty business, but I want to return finally
home, after all!" Regelson, 192.

[22]See, for example, ibid., 514.

[23]Struve, 149-70. A passage from a letter from Sergii regarding a possible
candidate for the episcopacy from the ranks of the parish clergy throws some light
on the limitations on Sergii's freedom: "Fr. Mikhail Smirnov appeals to me very
much . . . Let him come to Moscow . . . If he leaves a proper impression on us and
if there is *no opposition from elsewhere* [italics ours], he can be consecrated."
Patriarkh Sergii, 94.

empire by Alexander I. During the brief independence of Georgia following the Bolshevik seizure of power in Russia, the Georgian Church unilaterally declared autocephaly, which Patriarch Tikhon refused to recognize. Consequently, between 1919 and 1943 the Georgian Church had no canonical intercommunion with any other Orthodox Church.

It is with these successful efforts at rebuilding the regular structure of the Church and of the unity of the Orthodox in the whole Soviet domain that Sergii's apologists credit him most of all. They lauded him upon his death as a genius with unique spiritual and canonical intuition and erudition who alone had been able to preserve, revive and properly direct the ship of the Church in the extremely "difficult, crisis-laden, politically crucial years of our motherland." Some saw him as a man who succeeded in "whitewashing the church vestments," which is more than dubious in the light of his obviously insincere maneuvers and declarations regarding the Soviet state. Even such an outstanding theologian living in conditions of political freedom in France as Vladimir N. Lossky praised "the great churchman . . . the great Sergii in whose life everything was great . . . he lived by the dogma of the Church . . . raised everything to the basic truths of the faith."[24] In short, they saw the revival of the Orthodox Church in the USSR in the war years as the result of Sergii's lifetime policies and efforts.

The Soviet religiologist Shishkin's remark regarding the Renovationist legacy inherited and perpetuated by the Patriarchal Church, only couched in the language of Orthodox traditionalism, has already been cited in chapter 2. What Shishkin's cynical oversimplification and the above eulogies have in common, however, is that both credit Sergii with saving the Church from utter annihilation.

His Orthodox critics, however, claim that the reversal in the fortune of religions was caused by the war, by the need to win the support of the nation in the struggle against the Nazis, by the need to respond to the great religious revival on the German side of the front and to give the nation an unwritten promise, as it were, that Stalin would not persecute the Church anymore and

[24]Ibid., 92-8, 163-281.

that she could openly exist and develop in Stalin's land as well, not only in Hitler's.[25]

Indeed, the reopening of the churches on Soviet territory, even after September 1943, was much more limited in numbers than it was under the Germans, as confirmed by the Soviet press itself. And, following the reports in the *Journal of the Moscow Patriarchate* on episcopal services in the local churches, as well as other bits and pieces of information that mention parishes by name, one can see that the greatest number of open churches was on the territories that had been under German occupation, and next come the territories adjacent to the frontline—where the movement had to match what was going on immediately on the other side of the front and where the church reopenings were meant to encourage the local people to patriotic exploits.[26] But the territories east of the Volga and particularly in Siberia saw very few of their churches reopened. For instance, Krasnoyarsk and its suburbs saw the reopening of only two churches during Archbishop Luka Voino-Yasenetsky's time there (1943-1944). The city of Gorky, with its population of a million and a half by the end of the 1970s, had only three churches functioning; Sverdlovsk, with a population of a million, one church, etc.[27]

The New Face of the Official Church

The duality of the newly reconstructed Church, in its contra-

[25]See the comments of the above anonymous bishop, for instance, in Regelson, 187-8.

[26]Fletcher, *Study in Survival*, 114, including n. 123, which refers to a dissertation claiming that the total number of Orthodox churches newly reopened on the territory that had not been under the German occupation did not exceed two thousand. Fletcher thinks this is a gross underestimate. But the fact is that of the less than seven thousand Orthodox churches functioning by the end of the 1970s, about five thousand were in the Ukraine, Belorussia, the Baltic republics and Moldavia (data provided by Soviet Russian clerics in 1979), while the bulk of the churches closed during Khrushchev's persecutions involved the western territories. In the majority of cases they were closed under the pretext that their reopening occurred under the occupation, which was illegal under Soviet law. See also P. Sokolov, "Put' russkoi pravoslavnoi tserkvi v Rossii i SSSR," in *Russkaya pravoslavnaya tserkov' SSSR* (Munich, 1962) 67-9.

[27]On Krasnoyarsk, see Popovsky, 340-1; on Gorky, multiple *samizdat* documents, including AS 197 (Gorky, September 1968). For more details see below in chapter 12.

dictory and mutually exclusive functions of serving God and lauding a theomachistic regime, revealed itself most vividly at the 1943 Sobor and soon after it.

The very first patriarchal report at the sobor, delivered by Sergii, contains some rather risky hints: "We did not need to think long on which position to take during the war . . . the fascists attacked our country, ruining her, leading away our countrymen to forced labor . . . Thus, a simple sense of decency did not allow us to take any other position."[28] The suggestion here is that the Church is quite apart from the state and has the moral right to choose a position of either loyalty or disloyalty to it. It really begs the question: And which position would the Church have taken, had the Soviet Union been attacked by someone else, who would have behaved quite decently?

On November 7, 1943, a solemn liturgy on the occasion of the 26th anniversary of the Bolshevik Revolution was celebrated by the patriarch, but the prayers of the liturgy were in reality dedicated to the taking of Kiev the day before: thanksgiving and prayers for those who fell in the war. The liturgy also included a prayer for "the God-protected country of ours, and for those who govern her with the God-given leader at the helm. Let the Lord grant them power to continue their great service for many years to come!"[29]

Soon after the sobor, a division of functions among the three top hierarchs became evident: Metropolitan Nikolai became engaged in promoting Soviet foreign policy interests; Metropolitan Aleksii concentrated on patriotic appeals to the faithful, organizing collections for the needs of the armed forces and for war invalids, etc.; and Patriarch Sergii's messages were mostly dedicated to moral-theological and pastoral issues.[30]

Although Metropolitan Aleksii's first published act as patriarchal locum tenens upon Sergii's death was a letter to Stalin in

[28]Report of September 8, in *ZhMP*, no. 1 (September 1943) 7-8.

[29]*ZhMP*, no. 4 (December 1943) 13-5. A similar thanksgiving service, allegedly to commemorate the twenty-seventh anniversary of Soviet power, was celebrated in the following year in Moscow and Leningrad (*ZhMP*, no. 11 [November 1944] 19-22). There are no reports of such services in other cities and churches. By the 1950s, however, and certainly after Stalin's death, there are no more reports on any such services in the journal.

[30]Compare, for instance, the Christmas messages of the patriarch and of Metropolitan Aleksii in *ZhMP*, no. 4 (December 1943).

which he assured him of unswerving loyalty, nevertheless he made his priorities clear: ". . . on the one hand I shall adhere to the canons and regulations of the Church; and on the other [I will adhere] with steadfast loyalty to the fatherland and to you as the head of the government." Note, however, that the Church comes first; and under Khrushchev's persecutions of the Church he was to show that these were not only empty words.[31]

Under Aleksii as patriarch, although his expressions of devotion to Stalin were often couched in even more sycophantic terms than those of the late Sergii, the "division of labor" between him as the spiritual and pastoral leader of the Russian Church and Nikolai as her "foreign minister" and man in charge of supporting Soviet propaganda was quite obvious.

Details of Metropolitan Nikolai's controversial political activities are to be found in William Fletcher's monograph *Nikolai.* Here we should like to mention only a few of his most salient activities during World War II, in addition to the ones already discussed. One of the first of these was his leaflet addressed to the Soviet anti-Nazi partisans and the local resistance of the population to the Germans, written on the occasion of the first anniversary of the German attack, June 22, 1942, and obviously distributed on the other side by Soviet military aircraft. Beginning in November 1942 and through 1943, the metropolitan issued addresses-appeals to the Orthodox Church and soldiers of Romania and to the peoples and churches of Yugoslavia, Czechoslovakia and Greece; while Nikolai became a member of the Soviet state-created Pan-Slavic Committee, appealing to fellow Slavs to support the Soviet struggle against the Nazis. One such appeal by Metropolitan Nikolai contained an unusual phrase for a Christian: "The Church is full of . . . holy hatred for the enemy." But this feeling may have been quite genuine, for even the saintly Archbishop Luka was guilty of such statements.[32] In one article in the *Journal of the Moscow Patriarchate* he demanded the death penalty for the Nazis, citing the law of Moses and other parts of the Old Testament. And he added that Christ's commandment, "Love thy neighbor," did not apply "to the German murderers . . . it is absolutely impossible to love them."

[31]Spinka (107-14) likewise stresses this point.
[32]*Patriarkh Sergii,* 45-6; Popovsky, 401-5.

Much more tragic in the Soviet context is his exclamation: "How shall we now preach the gospel of love and brotherhood to those who do not know Christ, but who have seen the satanic face of the German who claims to be a Christian?"[33]

This confusion between the leaders and the led is indeed surprising in a Soviet citizen, particularly in one of the foremost Christian victims of communism, who certainly distinguished between the peoples of the USSR and their communist oppressors. Luka obviously wrote this in full sincerity, as his whole life gives ample proof of his unbending courage and fearlessness. This fact tells us something very frightening about the state of the minds and emotions of people toward the end of World War II.

As to the resurrected *Journal of the Moscow Patriarchate*, its wartime issues are full of highly patriotic articles emphasizing the patriotic tradition and role of the Orthodox Church throughout Russian history. There are also many reports on such activities of individual parishes as sending church choirs to hospitals to entertain the wounded with programs of secular songs, organizing voluntary (unpaid) services by church members as nurses' aides, orderlies and the like to take care of the wounded and invalids.[34] Strictly speaking, all this charity work was illegal in terms of Soviet law.

The Sobor of 1945 and the First Acts of Patriarch Aleksii

Although the European war ended in May 1945, there was still the war with Japan, and generally, as far as the Church was concerned, 1945 could be treated as one chronological unit.

The most important single event of 1945 was the sobor that met from January 31 to February 2, 1945, which unanimously elected Aleksii the thirteenth patriarch of Russia and promulgated the new Statute (*Polozhenie*) on the structure and administration of the Church. According to a reliable source, at the Coun-

[33]*ZhMP*, respectively, no. 2 (1944) 26-8, and no. 4 (1943) 25.
[34]See, for example, the reports from Kaluga, Tula and Penza in *ZhMP*, no. 4 (1943) 30-1; and T.M. Bogoslovsky, "Patriarkh Germogen—velikii patriot zemli russkoi"; anonymous, "Sv. svyashchennomuchenik Isidor"; and Mikhail Arkhangelsky, "Patriotizm pravoslavnogo dukhovenstva," all in *ZhMP*, no. 1 (1944).

cil of Bishops that met on November 21, 1944 to elect a Preconciliar Commission for the sobor, Archbishop Luka reminded the bishops that, according to the canons of the 1917 Sobor, elections of the patriarch ought to be secret, with a free choice of candidates. In view of the uncanonical promotion of Metropolitan Aleksii as the sole eligible candidate, he was voting against him. Consequently, the only Russian bishop not invited to participate in the actual 1945 Sobor, with its forty-one Russian and five foreign guest bishops, was Luka.[35]

It is curious that an authoritative publication of the patriarchate states that Aleksii was approved for the post because he had been appointed locum tenens by the late Patriarch Sergii in his will and because Aleksii was the most senior of the ruling bishops according to his year of consecration.[36] Obviously, none of the above grounds has anything to do with the canons, which, as mentioned earlier, expressly forbid ruling bishops to name their successors. This canon had been overruled by the Sobor of 1917-1918 only as an emergency measure for the troubled times. The fact that such an expert canonist as Sergii decided to break it once again seems to indicate that he feared worse times could come again and felt that his reconstituted church organization was insecure.

The Statute, which had probably been drafted still under Patriarch Sergii, differed considerably from the spirit and letter of the resolutions of the 1917-1918 Sobor and its legislation. The difference starts with the prerogatives of the patriarch. Whereas, according to the 1917 regulations, and in accordance with the regulations of other Orthodox patriarchates, the patriarch is primus inter pares in relation to other bishops, administers the Church collegially with synods of bishops and is accountable to them as well as to periodically elected sobors of the whole Church, the 1945 Statute imposes no limitations and accountability upon the patriarch. True, like the Soviet Constitution, it does pay lip service to church democracy, but that is all: ". . . the supreme authority in ministry, church administration

---

[35]Popovsky, 397-8. Characteristically, not a single church publication of the sobor gives any hint of either this incident or of Luka's absence from the sobor. See, for instance, A.I. Georgievsky's reminiscences on the sobor in ZhMP, no. 2 (1971) 18-21.

[36]Pr. G-y, "Patriarkhi moskovskie," ZhMP, no. 9 (1944) 16.

and ecclesiastical justice—legislative, administrative and judicial —belongs to the national sobor, which is to be elected periodically and to consist of bishops, priests and laymen." The difference between this formula and that of the 1917 regulations was that the latter had stipulated that the periodicity of sobor sessions had to be specified and that the sobors would have controlling powers over the patriarch and over all his other administrative institutions—i.e., the patriarch was to be fully accountable to the sobors. In addition, the 1917-1918 Sobor stipulated: a council of all bishops of the land to meet on special occasions (e.g., for the trial of the patriarch); a Synod of twelve bishops to be permanently in session under the presidency of the patriarch (the metropolitan of Kiev ex officio, in addition to the patriarch, plus six diocesan bishops chosen by the national sobor and five diocesan bishops called to its meetings by the patriarch and the permanent Synod members for half-year sessions on a rotation basis); and a permanent Supreme Ecclesiastical Council of three bishops chosen by the Synod and six priests and six laymen chosen by the sobor.

The 1945 Sobor stipulated that:

> the patriarch, with the permission of the government, convenes a council of all diocesan bishops, and presides over it, in order to solve particularly important church problems. When the need arises to hear the voice of the parish clergy and laity, and if external conditions permit this, the patriarch convenes the national sobor and presides over it.

It also set up a Synod consisting of: the patriarch as its president, the metropolitans of Kiev, Leningrad and Krutitsy (Moscow) — ex officio—plus three bishops chosen by the patriarch and the permanent members of the Synod for one half-yearly session according to seniority.

Thus, the only permanent collegial body common to both structures is the Synod of Bishops, but even this body was much more authoritarian in structure than its 1917 predecessor.

The Statute says nothing on how the clerical and lay delegates to the sobor are to be elected and in what proportion to their numbers in each diocese (presumably, every bishop participates in the sobor ex officio, as in 1917-1918). At the 1917-1918 Sobor, each diocese elected two priests and three laymen, in addition to the diocesan bishop; at the 1945 Sobor there were 46 bishops, 87 priests and only 37 laymen.

The weakest point of the Statute, however, was its total lack of delineations of functions and prerogatives of the different bodies of church administration, including those of the patriarch. The only clearly stated function of the sobor became the election of a new patriarch on the death or demise—in whatever form—of his predecessor. And, in fact, since 1945 the only time a national sobor did gather in the USSR was in 1971, to elect Pimen as the new patriarch.

As to the meetings of councils of bishops of the whole land, on several occasions instead of such a session the patriarch would simply send telegrams to all bishops with a request for approval of a certain decision, whereupon the resulting decree would appear as a conciliar decision of a council of bishops. Besides the sobors of bishops, which met to prepare the national sobors to elect the patriarchs in 1945 and 1971, one of the few actual physical sobors or councils of bishops took place in 1961.

Indeed, the 1945 Sobor regulations were incompatible with the law of 1929 and other Soviet laws on religion. To begin with, they introduced a highly centralized structure of church administration, clerically and episcopally oriented, with the authoritarian and autocratic figure of the patriarch at the top, resembling that of the Roman Catholic Church, and wholly incompatible with Soviet law, which, strictly speaking, recognized only a group of twenty laymen renting a church building from the state as the only legal religious body. No trace of the parson's or bishop's tenure, established by the 1917-1918 Sobor, is left in 1945. The patriarch appoints, removes and moves around bishops at will, albeit with the approval of the Synod. The bishops have to submit annual reports on their dioceses to the patriarch. He instructs them and issues orders to them as a supreme leader.

In the dioceses there is a similar authoritative relationship of the local bishop to the deans of groups of parishes, and of the latter toward the parish priests. At will, a diocesan bishop may organize a diocesan council consisting of parish priests, but he may just as well administer the diocese on his own via his chancery. Again, there are no regulations on how such a council ought to be chosen and of what proportion of priests in the diocese. Contrary to Soviet secular laws, the bishop is the sole superior of the local priests, who are accountable to him and whom he can, theoretically, remove and appoint at will.[37]

Even the prerogatives of the "twenty," so favored by the Soviets, were undermined by this "legislation," which now termed them "parish communities." The organs of the community are: the parish meeting and a parish council of three members, plus a three-member auditing commission—both elected by the parish meeting. In contrast to the 1929 legislation, according to which the priest was simply a hired employee of the "group of twenty," under the 1945 regulations he became the chairman of the parish community, as well as of the parish meeting and of the parish council[38] (only until 1961, however).

It is a paradox that the same Sergii who had advocated the maximum possible democratization, collegiality and lay participation in the Church in 1905 was now the author, or at least the inspirer, of the centralized and almost papist church structure advocated in 1905 by none other than Metropolitan Antony (Khrapovitsky), the future head of the émigré Synod and Sergii's greatest antagonist in the 1930s. Apparently, Sergii and Aleksii wanted to match the Soviet administrative structure by their church centralization, hoping that such a centralized Church would be stronger and could better withstand future trials and attacks of an ideologically incompatible and hostile state.

It may be of interest that the latest church *samizdat* voices have again begun to advocate decentralization of the Church,

[37]It is an open question to what extent the bishops and the patriarch really became autocrats and to what extent this formula in fact concealed the government manipulation of both. See the Tuchkov offer to Metropolitan Kirill in chapter 3 above, pp. 105-6.

[38]Although some of the comments and interpretation of the information on the Statute and its effects may be ours, the citations and the professional analysis are summarized from the following two works by the outstanding canonist, the late Prof. Alexander Bogolepov: *Tserkov' pod vlast'yu kommunizma*, 32-46; and "Pravovoe polozhenie russkoi pravoslavnoi tserkvi v SSSR," in *Russkaya pravoslavnaya tserkov'*, 113-46.

Such a detailed summary of these works is presented because they are not available in English. During our last meeting with the late professor he encouraged us to continue this work.

claiming that decentralized autonomous dioceses could be more dynamic and operational in reacting to the secular powers' pressures and in catering to the needs of the growing numbers of believers; and that it is easier for the state to control a Church with a centralized apparatus than a pluralist Church, with a multitude of independent units.[39] Although it is hard to pass judgment on these opposing views, it is worth noting that if the above motives were behind Sergii's and Aleksii's centralizing measures, they appear to have ignored the very important provisos, undoubtedly inserted by Karpov's council, which made the powers of the priests, bishops and even the patriarch himself rather nebulous and conditional, to say the least.

Article 16 of the Statute says that the patriarch, *not the patriarchate,* has an official stamp registered with the appropriate civil authorities. This means that, before a bishop is elected patriarch, the secular authorities must be asked whose stamp they will agree to register—i.e., the candidate for the patriarchal throne is thus predetermined. Hence, there were no contestants for the post at either the 1943, the 1945 or the 1971 sobors. The same applies to the stamp of a diocesan bishop or of a parish dean—none of them can be appointed to his post without advance approval by the Soviet authorities in charge of church affairs. Moreover, the diocesan bishop "must coordinate his actions with the . . . local representative of the Council for Russian Orthodox Church Affairs."

The highly authoritative Orthodox Church canonist, Professor Alexander Bogolepov, concludes that the controlling authority of the chairman of the state's Council for Russian Orthodox Church Affairs (henceforth, CROCA) is at least parallel to that of the prerevolutionary overprocurator of the Synod, with the important difference that the latter represented a state that was sympathetic to the Church, while the Soviet official represents a state at war with her.[40] In every province, the CROCA is represented by a local plenipotentiary and his staff.

Other acts of the Soviet government testifying to its de facto recognition of the Church as a legal person were the granting

---

[39]A good example is Nikolai Gerasimov, "Vkhozhdenie v tserkov' i ispovedanie Tserkvi v tserkvi," *VRKhD,* no. 128 (1979) 70-8.
[40]Bogolepov, *Tserkov',* 41-2 and 34.

of typographical equipment for religious publications and permission to open workshops or small factories to produce candles, icons and other objects of Orthodox worship and piety. Whereas the latter right was reflected in the Statute, the former was not.[41] It seems that in later years, probably in 1959-1964, the printing equipment was confiscated from the Church, and she was again forced to use the state printing establishments, by no means favorably disposed toward church orders.[42]

Indeed, the whole 1945 affair was highly deceptive. The Statute was clearly incompatible with the whole trend of Soviet laws on the Church from 1918 to 1931. Their toleration by Stalin and his successors between 1945 and 1961 gave the illusion that they might soon be followed by a major revision of the Soviet laws on religion to accommodate them to the new de facto situation. The proper way for the leaders of the Moscow Patriarchate was to raise the issue of amending the state laws on religion right during the meeting with Stalin in 1943, or at least on the eve of the 1945 Sobor, while the war was still on and Stalin was still flirting with the Church. As it turned out, the Soviet government orally approved the new church regulations (for otherwise they could not have been promulgated or even presented at the 1945 Sobor), and perhaps promised to amend its own legislation accordingly some time after the end of the war, but it never formally endorsed these regulations by any official act. It inserted the above provisos concerning the official stamp attached to the person of the bishop rather than to his office to avoid granting the Church de jure recognition as a legal person. Thus, it left the Church as a body still, strictly speaking, outside the normal Soviet legal structure, and therefore subject to attack at any time and to being deprived of the de facto privileges of the 1943-1945 era, which were never confirmed de jure.[43]

[41]Ibid., 48 etc.

[42]Recounting this incident to me in 1963 (in Geneva), the late Metropolitan Nikodim said with annoyance that the printing press had been lying about without being used, and that is why it was finally taken away. The real explanation might have been that its use was prevented by Soviet authorities by refusing to allocate printing paper, ink, lead, etc., so that the patriarchate was forced to use the state printing houses instead.

[43]A 1971 official internal manual "for business use," giving laws and regulations regarding "religious associations" in the USSR (revised to include the 1975

During World War II, the Church organized voluntary collections and donations not only for war needs, but also for war orphans and invalids, etc. This action was particularly prominent under Patriarch Aleksii, beginning in 1944. For obvious reasons, this was tolerated by the regime during the war years. Stalin even sent thanks to the Russian Orthodox Church for these activities,[44] although they were in breach of the 1929 legislation banning any church charities. The Statute, however, took advantage of the precedent and expanded somewhat on the financial rights of the Church. For example, article 41 obligated the parish executive organ "to contribute necessary sums for the upkeep of the diocesan bishop and his administration, . . . and for general needs of the Church: the patriarchal administration, . . . for the support of theological education."

This resulted in the opening of patriarchal, diocesan and parish bank accounts, formerly banned. The same article legalized church donations for patriotic needs,[45] which originally might

amendments), repeats several times that religious associations and "executive organs of religious congresses and conferences do not enjoy any rights of legal persons." (The Administrative Code of the Ukrainian SSR, chapter 2, article 360; Instruction . . . of the All-Russian Central Executive Committee Presidium's Permanent Commission on Religious Cults, article 13 [1931]). "The decisions and decrees of religious congresses and conferences and of their executive bodies and of the so-called spiritual administrations can be executed by the believers only voluntarily"— i.e., they have no legal force even over the believers, as far as Soviet law is concerned (ibid., article 12). Moreover, "Religious centers, religious associations and clerics are forbidden . . . to apply any disciplinary or punitive measures toward the believers" (March 16, 1961, Instruction . . . of the Council of Ministers of the USSR . . . On the Application of the Religious Legislation . . ., article 10/g). See Zakonodatel'stvo, 133, 111, 109, 80.

There is also a discrepancy between the sobor by-laws and Soviet legislation on the stamp. The former says that all executive organs of the Church have the right to possess a stamp and use it, as long as it does not contain the official slogans and emblems of the Soviet state—i.e., again it is outside of Soviet law, for without such emblems it has no legal value as far as Soviet state officials are concerned. See the 1929 legislation on religious associations, as amended in 1975, article 23, in ibid., 15 et passim; and information supplied us by Soviet Russian clerics on problems with state officials arising therefrom.

[44]Fletcher, Study in Survival, 110-1; Bogolepov, Tserkov', 53. A most notable single example of this is Archbishop Luka's donation to the War Orphans' Fund of 130,000 rubles out of the 200,000 he had received in 1944 as the Stalin Prize for his book Notes on Purulent Medicine (Popovsky, 385-6). The remaining 70,000 he gave to his children, relatives and needy members of his diocese. All charity work is expressly forbidden to the Church. See Zakonodatel'stvo, 13, 109 etc.

[45]Fletcher, Study in Survival, 46-7.

have been a euphemism for charities but with time became arbitrary removals by the Soviet authorities of huge sums of money from church bank accounts for the so-called Peace Funds.[46] Legalization of parish bank accounts brought the parish very close to the status of a legal person, although the Church continues to be deprived of the right to own a house of prayer (it still has to be leased by a "twenty" from the state free of charge but subject to property taxes levied in accordance with the highest tax scale). Nevertheless, the bank account was not in the name of the "twenty" but in the name of the parish, and checks had to be cosigned by the parish rector and the warden. Since 1961, the priests have lost all financial control functions. The checks now have to be signed by the three members of the parish executive and endorsed by the local village or town soviet. The tactic is often used, for instance, when major repairs of a church building are required. On the basis of the soviet's refusal to endorse the checks, the bank blocks the church funds, whereupon an architectural or fire-safety commission shuts the church as unsafe for use and the priest is deprived of registration, i.e., of the right to legally perform his priestly duties.[47] This, apparently, indicates the existence of unpublished secret instructions, which operate in all spheres of Soviet life in addition and often in contradiction to the written laws.

As we have already mentioned, both Sergii and Aleksii failed to win any real concessions in the area of religious education for children, although William Fletcher, somewhat erroneously, interpreted Karpov's press interview of 1944 as evidence that religious education for church classes of children had been legalized and had begun. In fact, all Karpov said was that parents could invite a priest to teach religion to their children or even send children to a priest's residence for this purpose. Professor Bogolepov rightly stresses that no changes were made in the 1929 legislation forbidding any religious instruction to groups of more than three children at a time; and, if the instruction is done by persons other than the children's parents, "their pedagogical qualifications must be verified and approved by the local Depart-

[46]Information orally supplied by a Soviet Russian cleric (June 1980).
[47]Same source as in n. 49 below.

ment of National Education."[48] The latter, being an atheistically programmed body, would never dare qualify a priest as a pedagogue. So, in practical terms, the priest is excluded from acting as a religious teacher to anybody but his own children. There were no amendments to this in the 1945 church regulations. The most that did happen in the religiously "most liberal" 1940s would be the occasional basic catechetical talks by priests for children after services in some churches with the aid of slides illustrating texts from the New and Old Testaments. Occasionally a family would invite a priest home for dinner, over which he would informally lead a catechetical conversation for interested adults or children as the case may be, or a child might receive answers to theological problems during confession.[49]

As soon as Metropolitan Aleksii took over as locum tenens, he assured Stalin in a telegram that he would continue Sergii's course of church direction and administration and would demonstrate his love and devotion to Stalin. Stalin's first public act of approval of Aleksii's activities was a telegram of October 24, 1944, in which he thanked Aleksii for his extensive patriotic work and generous church donations for war orphans. Soon after his election, the new patriarch was received by Stalin on April 10, 1945, in the presence of Stalin's foreign minister Molotov. On the Church's side, Aleksii was accompanied by Metropolitan Nikolai of Krutitsy, who became the head of the Russian Orthodox Church's Department of External Ecclesiastical Relations. Hence, apparently, the conversations dealt with foreign policy, and the

---

[48]Fletcher, *Study in Survival*, 114 (including nn. 122 and 123); Bogolepov, *Tserkov'*, 49.

[49]Vasilevskaya, 147-8; and oral testimonies by Fr. Konstantin Tivetsky and his wife (San Francisco, June 1980). Similar information on such informal talks was given to me by a recent émigré from Moscow, Valentina Las (Boston, July 1980). Fr. Tivetsky—who had begun his theological studies in 1945, was ordained priest in 1951, concluded his theological studies in 1955 and served as a priest in Moscow and three provincial cities in the period 1951 to 1979—has never heard of any priest teaching religion to any children but his own and said that such attempts would invariably result in the priest's losing his secular registration, without which he could not legally serve in any church. The 1929 ban on any special religious meetings for youth, children or women, as well as on any religious instruction, organization of study, art, literature circles, etc., attached to the churches, was once again emphatically restated in the above-quoted 1961 instruction on the application of laws of religious cults. See *Zakonodatel'stvo*, article 17/v in the 1929 legislation and article 8 in the instruction, pp. 14 and 79, respectively.

Church was requested to actively promote Soviet state interests on the international church front, for that seems to be the only correct description of the many subsequent speeches and Soviet propaganda activities by Metropolitan Nikolai, in particular.

On May 28, Patriarch Aleksii departed on a pilgrimage to the Holy Land, no doubt on Stalin's approval or even instigation during the recent meeting. This was the first ever pilgrimage of a Russian patriarch to the Holy Land, and it was at least as much political as religious. The purpose was obviously to impress the noncommunist world that the Russian Church was a genuine and "free" institution, i.e., that the Soviet state had changed for the better and that all anticommunist propaganda in this respect was grossly exaggerated.

On the way back from the Holy Land, the patriarch visited Egypt and the Patriarch of Alexandria. There an émigré Russian parish joined the Moscow Patriarchate. From Egypt he proceeded to Beirut, where he met the Patriarch of Antioch, and by the end of June he was back in Moscow. Throughout the visit he was received by heads of states and other political and religious dignitaries.

But the main foreign policy role, as already mentioned, was performed throughout by Metropolitan Nikolai, who, by the way, did not return to Russia with the patriarch but made an official return visit to Great Britain. There he made a speech on fascism as the greatest enemy of humanity, Christianity and civilization at London University. At a reception given in York, the Archbishop of York, dancing to the latest tune of the Moscow Patriarchate, attacked the Vatican as a common adversary of Orthodoxy and Anglicanism and claimed that theologically the latter two churches were practically the same. Metropolitan Nikolai was received by King George VI at the Buckingham Palace. He also officiated and preached at the local Russian Orthodox church, which had just joined the Moscow Patriarchate.[50]

CHAPTER 7

The Church during the Second World War: German-occupied Territory[1]

Nazi Church Policy for Russia

Hitler and the Emigrés

Hitler's earliest contacts with the extreme right monarchist circles of the Russian émigrés go back to his Munich days and Alfred Rosenberg, a Baltic German who had been a student at the Kiev University prior to enlisting in the Russian Army in

[1]The most authoritative books on this subject in English, utilizing practically all the documents available to a western scholar at the present time, are Harvey Fireside's *Icon and Swastika* and Wassilij Alexeev's and Theofanis G. Stavrou's *The Great Revival*. Most of the material and factual data in this chapter are taken from these two books, as well as from such earlier studies as Friedrich Heyer's *The Orthodox Church in the Ukraine,* John Armstrong's *Ukrainian Nationalism* and Alexander Dallin's *German Rule in Russia.* Fireside concentrates on the details of the German church policies, both in Germany and in the USSR, but is a little thinner on the actual church revival under the German occupation and, writing as an outsider, fails to understand some issues of the Orthodox Church and her dilemmas. Alexeev and Stavrou, on the other hand, concentrate on the religious response of the Soviet people under the German occupation and treat the internal church question with greater understanding and detail. Consequently, this chapter is largely a summary of Heyer's, Fireside's and Stavrou-Alexeev's books, supplementing their data only in places where we were not entirely convinced by their conclusions.

Since completing this chapter we have inspected the German war documents at the YIVO Institute of Jewish Culture in New York, on which much of the material in the above-mentioned books is based, and found no reason to revise this brief overview of the events. The more inquisitive reader is, of course, advised to read the above books and, indeed, the documents themselves for additional details.

World War I. Rosenberg had only returned to the nation of his ancestors in 1919, and eventually became a top Nazi ideologist.[2] In Germany, Rosenberg encountered members of the Russian émigré Supreme Monarchist Council, which had been formed in Bad Reichenhal (only a few miles from Berchtesgaden, Hitler's future "Eagle's Nest") in 1921. His other East European contacts included General Skoropadsky, the German-installed hetman ("monarch") of the Ukraine of 1918. Some of Rosenberg's contacts were wealthy and helped finance his Nazi newspaper, *Voelkischer Beobachter*, where they published their anti-Semitic articles.[3] It may be recalled that these same Bad Reichenhal monarchists had been responsible for the partisan monarchist direction and politicization of the 1921 Karlovci Sobor, which cost the Church in Russia so dearly.[4] In these early monarchist-Nazi contacts a plan was discussed to build up cadres of Russian clerics for future use in Russia.[5]

Such top extreme right monarchists as Makharoblidze, Count Grabbe and Rklitsky (the future Karlovcian archbishop and Antony's official biographer) soon became the top secular operatives of the Karlovci Synod. It was apparently through their intrigues and with Nazi support that the Synod uncanonically deprived Metropolitan Evlogy of Paris of jurisdiction over his parishes in Germany. After the Nazis had come to power, almost all Evlogy's remaining parishes in Germany were taken away from him and handed over by the Nazis to the Karlovcian Bishop

---

[2]Dallin, 24-5.

[3]Fireside, *Icon and Swastika* (Cambridge, Mass.: Harvard University Press, 1971) 59 and 77; Alen Bullock, *Hitler: A Study in Tyranny* (London: Penguin Books, 1975) 79.

[4]See chapter 3 above, and Evlogy, *Put'*, 384-5 and 396-7.

Ironically, one of the leading monarchists, the Grand Duke Kirill Vladimirovich, had been the first commanding officer in 1917 to lead his Volhynian Guards regiment to pledge an oath of loyalty to the Provisional Government and the first (probably, the only) member of the Romanov family to decorate his uniform with a red ribbon—a sign of support of the revolution. In the 1930s he endorsed the monarcho-national-socialist movement of the "Young Russians," who proclaimed themselves the "Second Soviet Party" and whose central slogan was the "Tsar and the Soviets." They elected Kirill's son, Vladimir (now the official heir-apparent of the émigré monarchists) their royal patron. Toward the end of the 1930s and during and after World War II many members of the movement became Soviet patriots and returned to the USSR, including their head, Kazem-Bek.

[5]Fireside, 77.

Tikhon of Berlin.[6] Moreover, in 1938 the Nazi government erected a beautiful Orthodox cathedral for the Karlovcians and also financed major repairs on nineteen other Orthodox churches in Germany. But by then the Nazis apparently wanted a German to head the Orthodox diocese of Germany, and one was found in the person of Archbishop Serafim (Lade), who had converted to Orthodoxy in Russia and was consecrated bishop by the Ukrainian Renovationists. It is curious that the Karlovcian Synod, which has always prided itself as a defender of strict Orthodoxy, found it possible to accept this man without questioning the validity of his episcopal consecration, whereas the Moscow Patriarchate, even during the worst years of persecution, never accepted any Renovationist clerics without repentance on their part, and always reducing them to the status they had been in prior to joining the schism.[7]

During the war, Archbishop Serafim was elevated to the title of metropolitan, and the Nazis named him "Leader of all Orthodox in the Third Reich and in all the territories it controlled." It was apparently in fulfilment of the already mentioned monarchist plans that in 1939 a Nazi government-sponsored Orthodox Theological Faculty was established in Breslau (Wroclaw), in eastern Germany, with the blessing of Metropolitan Anastasy, the head of the Karlovci Synod.[8] Although Serafim was technically a member of the Karlovci Synod, after the Soviet-German war had

[6]Evlogy, *Put'*, 646-8. Bullock (93) mentions General Biskupsky as one of the monarchist émigrés whom Hitler met in Munich in 1923. He was later directly involved in wresting the Evlogy parishes away from him, while also becoming the head of Russian émigré Nazis in Berlin.

[7]Fireside, 77; see also Archbishop Aleksii of Ufa's article in *Pravda o religii v Rossii*, 160-1, where it is stated that Serafim had been banned from conducting services for having joined the Renovationist schism. Bishop Leonty adds that Serafim presented to the Karlovcians a 1927 document, according to which the Ukrainian Renovationists had not gone to the extremes of the Moscow ones. Leonty's own descriptions of the Renovationists in the Ukraine do not bear out this claim. See his ms. *Political Controls*.

[8]Fireside, 78. In 1938 Anastasy sent a message of thanks to Hitler for the building of the Orthodox cathedral for the Russians in Berlin. The Karlovcians later denied that this was an act of approval of Hitler's regime, only a formal act of thankful acknowledgment of Hitler's action in this particular case. See: "Ot kantselarii arkhiereiskogo sinoda," no. 12 (August 1947) 1; and the English translation of the message below, appendix 5. During the war, however, when Hitler's policy toward the Slavs became known, Anastasy allegedly refused to yield to the German demand to appeal to the Russian people to support Hitler.

broken out the Nazi government showed itself in no hurry to permit the Synod to leave its virtual captivity in Yugoslavia—they wanted the racially more acceptable Serafim to head any church activities that might spring up on the occupied territory. Only in 1943, after the election of Sergii as Patriarch of Russia, did the Germans bring the Karlovci Synod in corpore to Vienna for a joint session with Serafim, in order to issue a resolution condemning Sergii and declaring his election null and void. Henceforth, the Synod would be kept in Germany, eventually to take care of the religious needs of the Vlasov Army and of other Russian anti-Soviet military formations.[9] But as far as the Soviet territory under German occupation was concerned, both the Synod and Metropolitan Serafim with his Breslau school proved irrelevant and obsolete. The religious revival there was spontaneous and took care of its own church needs, aided by the neighbor churches of Latvia, Poland and Romania.

The Nazi-Occupation Church Policies in the USSR

Before looking specifically at the religious revival, let us first have a look at the Nazi church policies for the occupied Russian territories. These, naturally, reflected the general Nazi-German policies and attitudes toward the Slavs in general and toward the Russians in particular. Fireside sees as many as seven mutually exclusive policies emanating from different German state agencies. But to simplify matters, we list only three obvious ones: (1) Hitler's, which saw the Slavs in general as subhuman, to be used as slaves for the German race; (2) Rosenberg's, which aimed at cultivating the loyalties of the ethnic minorities of the USSR by promising them their own national states and by instigating in all of them hatred toward the Russians as a nation, if necessary identifying the Russian nation with the communist ideology and communist oppression (which, of course, would have required differential treatment, granting some privileges to various minorities, for which Hitler had no use); and (3) the Wehrmacht's, which saw the Russians as potential allies against Bolshevism and

---

[9]For details on these forces, see Wilfred Strick-Strickfeld's *Gegen Stalin und Hitler* (Mainz, 1970).

therefore was against any mention of any future splitting of Russia and was in favor of setting up Russian anti-Soviet military forces as allies of the Germans. The Vlasov Army and the Cossack units were products of this latter policy, which was obviously incompatible with the other two policies and practices.[10]

Rosenberg's line, moreover, was incompatible with the hopes of his earlier Russian-monarchist associates. In addition, Rosenberg, as the chief party ideologist, was a militant atheist, a hater of Christianity in general and of the Roman Catholic Church in particular. His contempt for everything Russian and Slavonic was such that he saw no danger to his ideology in Orthodoxy, considering it only an " 'oriental custom with nice songs,' which amounted to little more than 'fetishism.' " Therefore, in his view, "German administrators could afford to be indulgent about such practices; they might even be fostered as a means of keeping Slavic subjects tractable."[11]

Although Hitler appointed Rosenberg the Reichskommissar in charge of the Eastern Territories, the actual commissars—Erich Koch of the Ukraine and Lohse of Belorussia and the Baltic area from Lithuania to Leningrad—were also Hitler's appointees. They had no use for the idea of courting the non-Russian nationalities and largely ignored Rosenberg. The spontaneous mass reopening of churches in the occupied areas, sometimes accomplished with material help provided by local Wehrmacht commanding personnel,[12] and the mass religious enthusiasm of the population, however, forced Rosenberg to revise his earlier views about the unimportance of the "eastern religion." At the same time, he tried to impress the German administrators in Russia (or Ostland, as it was officially termed) that he was still their boss by writing his "Tolerance Edict" of June 1942, which prescribed a policy toward the Church in that area. The edict was never published in full, owing to the opposition of Bormann, and shorter published versions were issued separately by Lohse and Koch. Since, in terms of party discipline, Lohse and Koch were responsible to Bormann

[10]Ibid. (Russian edition: *Protiv Stalina i Gitlera* [Frankfurt am Main, 1975] 40-52); Fireside, 76-80; etc., Dallin, 44-58.

[11]Fireside, 73. Fireside's confusion between things Russian and Soviet leads him to the misreading of Rosenberg's proseparatist and rabidly anti-Russian ideas as "pro-Russian" (79 and 82).

[12]Strick-Strickfeld, 25; Fireside, 120.

rather than to Rosenberg, their superior in the less important government hierarchy, the latter lost control even over "his" church policy.[13]

In essence, the "edicts" amounted to a proclamation of religious freedom and of the right of believers to form religious associations. At the same time, like the Soviet laws, they emphasized the individual religious association as a self-contained religious unit—in order to limit the administrative authority of bishops and to prevent the rise of powerful national churches. Much emphasis was put on the prevention of the rise and development of a Russian Church on the occupied territories, for fear that it might recognize the authority of the Moscow Patriarchate. Instead, all support was to be given to an independent or autocephalous Orthodox Church in the Ukraine, where "the basic rule must be that the language of all associations be exclusively Ukrainian and that all priests belong to the Ukrainian populace." Similarly, autocephalous Belorussian, Latvian and Estonian Orthodox churches were prescribed for the respective territories. In actual practice, however, while Lohse tolerated a well-organized and unified Russian church organization in the Baltic states, with active missions in the genuinely Russian areas immediately to the south and west of Leningrad, he kept Belorussia apart, trying hard, but with little success, to cultivate Belorussian church nationalism. Erich Koch followed the policy of "divide and rule" more closely in the Ukraine. At first he had supported the Ukrainian Autocephalist movement, but when this Church, although attracting a minority of Ukrainian believers, began to show signs of growing into a potent national body, "he had his staff give desultory aid to rival religious organizations," namely, the Autonomous Orthodox Church of the Ukraine.[14]

Berlin's "ire was aroused when, in violation of the regulations, the Army and Abwehr sanctioned the movement of émigré priests . . . into the East during the first weeks of the occupation." All such missionary activities, as well as any active aid by the Wehrmacht in reopening the churches and/or participation of German military chaplains and personnel in services in the reopened churches, were henceforth strictly prohibited by Berlin. This

[13]Fireside, 83-5; Dallin, 478-82.
[14]Fireside, 83-7.

greatly disappointed the Wehrmacht command, who argued: "No move could have helped German propaganda more than the first religious service held in a church . . ."[15] But let us now turn to the actual church revival under the German occupation.

The Great Revival

The Pskov Mission

During the interwar period, the Orthodox churches of Latvia and Estonia, under the pressure of their increasingly nationalistic governments, had broken with the Moscow Patriarchate and transferred their allegiance to Constantinople. As this change of allegiance was unilateral, without canonical release from the mother Church—i.e., the Moscow Patriarchate—the latter never recognized its validity. In Lithuania, on the other hand, where the Orthodox Church was limited almost exclusively to the Russian and Belorussian ethnic minorities, there was no such transfer. After the break between Moscow and Metropolitan Evlogy of Paris in 1931, it was the head of the Orthodox Church of Lithuania, Archbishop Elevfery, who was appointed by Metropolitan Sergii as his exarch for Europe, simultaneously being elevated to the title of metropolitan.

When the Soviet Union occupied the Baltic republics in 1940, the local Orthodox churches were urged by the Moscow Patriarchate to return to its fold, which the metropolitans of Estonia and Latvia (respectively, an ethnic Estonian and an ethnic Latvian) duly did. Metropolitan Elevfery died on January 1, 1941, whereupon Archbishop Sergii (Voskresensky), who had been the Moscow Patriarchate's "ambassador-at-large" in the Baltic area, was appointed the metropolitan-exarch for the region.

When the Germans approached Latvia, the younger Metropolitan Sergii ignored the Soviet order of evacuation and hid in the cellars of the Riga Orthodox cathedral, resurfacing only upon the German occupation of Riga. He left no clue as to why he chose to remain on German-occupied territory. Professors Alexeev

[15]Dallin, 476-8.

and Stavrou think that his decision may have been motivated by the desire to secure a safer future for the patriarchate in case of German victory and the consequent need for the patriarchate to work under the Germans.[16] The barely forty-two-year-old metropolitan struck all those who knew him as a very gifted and far-seeing administrator with considerable diplomatic gifts and carefully planned actions and policies. Thus, he was not the kind of person who would be likely to act on the spur of the moment. Moreover, his behavior under the Germans demonstrated a carefully thought out course of action.

As soon as the Soviets were gone, the Estonian Metropolitan Alexander and the Latvian Avgustin tried to reestablish their independence from Moscow. But exarch Sergii, in his memorandum to the Germans of November 12, 1941, argued that it would do more harm than good for the Germans to revive the Latvian and Estonian church dependence on Constantinople, as the Constantinopolitan exarch for Western Europe lived in London and was rather intimately connected with British government circles. He argued that it was in the German interest to accept the canonically more regular system of ecclesiastic dependence on Moscow, with Ostland as an exarchate of the Moscow Patriarchate and himself, Sergii, as the exarch. In the same memorandum he assured the Germans that "the Moscow Patriarchate had never been reconciled to the godless authorities . . . [it] submitted to the Soviet power only de facto . . . [and] therefore . . . he had the moral right to publish [his call] on the Russian people to revolt." Obviously unaware of the Rosenberg insistence on fragmentation of the Church along ethnic and regional lines, Sergii, moreover, argued that it would be wrong to break up the Church precisely along these lines, that it was necessary to observe canon law and that the structure of the church administration should be strictly hierarchical—in contrast to the former Estonian and Latvian churches, which were democratic in structure with weak and circumscribed bishops. The purpose of these suggestions was obviously to appeal to the centralizing dictatorial principles of Nazi Germany. Sergii further maintained that any German inter-

---

[16]*Great Revival,* 82. Sergii was held prisoner by the Germans for a few days on their arrival in Riga, but, apparently while in captivity, managed to convince them of his anticommunism and of the correctness of the propatriarchate line.

ference with the church structure, such as breaking it away from its canonical links with Moscow in favor of separate Latvian and Estonian churches, would be interpreted by Soviet propaganda as evidence of German control over the Church.

Sergii's memoranda to and conversations with the Germans resulted in their decision that all the Orthodox people of the Baltic republics (apparently, including the more than 100,000 native Estonians and 50,000 Latvians of the Orthodox faith) would eventually be resettled in the Reichskommissariat of Moscow after the Nazi victory. Therefore, once Metropolitan Alexander of Estonia finally broke with Sergii in the process of setting up dioceses in the Baltic in 1942, while the second bishop of Estonia, Pavel of Narva, remained loyal to the exarch, the Germans decreed that Alexander and Avgustin could bear only the title of Metropolitan of Revel and Riga, respectively, not of Estonia or Latvia as a whole, since Sergii already bore the combined title of the metropolitan of all three Baltic countries. Moreover, in an internal document, the German administration pointed out to their subordinates that, while all parishes in Estonia had the right to choose whether to register in Alexander's separate Estonian diocese or Pavel's Russian diocese under Sergii, the German preference was that as many as possible register in the Russian ecclesiastic administration.[17] And it appears that the majority of parishes in Estonia and Latvia and all parishes in Lithuania remained under Exarch Sergii.

Sergii's most remarkable achievement, however, was his mission in northwestern Russia—the whole area west, southwest and south of Leningrad under German occupation. The whole venture became known as the Pskov mission, and Sergii had obtained German permission to start the mission as early as 1941. The mission, sent out to Pskov from Riga in August 1941, consisted of fifteen priests. When they arrived at their destination they found only one or two functioning churches in Gdov and none in Pskov or anywhere else in the whole huge area. Wherever the missionaries came, the local population, with the permission of the local German administrators—who in some cases even provided building materials—opened and repaired churches and

[17]Ibid., 83-9.

packed them for every service. According to the missionaries' reports:

> When . . . we arrived in Pskov, parishioners with tears in their eyes approached us in the streets for our blessing. At the first service all worshipers confessed . . . it was not the priests who had come to strengthen the people—the people were there to strengthen the priests.[18]

Forty percent of the whole remaining population of Pskov (10,000 out of 25,000) participated in the Blessing of the Water procession on Epiphany (in January 1942) alone. Services had to be held every day from six in the morning until ten at night. The above-cited missionary priest alone baptized 3,500 children between August and November 1941. Almost all of the high school teachers, whose professional duty under the Soviets had been to conduct atheistic education and who had to be sworn atheists, returned to the Church.

Internal German SD reports confirm the stupendous success of the mission. One such communiqué "relates that in the cities of Pskov and Ostrov almost the entire population gathers for church services." Another says "that the religiousness of the population is so strong that it is possible to tear the Russian people away from the Soviet government by simply relying on it."[19]

By the end of the German occupation of the area the number of priests increased to 175, serving more than 200 parishes. The mission published a religious bulletin, ran catechetical courses for adults, reestablished religious instruction in all the schools functioning under the Germans and ran some pastoral-theological courses. But most of the candidates for priesthood from the local population were sent for instruction to Riga and Vilnius. The whole project, and all the parishes, were financed exclusively by voluntary donations of the populace. Ten percent of the income of the parishes was sent to Pskov for diocesan expenses, of which one-half was forwarded to Riga. The priests received no salary, existing entirely on donations by the parishioners. In contrast to

[18]Ibid., 100-1.
[19]Ibid., 101-3.

the situation on the Soviet-controlled territory, all church income was exempt from taxation.[20]

As the area was mostly within the diocese of Leningrad, the clergy were instructed by the exarch to elevate prayers for Aleksii, the Metropolitan of Leningrad, at the liturgy, although Aleksii was on the Soviet side of the front. However, after anti-German leaflets signed by Metropolitan Aleksii had been dropped over the territory from Soviet aircraft, the Germans forbade the mentioning of his name in public prayers.

As far as Moscow was concerned, the elder Metropolitan Sergii (Stragorodsky) was apparently reluctant to directly condemn his exarch and close personal friend in Riga. In his second message, of October 14, 1941, he speaks only about rumors of collaboration of Russian clergy on the German side with the enemy, "rumors . . . which I would not want to believe." The message only threatens such clergy with church trial, not mentioning any names.[21]

The exarch's situation became very precarious after the election of Sergii of Moscow as patriarch. The Germans, obviously, wanted Sergii's election and patriarchal title to be proclaimed invalid by some authoritative churchmen. The exarch Sergii refused to do this. At that point, the Germans suddenly remembered the Karlovci Synod, which up to then had been denied any participation in the religious renewal in the East. The Synod was brought to Vienna and was joined there by Serafim of Berlin for a special session of October 8-13, 1943, which issued a declaration condemning the newly elected Patriarch Sergii for his collaboration with the Bolsheviks—citing his denials of church persecution in the USSR—and calling the September Sobor and the patriarchal election a propaganda trick of the Bolsheviks, invalid from the Church's point of view. Exarch Sergii, however—despite the Moscow Sobor's explicit condemnation of all clergymen collaborating with the Germans, threatening them with excommunication and deprivation of all clerical ranks—continued his ecclesiastic loyalty to Moscow. In an unpublished interview with, or an investigation by, the Germans, he maintained that Sergii of

[20]Ibid., 104.
[21]Ibid., 79. See also above in chapter 6.

Moscow's validity as Patriarch of All Russia should be recognized, claiming that anti-Bolshevik propaganda should take the line that the election proved the ideological bankruptcy of Bolshevism, forced to tolerate a patriarch and forced to appeal to him. The proper propaganda line must emphasize that a true accommodation between Bolshevism and the Church is impossible because it will spell death for communism.[22]

On April 28, 1944, Metropolitan-Exarch Sergii, along with his driver and a friend, driving along a deserted road between Vilnius and Riga, was gunned down from a passing car. The murderers wore German military uniforms, but the German authorities blamed the act on Soviet partisans. Professors Stavrou and Alexeev think that the Germans were more likely the murderers, which is also the official view of Soviet authors. But a recent *samizdat* document, the authenticity of which seems to be beyond doubt, clearly indicates that the murder was a centrally planned act of the NKVD.[23]

Belorussia

The Rosenberg doctrine of divide and rule in relation to the Church could be more easily applied in Belorussia and the Ukraine, where the vast majority of the autochthonous population was Orthodox and therefore attempts could be made at creating and/or cultivating separate Ukrainian and Belorussian churches. Technically, the task was facilitated also by the fact that the exarch for the western Ukraine and Belorussia, Nikolai (Yarushevich), unlike Exarch Sergii, was in Moscow, on the other side of the front; hence, it was impossible for the churches under the Germans to continue to recognize Nikolai as their leader.

[22]Ibid., 93-7.
[23]Ibid., 98; and the Soviet version in Z. Balevits, *Pravoslavnaya tserkov' v Latvii pod sen'yu svastiki* (Riga, 1967) 78-87, as cited in *Great Revival*, 98.
    The story is told by Fr. Nikolai Trubetskoi, a Riga priest who had been active in the Pskov mission and after the war served ten years in Soviet concentration camps. There he met an ex-Soviet partisan who claimed to have been one of the members of the murder team dressed in German military uniforms. His details of the act completely coincide with the German documentary version, based on the testimony of a local shepherd. See Nikolai Shemetov, "Edinstvennaya vstrecha," *VRKhD*, no. 128 (1979) 249-50.

Western Belorussia also contained substantial numbers of Roman Catholics, whom the Germans saw, not without reason, almost as a fifth column of the Poles, and therefore preferred to support the Orthodox in order to prevent any Roman Catholic missionary activities in eastern Belorussia. The opportunity for western Belorussian Catholic activities was further reduced by the shifting of the borders by the Germans: the Grodno province was added to East Prussia, the Pinsk province was added to the Ukraine, while Belorussia received "in compensation" the Smolensk and Bryansk provinces.

Although the Germans imported Belorussian nationalists from Poland, Prague and other places in order to strengthen the separatist-nationalist Belorussian influence in the Church (as well as elsewhere in the life of the country), the Belorussian Church, particularly her bishops, fiercely resisted all attempts at separation from the Russian Church. In March 1942, a council of bishops of Belorussia elected the senior bishop Panteleimon as Metropolitan of Belorussia, but failed to declare the Belorussian Church autocephalous, contrary to the wishes of the Belorussian nationalists and of the German administration. The name of Metropolitan Sergii of Moscow continued to be elevated at services, and Metropolitan Panteleimon refused to use Belorussian in his sermons, on the grounds that Russian, not Belorussian, was the common language in the cities. The nationalists, through the German administration, confined Panteleimon to a monastery and transferred the church administration to his assistant, Archbishop Filofei (Narko), who at first also refused to introduce any changes, on the grounds that he had no right to make any decisions without Panteleimon's approval.[24]

Having received a written authorization from Panteleimon to hold a Belorussian church sobor, Filofei convoked one on August 30, 1942. Much manipulation was applied by the nationalists to make the sobor more amenable to them. (Some clerics were physically prevented by the German authorities from arriving in Minsk on time.) Although forced to introduce the principle of autocephaly for the Belorussian Church in the statute that was produced by the sobor, its members included a proviso stipulating that autocephaly would be announced only after it had been

[24]*Great Revival*, 107-20.

approved by all the canonical autocephalous Orthodox churches —i.e., implicitly, by the Moscow Patriarchate as well. Only a year later were the appropriate letters to all the autocephalous churches finally drafted, properly translated and handed over to the German authorities for forwarding. However, they were never sent, and the Belorussian bishops meanwhile continued to resist the de facto autocephaly and "Belorussification" of the Church as best they could, never mentioning autocephaly in any of their official documents or in the official seal of the Church. The Belorussian Council of Bishops in May 1944 rejected the statute enacted at the Sobor of 1942 on the grounds that the two most senior bishops of Belorussia had been physically prevented by the occupation authorities from attending. After emigrating to Germany toward the end of 1944, they all joined the post-Karlovcian Synod, which had reconstituted itself after the war in Munich, West Germany.[25]

The Religious Revival in Belorussia

The devastation of the Church was as complete by 1941 in eastern Belorussia as it was elsewhere in the USSR. Out of the original seventeen churches, a monastery and a convent in Minsk, none had remained open after 1937. But within four months of German occupation there were already seven churches working to capacity in Minsk, and 22,000 child and infant baptisms were performed. Of the 400 prerevolutionary parishes in the Minsk diocese, 120 were reopened during the first year of German occupation. The Germans did not allow the reopening of any of the two prerevolutionary Minsk seminaries, but did permit short-term pastoral courses of several months' duration, and each graduation added twenty to thirty priests, deacons or readers to the Church. The 1944 Epiphany procession was attended by more than 80,000 people—about 30 to 40 percent of the city's total inhabitants.

A similar picture is obtained from reports on the church

[25]Ibid., 122-32. In 1944 Rosenberg's *Ostministerium* thus summarized the Belorussian situation: ". . . the overwhelming majority of the Belorussian Orthodox clergy is Russian in spirit. The rearing of a Belorussian nationally conscious hierarchy meets with difficulties; it would be possible only if German initiative were deployed in the religious field." Dallin, 488.

situation in all the other towns, villages and cities under the Belorussian church administration. Smolensk, which before the war had a population of 150,000 and only one church still functioning, by 1942, with the population reduced to under 30,000, had five churches working to capacity and pastoral courses graduating forty priests in their first seven months of existence. Only eight to ten original priests had actually survived in the Smolensk province to resurface under the Germans. Because of the great shortage of priests, the rural clergy went on circuits, staying in each village for about a week, performing 150 to 200 baptisms daily, hearing confessions, performing services, etc., and then moving on. (Many priests also arrived as missionaries from former Poland.) Table 7-1 gives the statistics on reopened churches in some other towns of note in the dioceses of Smolensk, Mogilev and Vitebsk.

According to reports of both Russian and German witnesses, in those places where all the church buildings survived—and where the occupational authorities did not interfere—about 75 percent of the prerevolutionary congregations were restored. In many places, particularly in the bigger cities, churches and monasteries were blown up or burned down by the Soviet forces immediately prior to their retreat. But in Vitebsk, for instance, two churches were saved because a "Komsomol brigade consisting of girls," which was to set them on fire, was destroyed before carrying out its plan. In another town the Komsomol girl who was ordered to destroy the churches committed suicide rather than

TABLE 7-1
REOPENED CHURCHES ON GERMAN-OCCUPIED TERRITORY[26]

Town	Number of churches	Town	Number of churches
Roslavl	7	Mogilev	3
Bryansk	12	Orsha	10
Mstislavl	5	Shklov	7
Vyazma	8	Vitebsk (and suburbs)	8
Borisov	21	Polotsk	4

[26]*Great Revival*, 132-8.

fulfil the order. A census of the religious affiliations of the populations of Smolensk and Borisov taken by the Germans indicated
only one percent and under three percent atheists, respectively.
German reports confirm a very high degree of religiosity and
mention that although the first ones to flock to the churches
were older people, soon after a church reopened more and more
young people would turn up.[27]

The Ukraine

In the Ukraine the church situation was complicated by a
number of factors that did not exist in the Pskov-Novgorod area
at all and manifested only an embryonic presence in Belorussia.

First, there was the Uniate Catholic (or Roman Catholic of
the Eastern Rite) Church in Galicia. Although the Nazis supported Ukrainian nationalistic separatism in order to weaken any
Russian influences, and the core of Ukrainian nationalism was in
Uniate Galicia and therefore most of the Ukrainian nationalist
leaders were Catholic, the Germans categorically suppressed all
attempts to expand Catholic elements or missionary activities east
of Galicia.[28]

Second, there was the Orthodox Church of Poland, granted
autocephaly by the Ecumenical Patriarchate in 1923 without
canonical release from the Moscow Patriarchate—the mother
Church—on the shaky grounds that the Orthodox population of
Poland used to be a part of the Kievan metropolitanate, which,
until 1686, had been under the jurisdiction of the Ecumenical
Patriarch. Now, with the German occupation of the eastern
Ukraine, Metropolitan Dionisy, the head of the Polish Church,
was claiming jurisdictional rights over the Ukraine. Although a
pure Russian, before the war he had completely succumbed to
the pressures of the Polish government and the Ukrainian nationalists and had supported both Polonization of the non-Ukrainian
parishes of his Church and Ukrainization of the Ukrainian ones.
Consequently, Ukrainian nationalists, arriving in the eastern

[27]Ibid., 138-44.
[28]Dallin, 474-7.

Ukraine from Poland, retained contacts with Dionisy and supported his claims.[29]

Moreover, as he was prevented by the Germans from extending his control eastward (divide and rule), Dionisy now supported and blessed the reappearance of an anti-Moscow Ukrainian Autocephalous Church, promoting Bishop Polykarp (Sikorsky) of Lutsk to the rank of archbishop and administrator of this autocephalous Church in his (Dionisy's) absence.[30] While under Soviet occupation in 1939-1941, Sikorsky, although apparently recognizing the Moscow Patriarchate, refused to take the necessary trip to Moscow. He now claimed that he had never entered Moscow's jurisdiction and therefore was not breaking any canonical connection by continuing to receive orders from his prewar superior, the Metropolitan of Warsaw. The Autocephalous Church was formally reconstituted (since the demise of the Lypkivsky organization in 1930) at its first Council of Bishops in February 1942. Here they stipulated that they would accept the Lypkivsky clergy, which had resurfaced as a church organization at their church conference in Kiev in September 1941, without any reordination. The acceptance of the Lypkivskyites henceforth made the reconstituted Autocephalists canonically unacceptable to the rest of the Orthodox *oikoumene*.[31]

However, during the Soviet occupation, all the other bishops in the western Ukraine who had belonged to the Warsaw jurisdiction went over to that of Moscow, and most of them now refused to sever this canonical connection. On the basis of the decisions of the 1917-1918 Sobor, reconfirmed by Patriarch Tikhon in 1922, which had stipulated that the Church in the Ukraine be granted an autonomous status,[32] these bishops formed an Auton-

[29]See one of the most competent books on the Orthodox Church in Poland, Alexander Svitich, *Pravoslavnaya tserkov' v Pol'she i ee avtokefaliya* (Buenos Aires, 1959).

[30]Dublyansky, 26; also Svitich, 198-200.

[31]Dublyansky, 28-9; *Great Revival*, 153-7. Svitich (196) points out that during the Soviet occupation of the western Ukraine, Polykarp concelebrated with Metropolitan Nikolai (Yarushevich), the West Ukrainian exarch from Moscow, and even joined him in consecrating a new bishop—which he could not do unless he recognized himself as a member of the Moscow Patriarchate, since Moscow did not recognize the Polish autocephaly and banned all intercommunion with its clergy.

[32]Resolution of the all-Russian sobor of September 7/20, 1918, fully confirming the Statute on the Provisional Higher Administration of the Orthodox Church

omous Orthodox Church of the Ukraine at a council at the Pochaev Monastery in August 1941. Only their head, Aleksii (Gromadsky), proclaimed metropolitan-exarch by the sobor, would elevate the name of Metropolitan Sergii of Moscow as his superior; the rest of the bishops and clergy would elevate only the name of Aleksii. This Aleksii, formerly of the Polish Orthodox Church, argued that once he and his fellow bishops had returned to the fold of the Moscow Patriarchate following Metropolitan Dionisy's written abdication of his jurisdiction over Volhynia and the other parts of Poland that went to the USSR in 1939, Dionisy no longer had jurisdiction over the Ukraine. The latter, in turn, did not recognize the Autonomous Church.[33]

Thus, from the very beginning of the German occupation, two parallel Orthodox churches developed and competed with each other in the Ukraine. The Autocephalous Church recognized the validity of the Lypkivsky organization of the "Self-consecrators" (1921-1930), augmenting their ranks by accepting the surviving clergy of that uncanonical body without reordination. In the eyes of all canonical Orthodox churches, including the Autonomous Church of the Ukraine, the uncanonicity of the Lypkivsky Church that resulted from their break with the apostolic succession was thereby transferred to the whole Ukrainian Autocephalous Church. Consequently, the latter, now existing only in the Ukrainian diaspora in the West, has ever since been refused any liturgical contacts by all other Orthodox churches.

in the Ukraine, adopted by the sobor (*rada*) of the Ukrainian Orthodox Church in Kiev on July 9/22, 1918. This Statute is very closely modeled on the one adopted for the All-Russian Church in Moscow. The Ukrainian Church was to be headed by the Metropolitan of Kiev and Halych, who would be elected by a Ukrainian sobor and confirmed by the all-Russian patriarch. The Ukrainian Church would make her own appointments and consecrations, but the patriarch blesses her actions and remains the supreme arbiter in disputes between bishops and has the authority of the supreme court of appeal over them. Complaints against the Ukrainian metropolitan were likewise to be directed to the patriarch. *Sobranie opredelenii*, vol. 4, appendix 2, 15-9.

[33]*Great Revival*, 156-7. Svitich (184-91) mentions no such direct abdication, although he relates how on November 23, 1939, Dionisy wrote to Serafim of Berlin that since Poland has ceased to exist, the Orthodox autocephaly on that territory likewise should be subordinated to the Orthodox Church in Germany, and he abdicates in Serafim's favor. However, in 1940 he changed his mind and, on September 23, was confirmed by the Nazi Governor-General as Metropolitan-head of the Autocephalous Orthodox Church of the General-Government, i.e., of the German-occupied part of Poland only.

Twice in the course of 1941 the leading bishops of the Autonomous Church, including Metropolitan Aleksii, tried to come to an understanding with the Autocephalists, requesting only reordination for those of their clergy who had been originally ordained by Lypkivsky and his "bishops." That procedure, however, was turned down.[34]

Naturally, the Germans originally sympathized with the Autocephalists, in accordance with the Rosenberg instructions regarding the cultivation of anti-Russian sentiments in the Ukraine, but Erich Koch was not happy with a strong Ukrainian revival either, particularly when the nationalist Ukrainian partisan (guerrilla) movement began to grow in 1943. Hence, although according to Heyer and Alexeev-Stavrou only Autonomist clergy and bishops were murdered here and there on the German-occupied territory by the Bandera Ukrainian nationalist partisans, the Autonomous Church was able to develop, survive, outstrip the Autocephalists by far and grow by leaps and bounds, to a considerable extent because of this German policy of divide and rule. The Nazis came to see it in their interest to have the two rival churches compete and struggle with each other.[35]

Against Koch's wishes, a meeting between Metropolitan Aleksii and two bishops of the Autocephalous Church at the Pochaev Monastery in October 1942 resulted in an agreement of merger of the two bodies. The agreement, in fact, would have amounted to both a canonical and administrative capitulation by the Autonomists. It stipulated that the unified Church would be de facto autocephalous and would be headed by Metropolitan Dionisy, as the Kievan locum tenens, until the assembly of an all-Ukrainian sobor. Dionisy was to be assisted by a Synod of three bishops from the Autocephalists and two from the Autonomists, but with Bishop Mstyslav (Skrypnyk), the leading poli-

[34]*Great Revival,* 157. Gromadsky offered to invite Archbishop Illarion (Ohienko) of Holm in the General-Government to be the joint head of a united single Ukrainian Orthodox Church. The latter was a Ukrainian nationalist and former Minister of Religious Affairs under the Petlyura government in the Ukraine, but a regularly consecrated bishop. This plan misfired because the Germans refused to admit Ohienko (as well as Dionisy or other bishops from the West) into the eastern Ukraine. Ibid., 152.

[35]Heyer, 187-9, 201-3, 217-21. Dublyansky, however, cites cases of rural priests of the Autocephalous Church murdered by Soviet partisans and communist agents (43).

tician of the Autocephalists (and a nephew of the late Petlyura), as the Synod's responsible secretary. This submission of the Autonomous Church was not warranted at all, in view of its much more solid position with the Ukrainian population than that of the Autocephalists. It must have been the rising terrorism of the Bandera nationalist partisans, directed, among others, against the Autonomous Church, that must have stimulated Aleksii's submission. Aleksii's murder by the Banderists soon after his withdrawal from the agreement is a case in point.[36]

The overwhelming majority of bishops and clergy of the Autonomous Church, particularly those who were natives of the eastern Ukraine, refused to abide by this agreement. They argued that no merger was possible with the Autocephalists because: (1) like the Renovationists, they consecrated married family men as bishops (four of their bishops were in fact married men); (2) they accepted the Lypkivsky ordinations as valid; and (3) they placed politics, nationalism and divisions of the church organism ahead of real church interests.[37] Another factor was the German administration, which stated that it would tolerate no participation of Dionisy or of Ukrainian politicians in bishops' robes (Mstyslav Skrypnyk) in any Ukrainian church synod.[38]

By late 1942 the Autocephalous Church had fifteen ruling bishops, while the Autonomous had sixteen. However, as Heyer points out, the profiles of the episcopal bodies of the two churches differed vastly. The Autocephalous Church was but a spiritual branch of nationalist politics, and her bishops were deeply involved in such politics, acting in their behavior, dress (outside of services) and speeches predominantly as secular leaders. Many of them, like Bishop Mstyslav, were former secular politicians, others widowers or even married priests. In contrast, nearly all of the sixteen bishops of the Autonomous Church were genuine monastics, some of very high spiritual caliber and of ascetic disposition.[39]

[36]Heyer, 219 etc. See the complete text of the agreement in Heyer, 184-5, and Dublyansky, 46-7.

[37]Heyer, 181 (n. 17) and 185-7. He cites a long and moving letter by an East Ukrainian priest which implores the metropolitan not to merge with the uncanonical Autocephalists in the name of the countless martyrs who died under the Soviets defending the purity of the faith.

[38]Ibid., 187.

[39]Ibid., 181-3.

One of the bishops of the Autocephalists was Feofil Buldovsky, who had resurfaced in Kharkov soon after the German occupation and proclaimed himself the Metropolitan of Kharkov and Poltava. Buldovsky and Mstyslav Skrypnyk knew each other from the Petlyura days, and the negotiations between them now resulted in Feofil's joining the Autocephalists as a rather charismatic Metropolitan of Kharkov, also administering the war zones of Kursk, Voronezh and Donbas.[40]

It is an irony that of the fifteen bishops of the Autocephalous Church, two were ethnic Russians, although one of the bishops of the parallel Church stated that the Autocephalists wanted to be a Church for ethnic Ukrainians alone, while the Autonomists welcomed any Orthodox Christian of any nationality into their fold. The nominal head of the Autocephalists, Metropolitan Dionisy of Warsaw, whom they proclaimed locum tenens of the Kievan see, was likewise a pure Russian. All the bishops of the Autonomous Church, however, were ethnic Ukrainians.[41] Extreme nationalism often attracts the less nationally secure fringe elements.

The Church Revival

Let us now take a quick look at the religious progress of both church groups in the German-occupied parts of the Ukraine, and compare the achievements of both, which also reflect how the general population of the Ukraine felt about national separatism, or at least about its penetration into church life (see table 7-2).

No other eastern Ukrainian diocese reached such a high pro-

[40]Ibid., 240. Symptomatic of the sense of canonical insecurity of the Autocephalists is the fact that Dublyansky cites their recognition by Buldovsky—a bishop regularly consecrated by canonical bishops of the Moscow Patriarchate—but conceals the later Patriarchal ban regarding Buldovsky. See our second chapter on "The Lubny Schism," pp. 78-9.

[41]Names and data in Heyer, 182. Prof. John Armstrong wrongly says that "the bishops of Alexius's group were . . . predominantly of Russian origin." *Ukrainian Nationalism* (New York: Columbia University Press, 1963) 195-6. The intrinsic difference between the two, besides the canonical questions, was summed up by an official of the Autonomists: "The Autocephalists say: our Ukrainian Church is only for Ukrainians. We respond to this: everyone is free to pray with us; and if Russians or Germans come to us to pray the happier we are." Heyer, 190.

TABLE 7-2
CHURCH INSTITUTIONS AND CLERGY IN THE KIEV DIOCESE

	pre-1917	1940	1943 Autonomist	Autocephalist
churches/parishes	1,710	2	500	298
monasteries/convents	23	0	8	—
priests	1,435	3	600	434
monks/nuns	5,193	0	387	—

TABLE 7-3
PARISHES AND CLERGY IN GERMAN-OCCUPIED UKRAINE

pre-1917		1943 Autonomist	Autocephalist
Poltava diocese			
parishes	1,200	140	100 (approx.)
priests	?	140 (approx.)	102
Podolia diocese			
parishes	1,500	548 (approx.)	?
clergy	?	350	?
Zhitomir diocese			
parishes	800	300	100
clergy	?	300 (approx.)	?
Dnepropetrovsk diocese			
parishes	?	318	10
Chernigov diocese			
parishes	?	all open churches	0

portion of recovery (almost 50 percent of the prerevolutionary number of parishes and 70 percent of clergy) as the Kiev one. This ancient spiritual center of Russia was apparently attracting most of the missionary clergy arriving from the western Ukraine as well as surviving clergy on Soviet territory. Nevertheless, the recovery was remarkable everywhere (see table 7-3).

The above tables may, in fact, distort the real situation in *favor* of the Autocephalists. Heyer, on the strength of secret German SD reports, maintains that in the Poltava diocese, for instance, 80 percent of the faithful belonged to the Autonomous and only 20 percent to the Autocephalous Church, but the German-installed mayor of Poltava was a Ukrainian nationalist favoring the Autocephalists. Similarly, in Dnepropetrovsk, where the Autocephalists managed to establish only a few parishes, the German administration confiscated the bishop's residence from the Autonomists and gave it to the Autocephalists. In general, says Heyer, where the Autocephalists had the least support from the population they turned most often for support and protection to the occupational authorities. The latter, in general, actively obliged, until the anti-German activization of the Banderist partisans in 1943. Thereafter they began to favor the Autonomists and opposed any cooperation between the two church bodies.[42]

A Ukrainian Autocephalist publication complains that "in Kiev . . . in particular, the Russophile influence was strong . . ."[43] But what is more likely to have happened is that, because the nationalist potential was greater in Kiev than in most other areas of the eastern Ukraine, the Germans from the very beginning gave preference to the Autonomists—as demonstrated, for instance, in the solemn granting of St. Vladimir's Cathedral to the Autonomists by the German administration in 1942.[44]

German reports, as well as testimonies from church circles, claim that despite the terror unleashed by the Banderists, the vast majority of the Ukrainian population supported the Autonomists. Some reports even claimed that there were no separatist-nationalist sentiments among the eastern Ukrainian population.[45] While this might be an exaggeration, Heyer's observation is much more plausible: the further east you went from the Galician area the weaker was the national sentiment of the Ukrainians.[46] Indeed, the mass movement of the Banderist and Melnykite Ukrainian nationalist partisans was practically limited to Galicia, Volhynia and parts of Podolia—i.e., to the former Polish Ukraine.

[42]Heyer, 188-209. Dublyansky cites the following Autocephalist statistics by the summer of 1942 for the whole of the occupied Ukraine: 513 parishes, 298 of which in the Kiev diocese; and 455 priests, 226 of them originally from the Moscow Patriarchate, and 93 former Lypkivskyites (44-5).

[43]Ibid., 43.

[44]Heyer, 212-8 et passim; Dublyansky, 42-3.

[45]*Great Revival*, 167-8. One German report also complained that the Ukrainian people were complete strangers to a purely racial anti-Semitism. Ibid., 171.

[46]Heyer, 189, 194 et passim.

After the refusal of the Autonomous Church to join the Auto-cephalists and to recognize their canonical validity, the Banderists unleashed a vicious terror campaign against the Autonomist clergy and lay activists. The murder of Metropolitan Aleksii was followed by the murder of Bishop Manuil (Tarnavsky) of Vladimir-Volynsk, a former Autocephalist who had gone over to the Autonomists in 1942. In addition, Heyer lists twenty-seven priests of the Autonomous Church who were murdered by the Banderists in Volhynia alone during the summer of 1943. In some cases their families and guests who happened to be at their homes at the time were likewise murdered on the spot. The list is by no means complete. This campaign of murder and terror resulted in a "sudden" growth of the Autocephalous Church in the course of that year, particularly in Volhynia, where over six hundred parishes went over to them. Only city churches dared to remain faithful to their Autonomous hierarchy.[47]

The general consensus of German reports is that as many as 70 to 95 percent of the population in the Ukraine turned to the Church. Some reports maintained that the majority of church-goers were elderly; others spoke about a high degree of religiosity among the young as well. All report absolutely packed churches, a shortage of priests, mass baptisms, mass church weddings, etc. Stavrou and Alexeev point out that, although in the two short years of German occupation the number of reopened churches made up between 20 and 70 percent of the prerevolutionary total, the total number of those attending may have been no less than the prerevolutionary figure owing to the fact that before the revolution few churches had ever been filled, while now they were literally bursting at the seams.[48]

Well over twenty monasteries and convents functioned within the Autonomous but only two in the Autocephalist Church. As admitted by the Autocephalist Archbishop of Kiev Nikanor (Abramovich), the monastics on the whole refused to recognize the canonicity of the Autocephalous Church. Convents, on the whole, grew much faster than monasteries because the German authorities banned tonsure of males of working age. The total number of nuns and monks in the Autonomous Church may have

[47]Ibid., 218-23.
[48]Great Revival, 162-74.

reached some two thousand by 1943, while that of the Auto-cephalists was under one hundred.[49]

In 1943, the Autonomous Church reopened a seminary in Kremenets in the former Polish Ukraine (which had been closed by the Soviets in 1939) with 160 students in its first two years. An Autonomist seminary was about to begin classes in Kiev when the city was recaptured by the Soviet armies. Pastoral courses were run in a number of cities by both churches. The Autocephalists wanted to start a seminary and a theological academy in Kiev, but were prevented from doing so by the Germans.[50] There seems to have been well over four hundred new priestly ordinations in the Autonomous and at least two hundred in the Autocephalous Church in this short interval.

Two surviving old bishops in the South Russian territories adjacent to the Ukraine—Rostov and Taganrog—approached Metropolitan Aleksii in 1942 and brought their dioceses under the jurisdiction of the Ukrainian Autonomous Church.[51] In addition to the Orthodox Church, the Uniates tried to penetrate from Galicia, and in some isolated cases the remnants of the Ukrainian Renovationists tried to raise their heads—e.g., in the city of Berdichev. Both, however, were categorically suppressed by the Germans. Just as in Belorussia, they did not want any extension of the Church that had her center in the Vatican. As for the Renovationists, they were banned as Soviet agents.[52]

Although Alexeev and Stavrou conclude, on the basis of secret German reports, that "efforts to disseminate Ukrainian separatism met with complete apathy in the circles of Orthodox clergy,"[53] the actual situation was not as clear-cut as that in the Ukraine. This is evident from the contrast in German attitudes toward Belorussian and Ukrainian nationalism. In Belorussia, the German authorities deliberately imported Belorussian nationalists from

[49]Heyer, 201-4, and this author's mathematical calculations. Nikanor added that the future Autocephalist monasteries would be built on the model of Roman Catholic orders and would be working communes rather than monasteries. Compare this with the Renovationists' program (chapter 2, above).

[50]Heyer, 196-9; Dublyansky, 40-1.

[51]Heyer, 183, n. 21.

[52]Ibid., 188. They also made limited attempts at resurfacing in the northern Caucasus, where they had been particularly strong in the 1920s and early 1930s. *Great Revival*, 197-8.

[53]Ibid, 167.

the former Poland to foment nationalism and to weaken the Russophile tendencies; in the Ukraine, German communiqués complained about the overactivization of the Galician nationalists and about their attempts to take over social and cultural life in the eastern Ukraine. The much greater success of the Autonomists when compared to the Autocephalists testifies to the partial truth of the above Alexeev-Stavrou statement, but had there been "complete apathy" the Autocephalists would not have made the rather considerable gains discussed above. It was precisely because of the weakness of national separatism in Belorussia that the Germans artificially supported the nationalists, prevented the appearance of two parallel church organizations and insisted on autocephaly (failing in this, as we know), for they realized that, lacking roots in the country, such separatist and autocephalist bodies would have to rely on German support and hence could be manipulated. In the Ukraine, where nationalism had a greater potential, the Germans supported it as long as it fomented anti-Russian feelings, but when it threatened to develop into something more than just a tool for the Germans, the latter allowed the parallel development of non-nationalistic bodies— e.g., the Autonomous Orthodox Church, even though she quietly recognized the authority of the Moscow Metropolitan Sergii over herself.

In conclusion, it may be pointed out that whereas all Autocephalist bishops except the octogenarian Feofil (Buldovsky) evacuated with the Germans to the West, of the surviving fourteen Autonomist bishops, six remained with the people—at least three of them suffering long spells of incarceration by the Soviets —and a seventh one returned from Germany after the war.

Although Metropolitan Sergii of Moscow, as already mentioned, was forced to condemn all ecclesiastical collaboration with the Germans in his official wartime encyclicals, the real attitude of the Moscow Patriarchate to the Autonomists was one of understanding and approval. This is illustrated, for instance, by an official obituary on Archbishop Venyamin (Novitsky), formerly of that Church, who subsequently lived through some ten years of the most horrible of Stalin's concentration camps only to become one of the patriarchate's most outstanding bishops until his death in 1976. Among other things, the obituary said: "The

Ukrainian Autonomous Church, although in most strained circumstances, was nevertheless the only legal organization around which the popular forces could gather and in which they found support in the period of the nation's greatest trials."[54] Could this not also be said about the Moscow Patriarchate and its enforced collaboration with the communist regime?

Church Revival in the Romanian Zone of Occupation and Areas Adjacent to the Ukraine

The situation of the Orthodox was much more fortunate in the Romanian zone of occupation—i.e., the Black Sea littoral from the Dniester River to the Crimea, of which the area west of the Crimea with Odessa as its focal point was annexed to Romania under the name Transnistria. The state religion in Romania was Orthodoxy, hence a regular church life was organized in Transnistria by the Romanian Orthodox Church. The area was divided into three dioceses served by two bishops and one bishop-candidate from Romania. Of the original prerevolutionary 1,150 churches in the area, nearly 500 were reopened by 1943, served by up to 600 clergy of all ranks. Most of the priests were Romanians, who would be sent for six months of duty in Russia from the Moldavian Metropolitanate of Kishinev, where most of the population was bilingual. Some priests were local Russians. In fact, a seminary was set up in Dubosary with over eighty students, and several pastoral courses were run elsewhere. A church newspaper was published in Odessa in Russian. Twelve monasteries and convents began to function. Religious instruction was introduced in all schools, and cultural circles were established in many villages by the priests.

The drawback was the attempt by the Romanian government to use the church as an instrument of Romanization of the population. For instance, religious broadcasts for the population began to use Romanian; there were likewise attempts to use Romanian in church services (which was resented by the population and, apparently, discontinued). Reports of Romanian bishops noted

---

[54]"Arkhiepiskop cheboksarskii i chuvashskii Venyamin," *ZhMP*, no. 1 (1977) 18-20.

the exceptional religious intensity of the Russian population and said that Romanian clergy should go to Russia for spiritual self-enrichment.[55]

A similar religious upsurge was reported in the front areas of the northern Caucasus and the German-occupied Great Russian areas from the mouth of the Don to Orel. However, no accurate statistics on these areas exist. All that is known is that in place of the sole surviving functioning church in Rostov-on-Don, eight began to function, each celebrating two liturgies every day of the week, plus other services. Sixty churches were opened in the Rostov diocese, and all the churches in the Cossack city of Novocherkassk. As elsewhere, the churches were packed and baptisms were conducted daily for the population. One observer remarks that, to his amazement, most of the intelligentsia, including school teachers, went to the churches in Novocherkassk, even those who, he thought, were atheists. According to a German SD report, in the Crimea alone 200,000 people were baptized by December 1942.[56]

Such was the Christian potential in the Soviet Union after twenty-three years of persecution and of intensive atheistic education. At least one wartime missionary priest who, after returning from a long spell in Soviet prisons, served in a church in Riga until his death in 1978 said that little has changed since the war, and a similar missionary effort today would produce similar religious zeal and upsurge.[57]

[55]Heyer, 209-12; *Great Revival*, 187-92.
[56]Ibid., 193-9.
[57]Fr. N. Trubetskoi, in Shemetov, "Edinstvennaya vstrecha," 247.